T0093736

HEALTHCARE TECHNOLOGIES SERIES 46

Digital Twin Technologies for Healthcare 4.0

Other volumes in this series:

Digital Twin Technologies for Healthcare 4.0

Edited by
Rajesh Kumar Dhanaraj, Santhiya Murugesan,
Balamurugan Balusamy and Valentina E Balas

The Institution of Engineering and Technology

Published by The Institution of Engineering and Technology, London, United Kingdom

The Institution of Engineering and Technology is registered as a Charity in England & Wales (no. 211014) and Scotland (no. SC038698).

The Institution of Engineering and Technology
Futures Place
Kings Way, Stevenage
Hertfordshire SG1 2UA, United Kingdom

www.theiet.org

British Library Cataloguing in Publication Data
A catalogue record for this product is available from the British Library

ISBN 978-1-83953-579-6 (hardback)
ISBN 978-1-83953-580-2 (PDF)

Typeset in India by MPS Limited

Cover Image: Paper Boat Creative/Stone via Getty Images

Contents

9   Digital twin in prognostics and health management system   145

S. Malathy, C.N. Vanitha and Rajesh Kumar Dhanaraj

About the editors

Dr Rajesh Kumar Dhanaraj is a professor in the School of Computing Science and Engineering at Galgotias University, Greater Noida, India. He received the B.E. degree in Computer Science and Engineering from the Anna University Chennai, India in 2007 and the M.Tech. from the Anna University Coimbatore, India, in 2010 and Ph.D. degree in Computer Science from Anna University, Chennai, India, in 2017. He has contributed 35+ authored and edited books on various technologies, 21 patents and 68 articles and papers in various refereed journals and international conferences and contributed chapters to the books. His research interests include machine learning, cyber-physical systems and wireless sensor networks. He is a senior member of the Institute of Electrical and Electronics Engineers (IEEE), member of the Computer Science Teacher Association (CSTA); and International Association of Engineers (IAENG). He is serving as an Associate Editor and Guest Editor for reputed journals. He is an Expert Advisory Panel Member of Texas Instruments Inc., USA.

Website: https://sites.google.com/view/drdrk
Orcid id: https://orcid.org/0000-0002-2038-7359
Linkedin: https://www.linkedin.com/in/dr-rajesh-kumar-dhanaraj-89578423

Santhiya Murugesan completed her Bachelor of Engineering in Electronics and Instrumentation in 2012 and did her master's degree in Instrumentation Engineering at Madras Institute of Technology in 2014. Currently, she is working as Assistant Professor in Kongu Engineering College. She has academic experience of 8 years, and her specialization areas include Internet of Things, Sensors and Transducers and Process Modelling. She contributed research works related to the control of pressurized water nuclear reactor. Recently, she is pursuing research in the area of autonomous underwater vehicles.

Prof. Balamurugan Balusamy is currently working as an associate dean student in Shiv Nadar University, Delhi-NCR. Prior to this assignment he was Professor, School of Computing Sciences & Engineering and Director International Relations at Galgotias University, Greater Noida, India. His contributions focus on Engineering Education, Block chain and Data Sciences. His academic degrees and 12 years of experience working as a faculty in a global university like VIT University, Vellore has made him more receptive and prominent in his domain. He does have 200 plus high impact factor papers in Springer, Elsevier and IEEE. He has done more than 80 edited and authored books and collaborated with eminent professors across the world from top QS ranked university. Prof. Balamurugan Balusamy has served up to the position of an associate professor in his stint of 12 years of experience with VIT University, Vellore. He had completed his bachelors, masters, and Ph.D. degrees from top premier institutions from India. His passion is teaching and adapts different design thinking principles while delivering his lectures. He has published 80+ books on various technologies and visited 15 plus countries for his technical course. He has several top-notch conferences in his resume and has published over 200 of quality journal, conference and book chapters combined. He serves in the advisory committee for several start-ups and forums and does consultancy work for industry on Industrial IOT. He has given over 195 talks in various events and symposium.

 Prof. Valentina E. Balas is currently a professor in the Department of Automatics and Applied Software at the Faculty of Engineering, University "Aurel Vlaicu" Arad (Romania). She holds a Ph.D. in Applied Electronics and Telecommunications from Polytechnic University of Timisoara since 2003. She is author of more than 140 research papers in refereed journals and International Conferences. Her research interests are in Intelligent Systems, Fuzzy Control, Soft Computing, Smart Sensors, Information Fusion, Modeling and Simulation, Electronics, Measurements and System Theory. She is the editor-in-chief to *International Journal of Advanced Intelligence Paradigms* (IJAIP), member in editorial boards for national and international journals, serves as reviewer for many international journals and conferences and is evaluator expert for national and international projects. She participated in many international conferences as General Chair, Organizer, Session Chair, and member in International Program Committee. She was the mentor for many student teams in Microsoft (Imagine Cup), Google and IEEE competitions in the last 6 years. Dr. Valentina Balas has a great experience in research projects. She is a member of EUSFLAT, ACM and a Senior Member IEEE, member in TC – Fuzzy Systems (IEEE CIS), member in TC – Emergent Technologies (IEEE CIS), member in TC – Soft Computing (IEEE SMCS) and also a member in IFAC – TC 3.2 Computational Intelligence in Control.

Chapter 1

Introduction: digital twin technology in healthcare

*M. Santhiya[1], V. Vishnu Priya[1] and
Rajesh Kumar Dhanaraj[2]*

1.1 Introduction

Ever since the emergence of digital and modern healthcare, the globe has rushed to implement numerous technologies in this sector in order to improve health operations and patients' health, extend survival rate, and lower healthcare expenses. New methods, strategies, and devices have emerged as a result of advancements in technology throughout history. Such advancements have resulted in significant advances in a multitude of sectors, including industry, agribusiness, education, and now even in healthcare. The emergence of personalized health tracking devices and wearables connected to smartphone apps or inbuilt sensors may continue to observe individuals' health-related metrics, such as the electrocardiogram (ECG) signals, blood pressure, respiratory rate, and blood insulin level, reducing the hazard of data recording inaccuracies. Such sensors that collect and securely send information to the cloud, where it may be compared to past data to look for indicators of any sickness or alert the right medical experts. Reduced errors imply improved functionality, cost, productivity, and quality in medical services. The combination of technology and healthcare has entered in a smart context-aware IoT medical age. The applications of digital twin in various sectors are illustrated in Figure 1.1.

The attributes of intelligent healthcare systems are listed below:

1. **Frameworks:** Using a multilevel modular structure to enable information exchange and maintenance simple via "centrally controlled" channels and to provide quick and flexible implementation via "decentralized" channels.
2. **Business model:** Cloud computing has created a shift in the medical business concept, such as cloud healthcare facilities and cloud diagnostic imaging

[1]Department of Computer Technology, Kongu Engineering College, India
[2]Department of Computer Science & Engineering, School of Computing Science and Engineering, Galgotias University, India

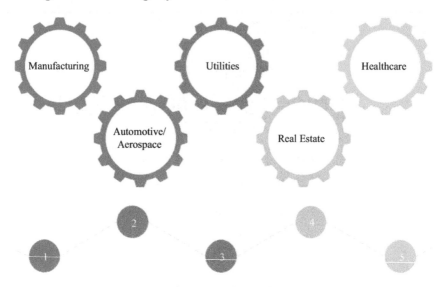

Figure 1.1   Applications of digital twin technology

technologies, that have reduced total infrastructure expenses and increased resource utilization rates.
3. **Regulatory criteria**: To accomplish individualized design, a blend of global criteria, national regulatory frameworks, and local factors is used.
4. **Interoperability between devices:** Combining IoT and wireless Internet in medical IoT to increase the tracking and alarming functions of fitness trackers and establish interoperability of clinical equipment.

1.2   Digital twin – background study

Digital twin is a revolutionary concept and a great challenge in this sector. Digital twin is predicted to revolutionize the digital healthcare industry and propel it to new heights never had before. A digital twin is a virtual clone of a physical object which actually uses real-time knowledge to replicate its current state. The Internet of Things is one of the greatest types of evidence of such technical advancements [1]. Artificial intelligence, big data analytics, the Internet of Things, and virtual and augmented reality with digital and physical things are all aspects of digital twin. This linkage enables real-time data processing, system surveillance to prevent issues from arising financial planning, reduction in costs, and forecasting future possibilities. Introducing a digital copy of a patient in a healthcare system might be an ideal option for promoting health, increasing control over disease, and improving healthcare activities. The simulation will aid in the monitoring of the patient's present health. Furthermore, medical history can also be used to anticipate the upcoming abnormalities, among other things.

Digital twin healthcare (DTH) is a novel medical simulation technique for the clinical activities or a medical system that uses digital twin technique with multi-science, numerical simulations, and multi-scale representations to deliver rapid, accurate, and efficient clinical attention. Physical objects, virtual objects, and health records are the three core components of DTH. The physical objects can be wearable devices, a human or an external attribute. The implantable devices model, fitness tracker model, digital person model, external aspect model, and digital simulation model are the virtual objects, correspondingly. Tracking data from medical implants or physical devices, real-time monitoring data from wearables, simulation information from virtual objects, chronological data and medical history from medical centers, and service information from services and applications or structures that connect the physical and digital spaces are included in the health data.

DTH's working methodology is divided into four parts. First, using sophisticated modeling techniques or tools. Some of these tools are SysML, Modelica, SolidWorks, 3DMAX, and AutoCAD. These tools precise the digital twin models equivalent to actual entity objects. Second, in order to preserve real-time interaction between physical and virtual objects, data should be connected via healthcare IoT and mobile network platforms. Third, to guarantee that the model is accurate, simulation is evaluated by fast implementation and validation. Fourth, model adaptation must be conducted out on a continual basis according to the demands and real situations in order to optimize and improve the digital twin models. The information from the models is then transmitted to the physical things and service operations, resulting in better aged healthcare solutions.

In healthcare, the digital twin may be used for two different purposes: hospital administration and planning, and patient care. Various probable solutions, including bed allocation, staff appointments, medical simulation, and virtual drug studies, may be tried in virtual settings using the DTH prior to planning and executing actual changes. The various elements of digital twin in healthcare are depicted in Figure 1.2.

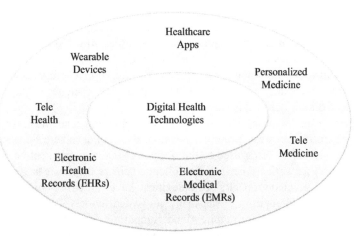

Figure 1.2   Digital twin technologies in healthcare

The characteristics of the digital twin are defined in the following points:

1. **Real-time response:** Different forms of physical object data must be connected, and real-time routing of physical objects can be possible.
2. **Interface and interconnectivity:** It occur throughout the lives of physical items and evolves with it.
3. **Adaptation and refinements:** Depending on an adaptive virtual modeling, it will describe and also improve physical objects characteristics.

1.3   Research on digital twin technologies

From its very start of invention, digital twins have shown to be a valuable and viable technology, particularly in healthcare. With the growing attention in combining digital twins with medical field among researchers and industry in latest years, this subsection compiles the most up-to-date investigations in this area.

The authors [2] suggested a general framework for digital twin in medical systems relying on self-adaptation and autonomous computing concepts, which allows for persistent monitoring and prognosis of the patient's state. They illustrated a persuasive case in controlling diabetic chronic illness to support their strategy. But they did not implement it in terms of operational effectiveness.

In [3], they have developed a digital twin system using cloud storage system for monitoring the elderly medical care services. By merging the cloud-based platform with the D4 model that was first introduced, they created a reference framework named Cloud-DTH. The goal of this combination is to make calculation and administration in healthcare systems easier. There are also two case studies that show how such cloud-DTH type paradigm offers personalized healthcare. Furthermore, there was no assessment of performance or outcome in the case studies. It also did not say if the forecast was based on AI or machine learning methods. The use of self-learning approaches to control the formation of digital twin in smart healthcare systems has been unproductive.

Karakra *et al.* [4] have presented an implementation to monitor quality healthcare. Employing discrete-event modeling techniques and IoT applications, the authors had created new hospital digital twin platform. Using actual information and a forecast decision support framework, the hospital's facilities system has been streamlined. With numerous scenarios, the FlexSim HC program was utilized to assess the practicality of the suggested technique. In the suggested paradigm, the presence of digital twin is unclear.

Zarrin *et al.* [5] proposed the concept of employing machine learning algorithms to identify seizures before they develop. Examining seizure signals obtained from DRE victims is being used to build this. A simulated gradient-based deeper spiking neural network framework for epileptic seizure diagnosis has indeed been created. The created model's complexities have still not been evaluated. Furthermore, the integration of the many suggested models with artificial neural circuits is safe and does not require cloud computing. Furthermore, the algorithm was trained with a small collection of data, which might lead to an overestimation of the performance of the system.

The study reported in [6] used digital twin to construct a robust, efficient, and reliable platform for individualized medicare. As a result, a digital twin paradigm for lung cancer victim behavior is being developed, with the goal of giving precise diagnostic data. The suggested structure additionally includes generative adversarial networks (GANs), which allowed for total confidentiality of health information as well as the creation of adaptable models for creating fake patients.

In [7–9], they employed wearable devices and artificial intelligence for obtaining and analyzing human data to imitate aspects of health including emotion detection, user intent detection, and behavioral motivational comprehension. Additionally, facilitated new games that assist artists in shaping their originality. Eventually, conduct long-term monitoring systems and provide suggestions to assist consumers in improving their wellbeing.

For the medical IoT and big data challenges, Ma *et al.* [10] presented a design methodology. It features remote health monitoring, clinical diagnosis services, mobile health equipment, LTE-based telehealth, and robot-assisted emotional contact. Those researches are lacking in their applicability to digital twin and duplication.

Similarly, Piacentino and Angulo [11] suggested utilizing GANs to create fake imagery to anonymize patient records in the health industry and to prevent the danger of critical data leaks. For false data creation, various GAN networks have really been trained. According to the study, multilayer neural networks can assist with unpredictable data that requires a complex GAN structure.

Ref. [12] proposes a wearable medicare platform to increase both QoE and QoS of the health sector professional. This idea proposes smart clothes that can be washable with detectors, transducers, and cables which acquire biological parameters and use cloud-based advanced algorithms to anticipate emotional condition.

Various health-oriented research [13–15] were suggested in the field to see if handling health records, participatory patient-centric health services provision, and edge computing medical service may help with resource management.

Different sectors, including visualization tools and industries, have included digital twin [16, 17]. Researchers revealed a digital twin architecture for industry that replicated the operations of an actual production line. Digital twin was already embedded inside the physical system's interconnects to provide additional services, such as scheduling orders and specifying product specification. As can be observed from these works, digital twin investigation has grown in recent years, with contemporary publications mostly proposing conceptual frames and models [18]. Various publications have addressed the issue of the digital twin in smart healthcare systems to date.

1.4   Digital twin sectors in healthcare

In four primary areas, we will focus on digital twin clinical activities:

- Digital patients
- The pharmaceutical business
- Healthcare facilities
- Smart wearables

1.4.1   Digital patient

In 2018, Chinese researchers published studies to better understand how memory and neural systems are linked, as well as to develop a precise multi-dimensional brain (i.e. three) model of the mind of human. They carried out various experiments in the disciplines of neuroscience analytics and artificial intelligence to understand much related to the challenging issues in the study. Simultaneously, two American programmers, the Brain Initiative and the Human Brain Project, have been launched to understand the biological brain's anatomy and interconnections and transfer them to computers. The Human Brain Project has a subproject called the Blue Brain Project [19]. The Blue Brain Cell Atlas initiative seems to be the most significant and easily available resource for documenting the quantity, classifications, and positions of cells in the entire parts of the mouse brain. This project team was the first research group to publish a three-dimensional anatomy of the entire mouse brain [20]. Figure 1.3 shows model of the blue brain.

A further project in the area of medical involves the US Military and the University of Nevada collaborating to construct virtual twins of servicemen. Different imaging modalities, like MRI, can be used to generate digital twins of servicemen. As a result, it has been stated that organs could be printed using the 3D printing technology using digital twins replicas in the event of an impairment/injury. Sim & Cure is the first firm to commercialize a patient-based simulation

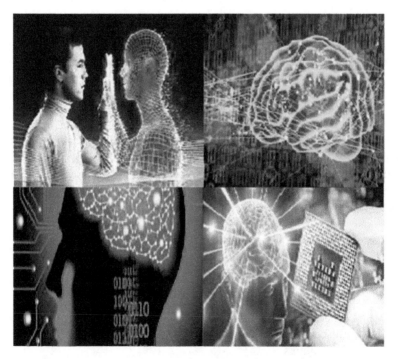

Figure 1.3   Blue brain model in digital twin technologies

model that predicts the implantation of medical equipment for aneurysm therapy (flow guidance, intravenous device, laser beam stent). Sim & Size replicates every dimension and device information depending on the patient's specific anatomy to offer the information needed prior to implant sizing. Over than 250 medical centers and 2,000 surgeries were modeled in 25 countries with the goal of reducing the error margin. The company's first and second key ambitions are individualized medicine and developing a treatment plan by securing the therapy administered to the patient. After that, the patient is prepped for surgery, and Sim & Cure's novel technology [21] uses 3D rotating angiography to produce a three-dimensional model of the aneurysm and adjacent blood arteries. Sim & Cure tool integrates the artery model and displays it to the surgeons, who selects the points that define the appropriate ideal spot on the arteries and the dimensions of the implant to be positioned.

The clinician may rotate and magnify the images using ANSYS software to properly comprehend the link between implants and aneurysm. Color labeling can be utilized to illustrate where implants make contact with the embolism. Any gap between the implants and the arteries is visible in a cross-sectional image. Based on the hardware, every simulation takes about 10–25 sec. Other devices and sizes can be simply selected and simulated by the surgeon for studying to see which will deliver the greatest results. The doctor can conduct the simulation procedure, choose the best gadget, and start the operation in less than 5 min [22]. When physical parts in devices had to be replaced, the digital twin method can identify this early.

Furthermore, Philips developed the "HeartModel[A.I.]," an individualized digital twin of the human heart, that is a significant advance toward the advancements in the digital patient, beginning with the problem of whether this idea is feasible to detect and treat diseases in the inner organs earlier they arise. Heart model converts the general model to an individualized model depending on the distinct photos of the heart. The Philips Heart Navigator software, which was also devised by Philips, integrates computed tomography (CT) images acquired prior to the clinical operation in a single view of a patient's heart structure with a layer of live X-ray information obtained throughout clinical surgery. This feature is useful for the surgeons in assisting and choosing the proper device by reducing prior operation planning thereby it allows for real-time 3D positioning of the gadget during surgery [23]. Figure 1.4 illustrates the framework of the Philips Model.

Siemens Healthineers develops smart algorithms capable of creating digital organ designs from vast volumes of data. Various methods for cardiovascular resynchronization treatment were evaluated by medical experts at Heidelberg University as a part of a research effort. Patients with persistent heart problems may benefit from this therapeutic approach. Cardiologists used electrodes to imitate the heart's electrical impulses in a computer environment, using an artificial intelligence framework to build the digital twin. First and completely mimicked heart was generated using MR scans and ECG readings. It reduces effort in order to receive a clear assessment as well as conducting several medication trials owing to the digital twin.

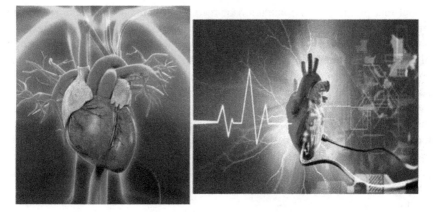

Figure 1.4   Framework of Philips Model in digital twin technologies

Siemens Healthineers Turkey talks over innovative medical technology and imaging solutions that will help to digitize the worldwide involvement. TURKRAD, the 40th National Congress of Radiology, was established in 2019. Siemens Healthineers, which is taking part in this activity under the phrase "We are Shaping the Future in Health," fascinates many people and helps to explore more about this digital twin technology and several other products, and endures to work to bring this technology in other industries supporting the health sector. After the first research in the digital twin, which involved heart modeling, the business is now working on constructing digital twins of all other parts, such as the brain. Because of pre-operative visualization and 3D imaging, digital twins, that are commonly employed by cardiologists, produce superior results. This device, which offers practitioners and cardiac surgeons a lot of convenience, especially when it comes to treating structural heart problems in neonates, was demonstrated at TURKRAD 2019.

For participants who wish to witness their basic digital twins, Siemens Turkey Healthineers had established a showcase. The app, which received a lot of courtesy, has been portrayed as a pictorial demonstration of the digital revolution of healthcare, also a path of complex and individualized medicine. While looking at researchers working for digital patients, the most of them are focusing on creating digital twins of specific organs rather than producing a digital twin of the whole human biological system. It is hardly too far away from doing research on unified digital twins, in which the volume of investigations on the subject tends to grow and linkages among various organs may be observed.

1.4.2   Pharmaceutical industry

Longevity companies and academics are observing the biological processes from the molecular layer to discover in what way the ageing proceeds and they are trying to identify the correct drugs as well as therapies to slowdown the aging process. Various researches are also done on improving drug manufacturing procedures and customized medicine challenges. In parallel to these areas, the University of Amsterdam's Computational Science Laboratory researches urban complex networks, computational financing, bioinformatics, complex adaptive theories, and cognitive bio-medicinal factors.

The European CompBioMed project [23], where an experimental research group contributed, is apprehensive with the application of digital human, because every individual's natural life and their metabolism is unique, treatment processes and medications should be tailored to the individual, and variations in the effectiveness of the internal organs could even be observed with the help of a virtual twin formed by using the genetic code present in the people's DNA. A short video was produced to provide knowledge in this topic. Because the impacts of drugs on patient's physical system, these are first viewed through the virtual twin, the video also offers advice on how to apply proper therapy to them.

A virtual twin explains how pharmaceuticals influence the proper places, what food, exercising, and behaviors are required to increase quality of living, and even how bones may be reinforced. Dassault Systèmes together with the US Food and Drug Administration linked a 5-year collaboration in 2014 for the SIMULIA Living Heart proposal, which is the first research in employing digital twin technique expressly to investigate how an organ interacts with drugs. It is hoped that this study would minimize the number of animal testing drug trials. SIMULIA Living Heart is considered as one of the digital twin simulations which was produced by mimicking a human heart and has been verified against a number of clinical metrics.

Educators, cardiology researchers, medical products developers, doctors, and many other organizations collaborated to build the model. Doctors used computer simulation to observe what they could not see owing to the movement of heart tissue and to investigate the heart's intricate anatomy by testing with the very same organ replica. By providing patient-specific physical signs, it leads to tailored therapy and potential investigation in future medical therapies. IBM hopes to replicate biochemical body functions by using the artificial intelligence approaches to identify malignant tissues and cells in previous health data using the supercomputer named Watson.

The interrelationship between the 37 trillion cells which constitute the human body, on the other hand, is a tough to comprehend and track process. Although each cell has its own unique traits, it all shares the same hereditary data. Cells that have been damaged for a variety of causes might divide and grow uncontrolled, leading to tumor development. Using 800 genes plus 45 biochemical processes, the Alacris computer model can analyze the evolving conditions by determining why and how the cell develops and the factors that lead to its demise. Thus, these digital twins from patients may be used to test which drugs can prevent harmful cells from proliferating excessively.

The nasal mucosa tumor in the frontal sinus cannot be eliminated by chemotherapy, immunology, or radiotherapy during the typical treatment procedure in a cancer case group. However, after administering a drug produced specifically for breast and bowel cancer and developed using the concept of digital twin, the frequency of dividing cells reduced to 15%. Data acquired from biopsies of the tumor after several months reveal that the frequency of dividing cells dropped to 70%. Depending on collected data and medical records, Semic Health's Digital Body Total has evolved the digital twin of Artificial Intelligence-based patient's bio components, parts, or molecular structures to assist diagnose present medical disorders and anticipate potential health concerns.

Testing eventualities such as modifying pharmaceutical doses for the cure of diseases like various cancers, hepatic sclerosis, Acute Myocardial Infarction, and Alzheimer's Disease in Digital System can help make realistic forecasts. Takeda Pharmaceuticals has converted to digital twin system manufacturing to reduce pharmaceutical procedures that require years to achieve in market. Takeda Pharmaceuticals has also undertaken several endeavors to give transformational treatments to patients all around the world. It can produce accurate input–output predictions regarding biological events that are hard to simulate using machine learning approach by establishing digital twins of entire functions.

With such an innovative approach focused on the digital clone of this pharmaceutical production process, Atos and Siemens are collaborating in this sector to optimize the processes in the manufacturing. It strives to deliver improved flexibility and agility for complex causes in the development of medicinal commodities with the "Process Digital Twin" for medicine manufacturing, which is now being used in various healthcare industries and assisted by IoT, artificial intelligence, as well as in the advanced data analysis. The project produced digital twins of physical systems with the goal of exploiting real-time data to tackle challenges in medication manufacturing and efficiency. The various parameters used for sensing the physical factors are shown in Figure 1.5.

To take advantage of the digital twin model's performance in the field of pharmaceutical business, extensive research has been conducted in areas where

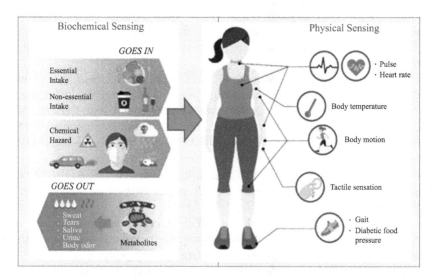

Figure 1.5   Health's digital body predictions

parameters are represented, such as the medication supply chain, human DNA, parts, and cell biology. Improvements in such areas are likely to aid in the pharmaceutical industry's projected customized medicine and product launch procedures.

1.4.3 Hospital

In the clinical setting of Mater Private Hospitals from Ireland, digital twin research was conducted with Siemens Healthineers [23] to enhance hospital procedures owing to rising patient needs, increased waiting times, and other factors. A digital twin for the radiology unit was developed as a part of the project and that was supplied with real data. Several predictions have been achieved using the digital twin, and potential conflicts were explored on this twin. From the results obtained by the digital twin, the modifications that needed to happen in the hospital's radiology department's management and coordination were defined. The 3D model of the hospital is picturized in Figure 1.6.

Many medical systems and asset management, including this study, are projected to adopt digital twins. It may be employed in a variety of situations, including resolving resource shortages in medical services even during COVID-19 epidemic.

1.4.4 Wearable technologies

General Electric Health Innovation Village largely encourages 26 indigenous businesses in various domains of the healthcare in Helsinki. This unit works in

Figure 1.6   3D animation (hospital)

collaboration with Startup Health, which is one of the world's biggest health centers, situated in the United States. In addition, GE takes a unique strategy by delivering healthcare to the cloud. Scientists in Helsinki are keeping a close eye on patients and developing wireless gadgets which will not surpass a bandwidth limit in the near future and continually communicate data like pulse rate, blood pressure, and breathing to the cloud. Digital twins of every person may be generated using this data to be examined by software, and the network is striving to build software that can notify clinicians in unanticipated situations.

Sooma, a smart wearable firm that develops gadgets that imitate brain electrical impulses to treat mental illness and other neuropsychiatric diseases, is one of the entrepreneurs who provides some meaningful information which will alter the user's experiences in the healthcare market. For 2 weeks, patients used these gadgets for 30 min every day, 5 days a week. The patient implants one electrode on each one of his temples which transmits the electrical impulses to the central brain. The positive electrode placed in the patient's body stimulates instantaneous activity in the brain, that is beneficial in the treatment of depression. Research suggests that cerebral activity and metabolism in depressed people is diminished or hindered. It is feasible to resume normal brain processes and lessen depression symptoms by simulating these regions.

Patients can sometimes be tracked at home using the Sooma Software Suite. On the patient's phone, an application is deployed that allows him to submit data on his everyday emotions and sentiments. All of this information is updated and transferred to a cloud that the physician may view remotely. The doctor may track the therapy progress and make modifications to the treatment regimen by evaluating these information and simulations. While Sooma expects this technology to be used in hospitals shortly, it hopes to provide an alternative to antidepressants and to reduce medication adverse effects by lowering drug consumption.

Myontec [23] develops products which utilize muscle stimulation system and electromyography (EMG) to find a novel aspect in recognizing muscle behavior. The company analyzes muscle activity and responses to workouts in relation to the overall functioning of the human body, then transmits the data to a digital environment using equipment positioned between the threads, and creates most appropriate exercises based on the available information. The firm analyzes the user's actions using custom shorts, determines the muscle performance threshold, improves training effectiveness, and also offers data about warming and cooling intervals while lowering the danger of damage in the muscles.

The Myontec Mbody Pro product's technology monitors the electrical impulses of the muscles while training and offers information on how these will behave in different situations. This product consists of fusion of sensors that captures and analyses EMG data from the muscles, as well as pulse rate and heart rhythm from the cardiac side. It helps consumers to perform their working approaches healthy and productive, as well as to find and avoid the physical health issues like muscle imbalances and irregularities. Extending and merging wearable technology that would allow patients for continuous monitoring of both physical and psychological factors and this can also help to construct and develop more inventive and

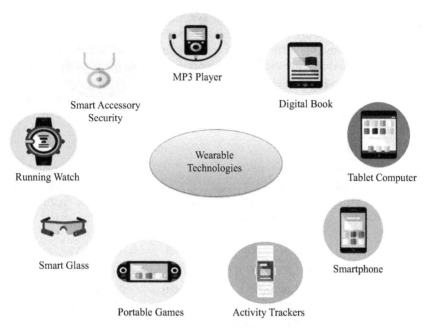

Figure 1.7 Wearable technologies in realistic world

comprehensive digital twins. Wearable digital twin innovations will be used in the future years to investigate modifications in the musculoskeletal system of individuals with flexibility problems and even paralysis. The various forms of wearables for the healthcare are shown in Figure 1.7.

1.5 Challenges and issues in implementation

1.5.1 Trust

Because the digital twin depends on gadgets to transport data, the digital twin prospect of using a virtual duplicate for a real thing has a possible void always because these gadgets may crash or disconnect for any cause. Digital twin also needs the participation of field personnel. To provide correct feedback, modify, and safeguard data, these people must be competent and ethical. Furthermore, applying AI to real-world situations poses a significant hurdle. As a result, establishing trust at all levels and for every component will help to establish trust in the digital twin idea in general. This necessitates the establishment of standards, increased awareness, and technological advancements, all of which need time and effort.

1.5.2 Security and privacy

As with information management, protecting the digital twin systems against illegal access, misuse, alteration, or disclosure are the main issues. Malicious hackers and digital intrusions will focus digital twin systems because they process enormous amounts of personal and confidential data. Furthermore, the inclusion of IoT sensing devices will increase the difficulty of implementing effective security because standard security measures may not always work with them. Management of specific user data might lead to regulatory issues. Compliance with privacy standards like the GDPR in Europe or constraints imposed by relevant national protection laws could constitute a need, adding to the design challenges of digital twin systems.

1.5.3   Standardization

Another major issue is a lack of regulations. Confidentiality, transparency, communications, rights, contributor procedures, data transfer, and synchronization between the virtual and real worlds are all affected by this aspect. Setting worldwide standards would assist to accelerate the spread of the digital twin trend and bring it closer to reality.

1.5.4   Diversity and multisource

Another issue that digital twins face is data variety and numerous sources. This is owing to the many sources via which data is collected, as well as the variety of data kinds. Due to the heterogeneity of the data, it is difficult to analyze and develop machine learning models.

Despite developments in smarter healthcare services, the four issues listed below continue to exist.

- Healthcare centres and patients do not have regular real-time contact.
- There has yet to be a true convergence of healthcare physical systems and information systems.
- The precision of the senior patient emergency warning function is insufficient, and there is no smart supervision, involving adaptive monitoring, analysis, and administration.
- Current methods or platforms do not offer ongoing healthcare management services to the elderly throughout their lives.

References

[1]   H. Elayan, M. Aloqaily and M. Guizani, "Digital Twin for intelligent context-aware IoT healthcare systems," *IEEE Internet of Things Journal*, vol. 8, no. 23, pp. 16749–16757, 2021, doi:10.1109/JIOT.2021.3051158.

[2]   L. F. Rivera, M. A. Jiménez, P. Angara, N. M. Villegas, G. Tamura, and H. A. Müller, "Towards continuous monitoring in personalized healthcare through digital twins," in *Proceedings of the 29th Annual International Conference on Computer Science and Software Engineering*, 2019, pp. 329–335.

[3]   Y. Liu, L. Zhang, Y. Yang, *et al.*, "A novel cloud-based framework for the elderly healthcare services using digital twin," *IEEE Access*, vol. 7, pp. 49088–49101, 2019.

[4] A. Karakra, F. Fontanili, E. Lamine, J. Lamothe, and A. Taweel, "Pervasive computing integrated discrete event simulation for a hospital digital twin," in *Proceedings of IEEE/ACS 15th International Conference on Computer Systems and Applications (AICCSA)*, 2018, pp. 1–6.

[5] P. S. Zarrin, R. Zimmer, C. Wenger, and T. Masquelier, "Epileptic seizure detection using a neuromorphic-compatible deep spiking neural network," in *Proceedings of International Work-Conference on Bioinformatics and Biomedical Engineering*, 2020, pp. 389–394.

[6] C. Angulo, L. Gonzalez-Abril, C. Raya, and J. A. Ortega, "A proposal to evolving towards digital twins in healthcare," in *Proceedings of International Work-Conference on Bioinformatics and Biomedical Engineering*, 2020, pp. 418–426.

[7] M. Chen, J. Zhou, G. Tao, J. Yang, and L. Hu, "Wearable affective robot," *IEEE Access*, vol. 6, pp. 64766–64776, 2018.

[8] M. Chen, Y. Jiang, Y. Cao, and A. Y. Zomaya, "Creative Bioman: Brain and body wearable computing based creative gaming system," 2019. [Online]. Available: arXiv:1906.01801.

[9] M. Chen, Y. Jiang, N. Guizani, *et al.*, "Living with I-Fabric: smart living powered by intelligent fabric and deep analytics," *IEEE Network*, vol. 34, no. 5, pp. 156–163, 2020.

[10] Y. Ma, Y. Wang, J. Yang, Y. Miao, and W. Li, "Big health application system based on health Internet of Things and big data," *IEEE Access*, vol. 5, pp. 7885–7897, 2016.

[11] E. Piacentino and C. Angulo, "Generating fake data using GANs for anonymizing healthcare data," in *Proceedings of International Work-Conference on Bioinformatics and Biomedical Engineering*, 2020, pp. 406–417.

[12] M. Chen, Y. Ma, Y. Li, D. Wu, Y. Zhang, and C.-H. Youn, "Wearable 2.0: enabling human-cloud integration in next generation healthcare systems," *IEEE Communications Magazine*, vol. 55, no. 1, pp. 54–61, 2017.

[13] P. Van Gorp and M. Comuzzi, "Lifelong personal health data and application software via virtual machines in the cloud," *IEEE Journal of Biomedical and Health Informatics*, vol. 18, no. 1, pp. 36–45, 2013.

[14] L. D. Serbanati, F. L. Ricci, G. Mercurio, and A. Vasilateanu, "Steps towards a digital health ecosystem," *Journal of Biomedical Informatics*, vol. 44, no. 4, pp. 621–636, 2011.

[15] S. Oueida, Y. Kotb, M. Aloqaily, Y. Jararweh, and T. Baker, "An edge computing based smart healthcare framework for resource management," *Sensors*, vol. 18, no. 12, p. 4307, 2018.

[16] J. Bao, D. Guo, J. Li, and J. Zhang, "The modelling and operations for the digital twin in the context of manufacturing," *Enterprise Information Systems*, vol. 13, no. 4, pp. 534–556, 2019.

[17] M. Raza, P. M. Kumar, D. V. Hung, W. Davis, H. Nguyen, and R. Trestian, "A digital twin framework for industry 4.0 enabling next-gen manufacturing," in *Proceedings of the 9th International Conference on Industrial Technology and Management (ICITM)*, 2020, pp. 73–77.

[18] X. Zhou, W. Liang, K. I.-K. Wang, H. Wang, L. T. Yang, and Q. Jin, "Deep-learning-enhanced human activity recognition for Internet of healthcare things," *IEEE Internet of Things Journal*, vol. 7, no. 7, pp. 6429–6438, 2020.

[19] "Blue Brain Project – EPFL," EPFL. www.epfl.ch/research/domains/blue-brain/ (accessed Sep. 27, 2020).

[20] Q. Luo, J. Wu, C. Erö, M.-O. Gewaltig, D. Keller, and H. Markram, "A cell Atlas for the mouse brain," *Front. Neuroinformatics*, www.frontiersin.org, vol. 12, p. 84, 2018, doi:10.3389/fninf.2018.00084.

[21] "Sim&Cure – Sim&Cure." https://sim-and-cure.com/ (accessed Sep. 24, 2020).

[22] M. Sanchez, "Brain Trust for Aneurysm Treatment | Ansys Advantage," *Ansys.* https://www.ansys.com/content/dam/resource-center/article/ansys-advantage-best-of-healthcare-aa-2018.pdf (accessed Sep. 24, 2020).

[23] T. Erol, A. F. Mendi, and D. Doğan, "The Digital Twin revolution in healthcare," in *2020 4th International Symposium on Multidisciplinary Studies and Innovative Technologies (ISMSIT)*, 2020, pp. 1–7, doi:10.1109/ISMSIT50672.2020.9255249.

[24] M. Sathyamoorthy, S. Kuppusamy, A. Nayyar, *et al.*, "Optimal emplacement of sensors by orbit-electron theory in wireless sensor networks,' *Wireless Network*, vol. 28, pp. 1605–1623, 2022.

[25] M. Arvindhan, D. Rajeshkumar, and L. P. Anupam, "A review of challenges and opportunities in machine learning for healthcare." *Exploratory Data Analytics for Healthcare,* pp. 67–84, 2021.

[26] R. K. Dhanaraj, K. Lalitha, S. Anitha, S. Khaitan, P. Gupta, and M. K. Goyal, "Hybrid and dynamic clustering based data aggregation and routing for wireless sensor networks," *Journal of Intelligent & Fuzzy Systems*, vol. 40, no. 6, pp. 10751–10765, 2021.

[27] S. Malathy, M. Santhiya, C. N. Vanitha, and R. R. Karthiga, "Diabetes disease prediction using artificial neural network with machine learning approaches," in *2021 5th International Conference on Electronics, Communication and Aerospace Technology (ICECA)*, 2021, pp. 1–5, doi: 10.1109/ICECA52323.2021.9676094.

[28] M. Santhiya, S. Saranya, S. Vijayachitra, C. B. Lavanya and M. Rajarajeswari, "Application of voter insertion algorithm for fault management using triple modular redundancy (TMR) technique," in *2021 Third International Conference on Intelligent Communication Technologies and Virtual Mobile Networks (ICICV)*, 2021, pp. 578–583, doi:10.1109/ICICV50876.2021.9388450.

[29] V. V. Priya, P. Natesan, K. Venu, and E. Gothai, "Improving convergence speed of the neural network model using meta heuristic algorithms for weight initialization," in *2021 International Conference on Computer Communication and Informatics (ICCCI)*, 2021, pp. 1–6, doi:10.1109/ICCCI50826.2021.9402415.

Chapter 2

Convergence of Digital Twin, AI, IOT, and machine learning techniques for medical diagnostics

M.N. Kavitha[1] and S. Sujitha[1]

In the recent years, Digital Twin (DT) has gained a remarkable place in the top ten technology trends. But digital twinning alone cannot provide solution to many applications. Hence, the integration of DT with the technologies like Internet of Things (IoT), Artificial Intelligence (AI), Cloud Computing, machine learning (ML), Big Data analytics, and Deep Learning (DL) techniques paves way to new opportunities and provides a solution to many research problems in diverse sectors. The DT provides an accumulation of data between the real and digital system in both paths. This chapter focuses on the definition, architecture, components, and different types of DT. It also emphasizes on the convergence of digital twinning with other technologies for solving many research problems and application areas in medical diagnosis, healthcare, and others. It also highlights on the issues and challenges pertaining to DT and its supporting technologies. Finally, a case study pertaining to manufacturing sector using DT is presented.

2.1 Introduction

An extremely worthy technological transformation is achieved because of the linkage among the digital and physical world. It has marked a vital role in improving the convergence with the support of technologies like Big Data analytics, Artificial Intelligence, IoT, and so on. In recent years, DT technology has set its foot in almost all domains. The progresses pertaining to industry 4.0 models has enabled its success primarily in the healthcare, manufacturing industry, aerospace, retail, and smart cities. The Internet of Thing's ridiculous environment combined with data analytics affords a vital resource for abnormality detection in patients, traffic management, fault detection, prognostic maintenance, and error detection in smart cities and manufacturing processes and so on. The seamless combination of IoT and data analytics has many challenges that can be handled by DT by the formation of a

[1]Department of CSE, Kongu Engineering College, India

connected physical and virtual version. A DT background permits fast assessment and also providing real-time conclusions prepared via precise analytics.

In recent healthcare practices, the digital devices with their services provides a vital part in supporting both patients and therapists for collecting the data for diagnosis and providing ways to decision making in disease diagnosis and others. In the healthcare domain, many research works are done that emphasis on refining diagnostics, drug efficacy, and treatment provision essential tasks like, data analytics and their modeling are as well driven by means of technology. The DT technology emergence has been primarily engaged by business and industrial enterprises, is been publicized as a stimulating and promising method which can add advance efforts in therapeutic discoveries, and also progresses medical and public health results. The goal of DT is revolutionizing healthcare for the benefit of individuals and the world through DT creation i.e. virtual models of individuals that permit analysis of the individually best treatment, health prevention, or maintenance measure. In healthcare, DT can be used for many purposes like diagnosis and treatment decision support, patient monitoring, surgery simulation, drug development and discovery, medical devices design and optimization, and so on. DTs have on the go to support physicians recognize their patient situations, even the novel ones such as COVID-19's influence on the lungs. In healthcare areas like cardiology department, the DT technology is considered as a blessing to better treat hereditary heart defects. Using this technology, we can duplicate unusual heart conditions like valves that are retreated from a healthy heart, and also virtually check certain treatments as an imitation before administering them to a patient. DTs are employed to create digital representations of healthcare data, such as human physiology, lab results, and hospital environments using computer models.

2.2   DT technology

The idea of living in the virtual simulation of the real world has become a reality. Appreciation goes to DT technology using which the engineers can produce virtual models of objects or systems. A DT can be defined as a digital duplication of physical entities like people, devices, systems or processes which support industries perform model-driven decision making. There are multiple goals of a DT and has set its foot in almost all domains and it can run economic simulations which may otherwise be expensive to simulate without a DT. The IT professionals and data scientists are using the data to create models that imitates the real-world resources in digital space. The IoT sensors and other information are used by DT to assemble real-time data for exact modeling of resources which are then combined with AI-driven analytics tools in a digital setting.

Diverse types of DTs be present; however, the conceptual model consists of three parts: the real component in the physical space, the digital representation of the real component in the digital environment, and the relations between the two i.e. the data and information transferred between the physical and digital components (Figure 2.1). Data perceived from diverse measures are required to construct

REAL WORLD   **DIGITAL TWIN**

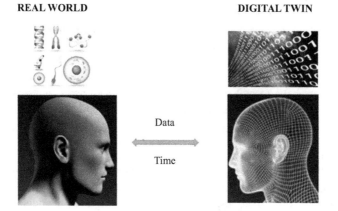

Data

Time

Figure 2.1   Components of DT

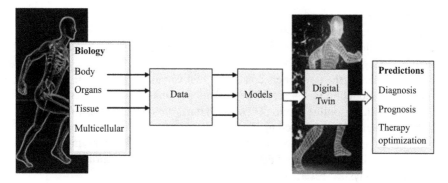

Figure 2.2   Diverse types of DTs may be perceived, enclosing the entire human body, a body system, an organ or a cell and can be employed for different predictions

digital illustrations of biological systems and human body. These models can be integrated with experimental data from individual patients. The predictions about diagnosis, prognosis, and optimization of therapeutic inventions can be derived using the DT (Figure 2.2).

The basic architecture of DT consists of sensor and other measurement technologies coupled with Internet of Things, Cloud Computing, ML, etc. The developers who build digital twins confirm that the virtual model can accept response from sensors which collect data from the real world. Thus the digital version can mimic and simulate the real-world version. A DT may be as complex or as simple as required, with different amounts of data shaping how precisely the model simulates the physical version.

2.2.1   Steps in DT creation

The digital resources can be built even before a resource is built actually. The process of creating a digital twin has basic steps:

Data collection

The developers have to collect a diverse data about an asset: physical characteristics, behavioral look, under specific conditions, support with similar assets, and more.

Constructing the model

A mathematical model is created using the gathered data and modeling software which precisely projects all the requisites of its physical equivalent. Model will have a matching form to the respective object, counting even the negligible details, and behaviors of the physical object. Virtual reality, augmented reality, 3D technologies, and many supports for visualization.

Fusion

The asset is then combined with the digital model to allow constant supervision in real time. For accomplishing this, the asset will have devices like sensors, trackers, and others which can transfer data to the IoT platform. It is then analyzed and visualized using the IoT platform.

    To summarize, the developers create a virtual version of a real-time product by using virtual modeling techniques. The sensors are linked to the objects to gather the diverse data in online mode. Then the data is uploaded to the IoT platform which is supported by cloud computing for processing, along with the ML or AI algorithms to assess and figure out the possible scenarios. By applying analytics into such models, engineers, and data scientists can acquire appropriate perceptions regarding the physical asset.

2.2.2   DT types and functions

DTs are categorized based on what they simulate (Figure 2.3). Product twins are the one which simulate distinct entities. Consider the example of manufacturers using a digital prototype for a particular product prior to developing the production line to examine the environment conditions and also the various issues that may occur. This inference helps to make the desired changes and build a more effective design

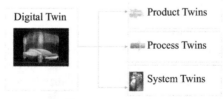

Figure 2.3   Types of DT

of products. These product twins may be employed to regulate the performance of the product in the real world. On the other hand, process twins are used for the simulation of processes; for example, manufacturing processes. There are various scenarios created of a production process in the virtual environment, to identify the events in different circumstances. Such scenarios help the industries to build well-organized production methodology. It also aids the industries to perform preventive maintenance, and avoids financial downtimes. Engineering operations are finished safely, fastly, and also efficiently. The system twins are replicas of the entire systems like a factory which assemble huge operational data created by the devices and the products in system, to achieve the insights and build new industry horizons that can optimize every process and enhance the integrity of the system.

DTs can be useful at various phases of product building which includes the design, creation, operation, and clearance. The design stage involves in creating various virtual model for the product to be developed which can assess and identify possible optimal technical solutions. An appropriate model is selected among them which is termed as the DT prototype (DTP). It comprises the facts required to define and build the physical variations of product samples. Next, the production stage aids to achieve the requisite features of the outcome using the DTP. DT instance (DTI) is used in the operation stage, which is a digital copy of a definite instance of a product related to the twin throughout its lifespan. If we consider them in human DT, DTI can be termed as identical replicas of the digital twin such that altogether fitting to the same individual, such as for application in personalized medicine which answer questions like "which medicine can be most profitable for a specific patient?" The DTI are created based on DTP and furthermore contains past facts of product manufacturing, statistics of failures, quality control, and many. During its operation, the DTI experiences related deviations of its physical sample. The disposal stage also involves the DTI. The DT aggregate (DTA) has an efficient system for information management which can operate several DTs belonging to a product family. They are called the aggregates of DT instances which belongs to different individuals, like sets including one family, or a whole population.

DTs may face several complexities, based on the necessities and the desired extent of information needs processing. While building a digital twin, it is important to choose among its functions, like if it will only observe the prototype, or gives a signal on observing any malfunctioning and recommend solutions depending on the advanced data analytics. The DTs may be employed to monitor, assess, and optimize the performance of their counterparts. Based on their functions, DTs can be distinguished as (shown in Figure 2.4):

Basic-level DTs – they accomplish supervising, supported by the sensors and other devices to obtain the data and a software is used to visualize it.

Middle-level DTs – they are furnished with the what-if type models that can alter operational situations to detect the best process configuration or asset.

Advanced-level DTs – they exploit few intelligent algorithms to do learning from gathered data, check issues, discover various potential solutions and pick the best fitting optimal solution. They are intended to provide for predictive maintenance.

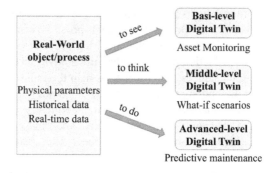

Figure 2.4   DT functions

2.3 DT and its supporting technologies – AI, Cloud computing, DL, Big Data analytics, ML, and IoT

DTs and AI have mutual relation and their integration contribute to build enormous applications. DTs can facilitate companies to produce simulation of data which may be applied to perform training of the AI or ML models. AI can be benefited from DTs since they can digitally build an environment for artificial learning test scenarios. Based on the utilities of these virtual environment, the engineers and data scientists make use of the AI/ML solutions. DTs can gain profit from artificial intelligence, i.e. AI–ML approaches enable industries to create few DTs and it also operates a huge amount of data gathered from DTs. For instance, by enabling the AI–ML capabilities with DTs, the engineers can speed up the design step by rapidly assessing the potential design alternatives. Artificial intelligence (AI) can be termed as the digital duplication of three humanoid cognitive abilities namely, learning ability, reasoning skill, and self-correction ability. Digital learning is defined as the assembly of guidelines, applied as an algorithm that translates the perceived facts into needed information. On the other hand, digital reasoning concentrates on picking exact guidelines to achieve the preferred target. The iterative steps in adopting to the results of learning and perception are focused in digital self-correction. All models based on AI tracks this method to create a smart system that implements a job that usually needs intelligence of human. Majority of AI-based systems depends upon the ML, data mining, DL, or other rules-based algorithms, while the remaining are based on knowledge and logic techniques. ML and DL are very famous subset of AI. ML is termed as a subset of AI that finds specific patterns in the real data to assist decision-making. If we are able to gather more data, the learning method tends to be much precise, placing Big Data significance [57–59,61]. ML can be categorized as:

1. Supervised learning method inputs data sets with the target being labeled for training the model to apply for classification or future predictions. Naive Bayes classifiers, Random forests, Decision trees, Regression, support vector machines (SVMs) are examples.

2. Unsupervised learning method that input unlabeled data sets and performs grouping or clustering of the datasets. Mixture models, K-means, and hierarchical clustering are examples.
3. Reinforcement learning method that inputs datasets without labels, performs specific actions, and it gives response to the AI system whether the action is reward/punish. Q-learning and Monte Carlo learning are examples of this method.

DL is termed as a learning technique and is also a subclass of ML which is inspired by biological neurons having the digital neurons in the hidden layers [56,60,63]. In this method, the perceived data are handled recursively by various layers, creating connections, and adjusting the weights of the neuron inputs for getting optimal results.

The primary domains where DTs are produced using the integration of AI–ML techniques include Prognostics and Health Management (PHM), healthcare, smart cities, smart manufacturing, automotive and transport, power and energy, and others. Big Data is considered as the top research trends in the recent years. Big Data analytics is termed as a method that examines "Big Data" and changes it to valued information, applying probabilistic, statistical, mathematical, or AI/ML model. It varies from a real data due to its huge velocity, heterogeneous variety, and huge volume. Generally these characteristics are called the "3Vs of Big Data." Veracity and Value are the additional two Vs appended to the list. The significance of big data is highlighted with the fourth V (value) which is an asset to the organization. Hence, to conclude a data as Big Data, it should be formed at very high-speed (velocity), enormous size (volume), and dissimilar with unstructured, semi-structured, or structured style (variety). But these 3Vs of Big Data also focuses on new challenges like storing, processing, capturing, sharing, analyzing, managing, and visualizing variety of data of high velocity and high volume. Different frameworks are considered for handling the big data and performing effective analytics and thereby supporting a wide range of applications [39–42].

Internet of Things (IoT) and the emerging sensor technologies in industrial environments have grasped their attention by many exciting applications, like monitoring of real-time devices, asset tracking at indoor, and outdoor. IoT devices enable the data collection during real-time which is significant for building digital twin of the real-time component, and also permit the performance improvement and optimization and also maintenance of the components by associating the real world to its digital version with the help of sensors and actuators. The IoT data is probably huge in nature, thus we can employ the Big Data analytics in the creation of a productive digital twin. There is high complexity in the industrial processes and the traditional techniques faces difficulty in detecting potential problems in the initial stages. Alternatively, these problems can be mined easily from the gathered data that provides knowledge and efficiency to industrial processes. Handling such huge data in the engineering and digital twin sectors need cutting-edge architectures, tools, algorithms, techniques, and frameworks. Zhang *et al.* [51] suggested a framework for big data processing that includes applications like smart

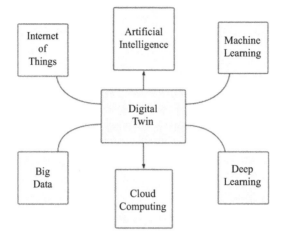

Figure 2.5   DT and its supporting technologies

production and maintenance for industries in a digital twin background. Cloud Computing technology is one among the top platform used for storing, processing, handling, and exploring big data [53]. Also, a DT system with knowledge and intelligence may be built using progressive AI/ML techniques on the composed data. Intelligence of such extent attained through letting DT to perceive better process strategy, fault detection, better resource allocation, etc. [54], forecast health and early maintenance [52], optimized planning, scheduling, assembly line, etc. [55], and performing decision making at real-time depending upon the real and/or DT data. IoT is applied to gather the enormous data or otherwise the Big Data from the real world. Then, this data is provided for AI model to construct the DT. Later, constructed digital twin is used to optimize other operations in the industry. Put together in a nutshell, the various technologies used to enable DT are presented in Figure 2.5.

2.4   DT integration with other technologies for medical diagnosis and health management

In healthcare, the major significance of DT using the AI–ML focuses on generating human DTs [38]. Constructing a complete imitation of the human body function-alities is impossible at present but we can construct the human DT emphasizing on biological aspects of the human body. Barricelli *et al.* [45] address on generating a DT for measuring fitness of athletes. Precisely, these DT classifies the athletes using the physical athlete data and their actions collected using IoT sensors and applying them to KNN [49] and SVM [50] for classification. Protein–protein interaction (PPI) networks applied to analyze a specific disease and give treatments to patients in the proposed work of Bjornsson *et al.* [36] where they implemented the model as AI-based system which observes the drug influence on the body using

ML tools, like decision trees, Naïve Bayes, DL, and others. Carson *et al.* [47] imitated the head actions of a human to perceive the sternness of carotid-stenosis that chooses constituents from a video of patient and applying principal component analysis to diagnose the sternness of carotid-stenosis, matching it to the digital version constituents. DL, ML, and other AI-based techniques can be employed to achieve better detection accuracy as recommended by the authors. Mazumder *et al.* [46] virtually duplicated the artificial PPG signals to build the DT of a cardio vascular system. Optimization of parameters are done to the DT created using Particle Swarm Optimization (PSO) algorithm that reduces the integral-squared error (ISE) available in the feature-set used to build artificial PPG signal.

The general data flow framework for constructing an AI-enabled DT is shown in Figure 2.6 that performs optimization, predictive analysis, fault detection, process planning, model design or maintenance by integrating with the Big Data, IoT, and cloud computing technologies.

Initially, the digital version is built by employing an AI model to the data perceived through the physical model. After producing DT, the facts from the physical and digital models are transferred to more AI models to attain desired business targets, like healthcare, optimization of the design, process planning, or prognostics and health management (PHM). Also, the outcomes can be additionally employed to improve the physical and DTs [36].

The digital-twinning provides larger opportunity in healthcare domain, since human-digital twins' support in daily physical fitness and its observing, premature disease detection, and observing the complete health of a person,

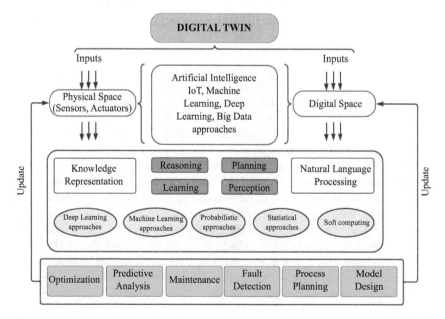

Figure 2.6   General data-flow framework of DT with its supporting technologies

specifically for the infants and aged people. Additionally, it is applied for treating the patients, by creating a DT for the patient. Constructing DT for particular body part or organic systems of human will definitely provide a revolt in the healthcare sector, like DT for heart, kidney, digestive system, endocrine system, female womb, liver, neural system, etc. The healthcare segment can be advantageous by generating digital twins for medicinal and surgical instruments, surgical processes, hospitals, etc.

The IoT devices are inexpensive and simpler to implement. In the healthcare sector, the improved connectivity is budding the DT use for many possible applications. A human DT gives a complete analysis of the body at real time. An important application of DT in healthcare is providing personalized medicine or drugs and simulation of the effects produced by certain drugs. Planning and performing surgical procedures are also an application of a DT fused together with AI/ML algorithms to perform smarter decision making and predictions. Most of the healthcare applications do not directly comprise the patients however are helpful for the patient's constant care and treatment. The simulation and act ability in real-time makes the DT backing with constant repair and prognostic maintenance of therapeutic equipment. The DT along with AI in medicinal setting have the prospective to make predictions or decisions based on past data as well as real-time data to save life and reducing risk. A digital twin of a person examines the daily health [43,44] and safety providing the prospective for a human, simulating the optimistic and destructive lifestyle changes and their impacts to the person. Like PHM [37] in manufacturing, a significant open research originates in removing the obstacles to model a human twin to monitor and maintain people's health. From daily-basis fitness monitoring to constant healthcare, the DT can act similar to PHM merging data analytics for ensuring the health and safety of the patients.

Cloud computing-based DT healthcare solution (CloudDTH) was proposed by Liu *et al.* [38] for aged people which offers a combination of real and digital systems to focus patients and health institution interaction in real time, and personalized drugs and treatment for the aged people. CloudDTH has a layered architecture issuing fitness resources, identifying therapeutic persons, virtualization, user-interface for efficient interaction between user and medical personnel, and providing security facilities to users. The CloudDTH records actual data at real-time using sensors for body temperature, ECG, pulse rate, BP, and executed in its cloud-based framework. Using TCP, the data perceived using sensors are transferred to the server in the cloud framework. If any deviations noticed like cardiac arrest, fainting, pressure variation, paralysis, etc., the detecting model makes examination on the obtained data, a high-frequency is transmitted to the doctors along with multiple feature observations of the patient. Researchers conducted a study involving the person with regular and irregular cardiac system. Initial inputs were sent to the system and processed to show an outcome with marks of arrhythmia in a patient along with the medication and medical suggestions. This cloud framework and their simulations gave a practical planning method for aged patients in clinics/hospitals, to avoid waiting in longer queues.

2.5 DT technology and its application

- DT technology has wide-range of immeasurable sectors like manufacturing industry, smart cities, retail area, automotive and aerospace, oil and gas, mining, and healthcare.
- There are huge circumstances in these spaces. Today in healthcare, all along with information from IoT.
- DT application in healthcare currently plays a significant part in the improvement of the health and medical sector.
- DT solutions can facility healthcare originalities and healthcare specialists to point out the behaviors to develop and streamline processes, promotion patient practice, reduce operating costs, and augment worth of care.
- The DT generates a physical prototype of spaces and developments where the charge, as well as the excellence optimization factors, are examined.
- The ultimate selected-based simulations leveraging a digital twin [8]. Additional, the DT usage in healthcare can advances with the up-and-coming technologies like real-time locating systems. That can propounds a powerful data resource and a means to test changes in the layout, process, etc.
- Although simulations and DTs both exploit digital models to replicate a system's several processes, a DT is actually the virtual environment, which makes it considerably comfortable for study [11]. The difference between DT and imitation is basically a matter of scale: although a simulation classically studies one particular development, a DT can itself run any amount of useful simulations in demand to review multiple processes.
- DT perception is the upcoming highest of the business areas, which helps to exactly predicting the current state and upcoming by analyzing their digital counter parts.
- By applying DTs, industries can increase better insights on product performance, improve client service, and make improved operational and deliberate decisions based on these insights [13].

Some of the on-going Digital Twin applications are shown in Figure 2.7. Some of the on-going Digital Twin application areas are discussed here.

2.5.1 DT application in manufacturing industry

2.5.1.1 DT for engineering

Earlier, developing a physical product is a difficult task but nowadays the DT tools makes it simple by using simulated prototype model that can be analyzed virtually via testing. This enhancement will help companies to validate and simulate each phase of their product growth and also can identify issues, potential failure once before the final product gets released [1]. The Twin Engineering will direct us to development sides that can be clearly understand the conceivable transforms in producing a product and their process can be influence production results also correct their producing operations regard this can be accomplish by the targeted enhancements. As an outcome, producers would be advance working processes and also decrease the overall charges on manufacturing.

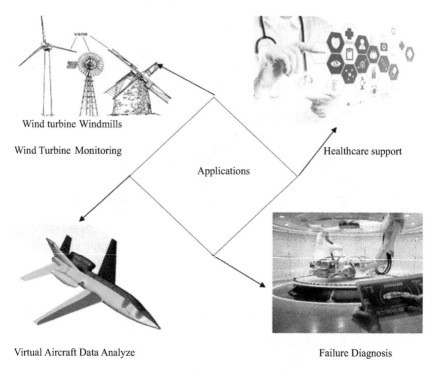

Wind turbine Windmills

Wind Turbine Monitoring

Healthcare support

Applications

Virtual Aircraft Data Analyze

Failure Diagnosis

Figure 2.7   Major application of DTs

2.5.1.2   DT for design customization

The clients get more suave, recent attention on demand of customized deliverable products on a rapid terms, the manufacturing industry converts more and modest. According to the Industry Week Special Research Statement convey that future industries of product manufacturing, industrial corporations which would be of any sizes can share a mutual energy on development of consolidation of customer relationships and production processes, where small industry emphasis their responsiveness to focus on client demand on product development with customization [12]. Also enabling the customization of process can permit the manufacturers to design and validate the items before manufacturing the real product which helps in satisfying the customer requirements.

2.5.1.3   DT technology for operations management

DT technology for the operations management (OM) OM can be used for predictive maintenance, developing operational effectiveness, and dynamic simulations as shown in Figure 2.8. The actual property is embedded with technologies like Internet of Things (IOT) where the sensors can dynamically link the data to the property in real-time scenario. Through this continuous data flow, the data gets updated and the digital replica can be built by using this real time data. Then, continually updated of dynamic information, based upon static information flow, that digital information replica can be built.

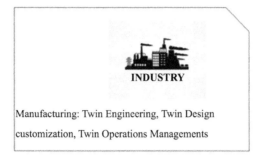

Figure 2.8   DT – industry

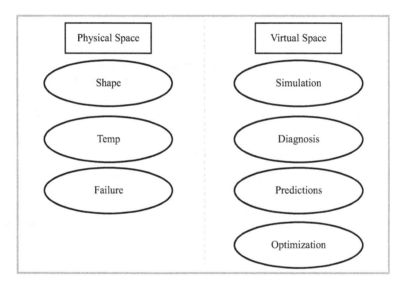

Figure 2.9   DT – automotive & aerospace

2.5.2   Applications of DT in automotive & aerospace

DT are extensively involved in aerospace and the automotive industries as depicted in Figure 2.9. DTs are used not simply in design customization and vehicle engineering, then are also for maintenance of aircraft and large transport are extensively. An aircraft tracking, weight monitoring, exact requirement of vehicle defect recognition and weather conditions, are the maximum projecting instances of the DT application in aerospace and automotive [31].

For example, in aerospace engineering, a physical twin is used before DT. In the 1970s, for instance, on Apollo 13, the earth was brilliantly used by NASA scientists to simulate the state of the ship and also discover responses when critical problems ascended. In Later 2002, the DT idea is introduced by John Vickers from NASA.

Nowadays the reputation of DTs in the automated aerospace industry is recognized by experts more than 76% of air force executives have thrown the vote for assurance in-favor to the digital twin, agreeing in Business Wire's survey report [11]. To predictive the forecasting any upcoming issue with the help of DTs, engineers can used including the engine, airframes, or other mechanisms to confirm the security of the people involved.

2.5.3   Medicine diagnosis and device development

DTs provides more efficiency solution in design healthcare products, development healthcare delivery, monitoring, and testing of novel based medications and medical products. Some of the examples are discussed below.

2.5.3.1   Diagnosis and treatment decision support – software as a medical device

The patient's DT feed from several health information sources such as image data, individual dimensions, laboratory report and results, and genetic will maintenance during diagnosis. The patient model will imitate the medical status of the individual patient as per taken from available data and suppose the misplaced parameters from statistical models [32]. A case, the pattern of cardiovascular imaging and control fluid dynamics permits non-invasive categorizations of flow arenas and the estimate the diagnostic system of measurement.

2.5.3.2   Patient monitoring – wearables sensors

Smaller and more easy wearables (sensors) drive be used to feed with real-time information our DT in the cloud. Through sufficient understanding of disease progression also continuous patient data gathering via heath monitor (biometric, behavioral, emotional, cognitive, psychosocial, etc.) [4]. Which can improve a models that identify indications at early phases, certain doctors also users the

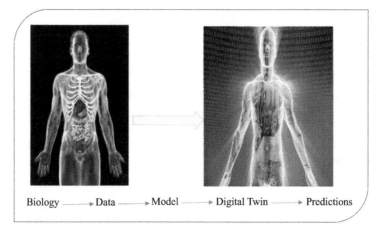

Biology ──→ Data ──→ Model ──→ Digital Twin ──→ Predictions

Figure 2.10   Medical – virtual infection – DTs

facility to analyze the patient earlier getting sick. Also, throughout the treatment, which will be capable of evaluating if the diagnostic is more effective.

There are already several sources of information that can feed digital twin, to adapt risk factors like medical records, report from the lab test results, pharmacy data, wellness, also disease management information, well-being device-generated information, and social determinants such as pin code, local weather, buying habits.

2.5.3.3 Surgery simulation – surgery risk assessment

Surgery by characterization is personalized. In the present state to the best outcome, surgery is tailored to the patient's requirements. Personalization is critical to develop intervention achievement and reduce patient risk. DTs is support by simulating an invasive clinical process to analyze the consequence before the treatment is selected [12]. From medical device choice (location, orientation, dimension, etc.) to surgical variable reasons (magnitude, angle, shape, etc.).

2.5.3.4 Medical devices design and optimization method – in MedTech

Two realms converge here. In one hand, which is the patient's digital twin that has to specific characteristic of the patient and, on the other hand, the medical device – DT that captures the device strategy as shown in Figure 2.10. Which can correlate both models to see suppose what happens when a particular device to be installed into a specific patient. This is because of populations which could be explored medically without harm, in such case who with infrequent syndromes or pediatric case.

DTs are also very useful to optimization tasks like the improvement of the device's performance by running hundreds of imitations with different conditions and different patients [14]. Also, with the emergence of 3D printing expertise, patient DTs can lead to a personalization of medical devices by designing unique designs for each patient.

2.5.3.5 Drug development and dosage optimization – silico clinical trials

We can treat computationally a digital twining with many of medications acceptable to recognize the best one or ones aimed that specific case. However, this does not need to stop at the medications that already exist. Which can create digital cohort of real-time patients data with different phenotypes, which share symptoms, also test new potential drugs to predict which one has more possibilities to accomplishment as well as the optimal dosage [34]. Advancing the first shoot will reduce the amount of clinical trials necessary.

The silico clinical trial will shed bright on processes that take years to remain observed in vivo or assess the danger of rare cases where is a randomized clinical study would need patients' thousands of observe just a few of such cases.

2.5.3.6 Regulatory decision making

Later 2016, both the European Parliaments and US Congress started to include modeling also simulation among the resources of proof that the governing procedure of biomedical products. Which a particular, the FDA has committed to change digital evidence into a valuable regulatory device because of its potential to cost-savings in evaluating medical devices.

Also, some healthcare organization have specified that the price for medical trials may be overtake profits, which will accelerate the shift of an industry toward reliable and other relevant information sources for indicating the efficiency and safety of medical products and pharmaceutical products.

2.5.4   Wind twin technology

- WT is specifically developed for wind twin-turbine industry.
- WT aimed is providing better solution to relieve the quickly increasing operational costs and maintenance related with consecutively wind turbines, and in return support to optimization of energy generated via wind by which provision of more reliable, in-service in the wind turbines.
- The project with connect digital twin expertise in the form of a digital software platform, high reliability, operational sensor are combined and provided information with virtual system prototype data for this drive of predictive maintenance of wind turbines (WT) [9].
- To facilitate this, the consortium members to be integrate and develop a number of acceptable technologies such as high-performance cloud computing, also a degradation model, system fault, visualization, and data analytics.
- "The data to be provided by which Wind Twin digital software platform has been potential to provide the wind-turbine manufacturing with many benefits," explains Senior Project Head, Condition and Structural Health Monitoring at the TWI.
- "It will enable wind-farm operators be a better diagnose performance variations of the complete wind turbine asset down to its integral individual components level; anticipate degradation also failures, and deploy condition-based maintenance as a substitute to schedule-based strategies."
- A sensor network system, using the optimized signal processing and condition monitoring procedures, will be applied to the live wind turbine (WT) to collect operational data that will then interface with a replica also the virtual 3D model, or DT of the wind turbine [7].
- "Improvements in delivering Wind Twin that can be supported minimize wind turbine (WT) downtime also maintenance costs and decrease inspection," said by Angulo.
- "Operators will enable to virtually examine maintenance improves previously better resistor and deployment of wind turbine setting, resulting energy output which is due to optimized wind-turbine performance."

2.6   Conclusion

In inference, DT applications display visibility into physical properties and potential production blockages in the manufacturing industry. Moreover, it streamlines processes to optimize operational and innovative product development. DT technology is merged with several technologies like ML, IOT, and artificial intelligence. This DT technology helps several companies across world to decrease the operational charges, increase performance, improve high productivity, and the alternating method of predictive conservation is complete. The product producers, in particular, DT technology, are critical to accomplishing more effective manufacture lines and faster period-to-market space.

References

[1] M. W. Grieves, "Virtually intelligent product systems: digital and physical twins," *Complex Syst. Eng., Theory Pract.*, pp. 175–200, 2019, https://doi. org/10.2514/5.9781624105654.0175.020.

[2] M. Grieves, "Digital twin: manufacturing excellence through virtual factory replication," *White Paper*, vol. 1, pp. 1–7, 2014.

[3] E. J. Tuegel, A. R. Ingraffea, T. G. Eason, and S. M. Spottswood, "Reengineering aircraft structural life prediction using a digital twin," *Int. J. Aerosp. Eng.*, vol. 2011, pp. 1–14, 2011.

[4] D. Cearley, B. Burke, D. Smith, N. Jones, A. Chandrasekaran, and C. Lu, "Top 10 strategic technology trends for 2020," Gartner, Stamford, CT, USA, Tech. Rep., 2019.

[5] T. R. Wanasinghe, L. Wroblewski, B. K. Petersen, *et al.*, "Digital twin for the oil and gas industry: overview, research trends, opportunities, and challenges," *IEEE Access*, vol. 8, pp. 104175–104197, 2020.

[6] Y. Lu, C. Liu, K. I.-K. Wang, H. Huang, and X. Xu, "Digital twin driven smart manufacturing: connotation, reference model, applications and research issues," *Robot. Comput.-Integr. Manuf.*, vol. 61, Art. no. 101837, 2020.

[7] C. Cimino, E. Negri, and L. Fumagalli, "Review of digital twin applications in manufacturing," *Comput. Ind.*, vol. 113, Art. no.103130, 2019.

[8] Q. Qi and F. Tao, "Digital twin and big data towards smart manufacturing and industry 4.0: 360 degree comparison," *IEEE Access*, vol. 6, pp. 3585–3593, 2018.

[9] F. Tao, H. Zhang, A. Liu, and A. Y. C. Nee, "Digital twin in industry: state-of-the-art," *IEEE Trans. Ind. Informat.*, vol. 15, no. 4, pp. 2405–2415, 2019.

[10] A. Rasheed, O. San, and T. Kvamsdal, "Digital twin: values, challenges and enablers from a modeling perspective," *IEEE Access*, vol. 8, pp. 21980–22012, 2020.

[11] B. Kitchenham and S. Charters, "Guidelines for performing systematic literature reviews in software engineering," Keele Univ., Durham Univ., Keele, U.K., Tech. Rep. EBSE 2007-001, 2007.

[12] B. Kitchenham, O. P. Brereton, D. Budgen, M. Turner, J. Bailey, and S. Linkman, "Systematic literature reviews in software engineering—a systematic literature review," *Inf. Softw. Technol.*, vol. 51, no. 1, pp. 7–15, 2009.

[13] C. Okoli and K. Schabram, "A guide to conducting a systematic literature review of information systems research," *SSRN, Tech. Rep.*, 2010. Available: http://dx.doi.org/10.2139/ssrn.1954824

[14] D. Cearley, B. Burke, S. Searle, and M. Walker, "Top 10 strategic technology trends for 2017: a gartner trend insight report," *Gartner*, vol. 23, Art. no. 6595640781, 2017. Available: https://www. gartner.com/doc/3645332

[15] D. Cearley, B. Burke, S. Searle, and M. J. Walker, "Top 10 strategic technology trends for 2018," Gartner, 2017.

[16] D. Cearley and B. Burke, "Top 10 strategic technology trends for 2019," Gartner, 2018.

[17] M. Grieves and J. Vickers, "Digital twin: mitigating unpredictable, undesirable emergent behavior in complex systems," *in Transdisciplinary Perspectives on Complex Systems*. Cham, Switzerland: Springer, 2017, pp. 85–113.

[18] E. Glaessgen and D. Stargel, "The digital twin paradigm for future NASA and US air force vehicles," in *Proc. 53rd AIAA/ASME/ASCE/AHS/ASC Struct., Struct. Dyn. Mater. Conf., 20th AIAA/ASME/AHS Adapt. Struct. Conf., 14th AIAA*, 2012, p. 1818.

[19] F. Tao, F. Sui, A. Liu, *et al.*, "Digital twin-driven product design framework," *Int. J. Prod. Res.*, vol. 57, no. 12, pp. 3935–3953, 2019.

[20] R. Söderberg, K. Wärmefjord, J. S. Carlson, and L. Lindkvist, "Toward a digital twin for real-time geometry assurance in individualized production," *CIRP Ann.*, vol. 66, no. 1, pp. 137–140, 2017.

[21] G. Bacchiega, "Creating an embedded digital twin: monitor, understand and predict device health failure," in *Inn4mech-Mechatronics Ind.*, vol. 4, 2018.

[22] R. Dong, C. She, W. Hardjawana, Y. Li, and B. Vucetic, "Deep learning for hybrid 5G services in mobile edge computing systems: learn from a digital twin," *IEEE Trans. Wireless Commun.*, vol. 18, no. 10, pp. 4692–4707, 2019.

[23] B. Björnsson, C. Borrebaeck, N. Elander, *et al.*, "Digital twins to personalize medicine," Genome Med. vol. 12, no. 1, pp. 1–4, 2020.

[24] J. A. Marmolejo-Saucedo, "Design and development of digital twins: a case study in supply chains," *Mobile Netw. Appl.*, vol. 25, no. 6, pp. 2141–2160, 2020.

[25] C. Zhuang, J. Liu, and H. Xiong, "Digital twin-based smart production management and control framework for the complex product assembly shopfloor," *Int. J. Adv. Manuf. Technol.*, vol. 96, nos. 1–4, pp. 1149–1163, 2018.

[26] R. Piascik, J. Vickers, D. Lowry, S. Scotti, J. Stewart, and A. Calomino, "Technology area 12: Materials, structures, mechanical systems, and manufacturing road map," NASA Office Chief Technol., 2010.

[27] P. Caruso, D. Dumbacher, and M. Grieves, "Product lifecycle management and the quest for sustainable space exploration," in *Proc. AIAA SPACE Conf. Expo.*, Aug. 2010, p. 8628.

[28] JETI. Which Technologies is Jeti Considering? Accessed: May 8, 2020. Available: https://jtc1info.org/technology/advisory-groups/jeti/.

[29] Automation Systems and Integration Digital Twin Framework for Manufacturing—Part 1: Overview and General Principles, Standard ISO/ DIS 23247-1, 2020. Available: https://www.iso.org/standard/75066.html.

[30] Industrial Automation Systems and Integration-Product Data Representation and Exchange—Part 1: Overview and Fundamental Principles, Standard ISO 10303-1, 1994. Available: https://www.iso.org/standard/20579.html.

[31] 2014 Cutting Tool Data Representation and Exchange—Part 3: Reference Dictionary for Tool Items, Int. Org. Standard, Standard ISO 133993,2014. Available: https://www.iso.org/standard/54168.html.

[32] O. Foundation. Unified Architecture. Accessed: 2008. Available: https://opcfoundation.org/about/opc-technologies/opc-ua/.

[33] R. Rosen, G. von Wichert, G. Lo, and K. D. Bettenhausen, "About the importance of autonomy and digital twins for the future of manufacturing," *IFAC-Papers OnLine*, vol. 48, no. 3, pp. 567–572, 2015.

[34] J. Vachálek, L. Bartalský, O. Rovný, D. Šišmišová, M. Morháč, and M. Lokšík, "The digital twin of an industrial production line within the industry 4.0 concept," in *Proc. 21st Int. Conf. Process Control* (*PC*), Jun. 2017, pp. 258–262.

[35] A. Fuller, Z. Fan, C. Day, and C. Barlow, "Digital twin: enabling technologies, challenges and open research", *IEEE Access*, vol. 8, pp. 108952–108971, 2020.

[36] B. Björnsson, C. Borrebaeck, N. Elander, *et al.*, "Digital twins to personalize medicine," *Genome Med.*, vol. 12, no. 1, pp. 1–4, 2020.

[37] A. Oluwasegun and J.-C. Jung, "The application of machine learning for the prognostics and health management of control element drive system," *Nucl. Eng. Technol.*, vol. 52, no. 10, pp. 2262–2273, 2020.

[38] Y. Liu, L. Zhang, Y. Yang, *et al.*, "A novel cloud-based framework for the elderly healthcare services using digital twin," *IEEE Access*, vol. 7, pp. 49088–49101, 2019.

[39] P. P. Shinde and S. Shah, "A review of machine learning and deep learning applications," in *Proc. 4th Int. Conf. Comput. Commun. Control Autom.* (*ICCUBEA*), Aug. 2018, pp. 1–6.

[40] A. S. Modi, "Review article on deep learning approaches," in *Proc. 2nd Int. Conf. Intell. Comput. Control Syst.* (*ICICCS*), Jun. 2018, pp. 1635–1639.

[41] K. E. Barkwell, A. Cuzzocrea, C. K. Leung, *et al.*, "Big data visualisation and visual analytics for music data mining," in *Proc. 22nd Int. Conf. Inf. Visualisation* (*IV*), Jul. 2018, pp. 235–240.

[42] S. E. Bibri and J. Krogstie, "The core enabling technologies of big data analytics and context-aware computing for smart sustainable cities: a review and synthesis," *J. Big Data*, vol. 4, no. 1, p. 38, 2017.

[43] F. Tao and M. Zhang, "Digital twin shop-floor: a new shop-floor paradigm towards smart manufacturing," *IEEE Access*, vol. 5, pp. 20418–20427, 2017.

[44] K. Xia, C. Sacco, M. Kirkpatrick, *et al.*, "A digital twin to train deep reinforcement learning agent for smart manufacturing plants: environment, interfaces and intelligence," *J. Manuf. Syst.*, vol. 58, 210–230, 2020.

[45] B. R. Barricelli, E. Casiraghi, J. Gliozzo, A. Petrini, and S. Valtolina, "Human digital twin for fitness management," *IEEE Access*, vol. 8, pp. 26637–26664, 2020.

[46] O. Mazumder, D. Roy, S. Bhattacharya, A. Sinha, and A. Pal, "Synthetic PPG generation from haemodynamic model with baroreflex autoregulation:

a digital twin of cardiovascular system," in *Proc. 41st Annu. Int. Conf. IEEE Eng. Med. Biol. Soc. (EMBC)*, Jul. 2019, pp. 5024–5029.

[47]   N. K. Chakshu, J. Carson, I. Sazonov, and P. Nithiarasu, "A semi-active human digital twin model for detecting severity of carotid stenoses from head vibration—a coupled computational mechanics and computer vision method," *Int. J. Numer. methods Biomed. Eng.*, vol. 35, no. 5, p. e3180, 2019.

[48]   F. Laamarti, H. Faiz Badawi, Y. Ding, F. Arafsha, B. Hafidh, and A. El Saddik, "An ISO/IEEE 11073 standardized digital twin framework for health and well-being in smart cities," *IEEE Access*, vol. 8, pp. 105950–105961, 2020.

[49]   N. S. Altman, "An introduction to kernel and nearest-neighbor nonparametric regression," *Amer. Statistician*, vol. 46, no. 3, pp. 175–185, 1992.

[50]   C. Cortes and V. Vapnik, "Support-vector networks," *Mach. Learn.*, vol. 20, no. 3, pp. 273–297, 1995.

[51]   F. Tao, J. Cheng, Q. Qi, M. Zhang, H. Zhang, and F. Sui, "Digital twin driven product design, manufacturing and service with big data," *Int. J. Adv. Manuf. Technol.*, vol. 94, nos. 9–12, pp. 3563–3576, 2018.

[52]   D. Shangguan, L. Chen, and J. Ding, "A hierarchical digital twin model framework for dynamic cyber-physical system design," in *Proc. 5th Int. Conf. Mechatronics Robot. Eng. ICMRE*, 2019, pp. 123–129.

[53]   J. Liu, X. Du, H. Zhou, X. Liu, L. ei Li, and F. Feng, "A digital twin-based approach for dynamic clamping and positioning of the flexible tooling system," *Procedia CIRP*, vol. 80, pp. 746–749, 2019.

[54]   F. Tao, H. Zhang, A. Liu, and A. Y. C. Nee, "Digital twin in industry: state-of-the-art," *IEEE Trans. Ind. Informat.*, vol. 15, no. 4, pp. 2405–2415, 2019.

[55]   O. Novo, "Blockchain meets IoT: an architecture for scalable access management in IoT," *IEEE Internet Things J.*, vol. 5, no. 2, pp. 1184–1195, 2018.

[56]   M. N. Kavitha, S. S. Saranya, K. Dhanush Adithyan, K. Soundharapandi, and K. S. Vignesh, "A novel approach for driver drowsiness detection using deep learning", in *Proceedings of the 4th National Conference on Current and Emerging Process Technologies e-CONCEPT-2021 AIP Conf. Proc.*, 2387, 2021, pp. 140027-1–140027-6.

[57]   N. Kanimozhi, N. V. Keerthana, G. S. Pavithra, G. Ranjitha, and S. Yuvarani, "CRIME type and occurrence prediction using machine learning algorithm," in *Proceedings of the International Conference on Artificial Intelligence and Smart Systems (ICAIS-2021)* IEEE Xplore, March 2021.

[58]   S. S. Saranya, C. Santhosh, and M. VijayaKumar, "Blockchain endorsement technology–a review of future smart paradigms," *Int. J. Aquatic Sci.*, vol. 12, no. 3, 2021.

[59]   M. N. Kavitha, V. Vennila, G. Padmapriya, and A. Rajiv Kannan, "Prevention of Sql injection attack using unsupervised machine learning approach," *Int. J. Aquatic Sci.*, vol. 12, no. 3, pp. 1413–1424, 2021.

[60]   M. N. Kavitha, N. Kanimozhi, and S. S. Saranya, "Face mask detection using deep learning," in *Second International Conference on Artificial Intelligence and Smart Energy (ICAIS)*, IEEE Xplore, 2022, pp. 319–324.

[61] S. S. Saranya, N. Kanimozhi, M. N. Kavitha, K. S. Atchayaprakassh, and K. K. Ragul, "Authentic news prediction in machine learning using passive aggressive algorithm," in *Second International Conference on Artificial Intelligence and Smart Energy (ICAIS)*, IEEE Xplore, 2022, pp. 372–376.

[62] K. Sathya, J. Premalatha, and V. Rajasekar, "A modernistic approach for chaotic based pseudo random number generator secured with gene dominance," *Sādhanā, vol.* 46, p. 8, 2021, https://doi.org/10.1007/s12046-020-01537-5

[63] K. Sathya, J. Premalatha, and S. Suwathika, "Reinforcing cyber world security with deep learning approaches," *IEEE Xplore Digital Library*, Sept. 2020, DOI:10.1109/ICCSP48568.2020.9182067

Chapter 3

Application of digital twin technology in model-based systems engineering

S. Chellam[1], M. Jajini[1] and M. Santhiya[2]

The paper introduces the concept, digital twin technology (DTT) which is a new and advanced technology that is used in all aspects of the electrical industry. In addition to simulation tools, the technology has been combined with multi-disciplinary, multi-physical, multi-scale, and multi-probability sectors. The simulation operations are carried out utilizing a physical model with sensors. The physical model was created in real-time, and the modeling was done in virtual space. In virtual space, the new DTT merged current power system simulation models and procedures. The use of DTT has been broadened to include power grid optimization, virtual power plants, grid fault modeling, intelligent monitoring of equipment, and other services.

3.1 Evolution of DTT

Grieves proposed an emerging concept – product life cycle management called digital twin for the first time in 2002. In 2003, it was known as Mirrored Pace Models, but in 2005, it was conceptually changed to Information Mirroring Models. It was eventually dubbed digital twins in the year 2011. The National Aeronautics and Space Administration (NASA) is a federal agency that oversees the re-examined the idea of the digital twin in 2012, describing it as a probabilistic and ultra-fidelity simulation model that represents the state of a corresponding twin-based data into real-time sensor-based data over the time. Any information in a physical space can be transformed into a virtual space, according to the definition of a digital twin.

The layers in DTT are depicted in Figure 3.1. Digital twins are same as computers which were present during 1950s. The computers were huge and dense objects that require a great deal of maintenance and manual professional assistance. But, digital twins are expected to become a well-established paradigm with

[1]Department of Electrical and Electronics Engineering, Velammal College of Engineering & Technology, India
[2]Kongu Engineering College, India

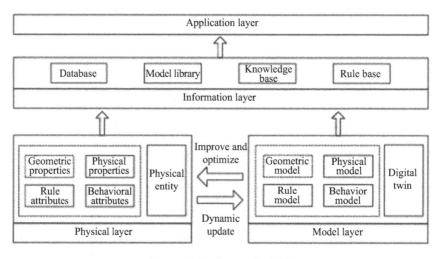

Figure 3.1   Layers in DTT

applications across a wide range of industries. When digital twins are deployed, expert input like model construction and validation will be replaced by data-driven procedures. Furthermore, the settings are analyzed, changes are identified automatically and accepted.

3.2   Basic concepts of DTT

A digital twin has been described as a subsystem that combines digital equipment design with real-time features. DTT is also utilized as a digital asset for PLM data management, modeling, and maintenance. Other specialized uses of the digital twin include data simulation, diagnostics, and prediction. The capacity to link data stored in many locations and shared data from the digital twin directory has enabled DTT. In the following paragraphs, we will go over the most important aspects of DTT.

Design: The components are modeled and evaluated in the design stage of DTT to check and inspect the final design. The solution was found by ensuring that all of the components were in good working order. Physical models are used to interpret the corrections between the simulated components.

Integration of systems: This section of DTT deals with system integration and 3D system-level visualizations of spatial footprints for linking and confirming physical relationships and constraints. Mechanical and electrical activities are examples of interactions between data transfer and capability. What-if scenarios can be used to simulate the interaction of components with the digital twin in system integration. As a result, the on-site integration effort has been reduced, as has the customer's downtime as a result.

Diagnostics: Non-observable data, such as section temperatures and material tension, can be diagnosed using simulations. The digital twin examination will aid in the troubleshooting of the 3D visualization. Field technicians have dependence on the physical equipment that allows them in imitation of the values related to virtual-reality glasses.

Prediction: Historical and current operating data can be predicted by providing an insight into the state of infrastructure. For various forms of failures, the predictive algorithm in conjunction with sensors has replied. It aids in the scheduling of reasonable repairs and the avoidance of unwanted downtime.

Advanced services: These services provide IoT connectivity parameters and analytical algorithms information. By authorizing equipment installation and subscribing the customer to the services, the parameters are preloaded into the digital twin. Furthermore, engineering is not required in the best-case scenarios.

The design and structure of the DTT are relatively straightforward. As a result, modeling ambiguity is reduced. DTT facilitates the use of a system to track specialized facilities and ensures their availability and stability. The ability to refer to data storage at several locations has been monitored from various aspects of a digital twin. Through remote accessing of data in the product lifecycle, the required data for numerous utilization cases is supplied by the digital twin. Data representation in digital form.

In the DTT, inclusion of calculated variables will map with digital variables. The fundamental goal of the digital twin is to make it easier to measure data and to put together the digital representation. As a result, communication between the infrastructures that must be engineered is required.

The technology of the digital twin is described in Figure 3.2. The digital twin includes the system description, data processing, and data management between applications. The digital doppelganger was connected to the system's real-time environmental data and process measures. The digital twin functioned between the initiation of the twin and operation/control.

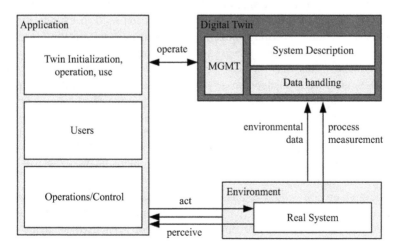

Figure 3.2 Implementation of DTT in power system

3.3   DTT implementation in power system

The deployment of DTT in the power system is based on a virtual system that is consistent with the real system. It will give accuracy by quickly comparing and modifying virtual values to real ones during the run time. Data-driven method, closed-loop feedback approach, and real-time interaction approach are the three basic DTT approaches.

(i) **Data-driven approach**
    The data-driven approach collects massive amounts of data from power grids and uses it to gradually improve the big data mining system. In the power system, DTT will make this approach more appropriate for the complex power industry.

(ii) **Closed-loop feedback approach**
    This method ensures that the system's data model adeptness is optimally analyzed by learning a significant collection of data which has been brought into action. The outcome of learning the digital twin has continuously improved over the increase in number of digital values.

(iii) **Real-time interactive approach**
    This method combines the benefits of both data-driven and closed-loop feedback methods. By leveraging power system digital twin (PSDT) technology to conduct virtual tests in real-time, this technique has improved real-time functionality and provided awareness. PSDT replicates decision-making practically and efficiently. Not just in ordinary operations, but also in emergencies, choices are made quickly and accurately.

Figure 3.3 shows how the physical items are linked to the digital twins via human machine interfaces. When compared to traditional power system simulation, the PSDT provides a lot of information. Mathematical equations such as algebraic, differential, or partial differential equations have been used to express the traditional power system, modeling model. These mathematical equations make the electricity system's operational process simple to comprehend. PSDT data also offers a large system status that includes pervasive sensor networks. The data-driven approach models were developed based on statistical learning and the synchronization between physical and mathematical models was established by measuring the data using historical data.

PSDT is a physical power network that contains digital space model information. Data and system knowledge are used to model and drive the network. PSDT stands for high-performance in digital simulation technology that is based on realization of complicated "information-energy-environment" systems. Simulating dynamic and precise values together is a precondition in the design of PSDT. Fusion of data in the digital space, artificial intelligence optimization decisions, and complex and dynamic behavior prediction have all been used to create digital technology in power systems.

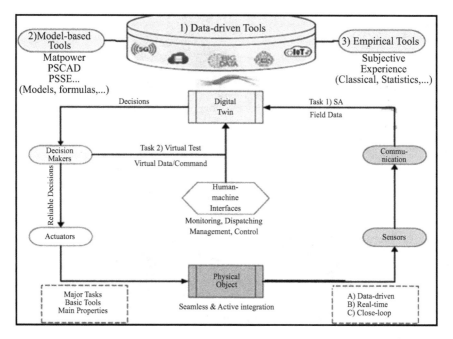

Figure 3.3 Structure of DTT in power system

3.3.1 Characteristics of DTT in power systems

(i)   In account of multi-scenario simulations with varying probabilities.

(ii) It works under circumstances including new energy generation, severity of AC system malfunction, DC converter misoperation, and so on.

(iii) To make the PSDT capable of simulating a variety of scenarios with varying probabilities of occurrence.

(iv) In addition to the events stated above, power systems can typically imitate this type of event chain as well.

Even though all of the needed data is correct, simulating the massive power system network is a difficult task. The components of the power system must be correctly organized and rated. Otherwise, the entire network will run inefficiently. Figure 3.4 depicts the use of cloud systems to connect the power system network utilizing DTT. Large amounts of data can be quickly saved utilizing cloud technology, and simulations may be done without delay.

3.4 Power system network modeling using DTT

The DTT concept is presented in two ways namely conventional design of experiments (DoE) method and model-assisted DoE (mDoE) method. DoE includes structural prototypes, flight dynamics models, and material state

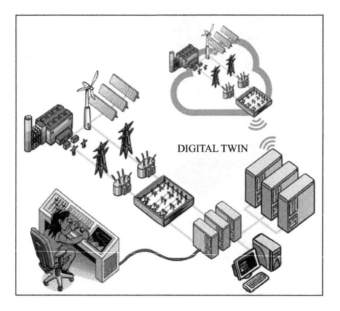

Figure 3.4   Connecting local facilities with cloud systems using DTT

evolution models. An airplane, high-performance wages, and computational reliability simulations with virtual health sensors are required for the DoE models. The DoE model can forecast how much maintenance is required for each aircraft. This method incorporated recent digital twin technological improvements. As a result, exponential growth can be seen in diverse industries 4.0 applications or power systems.

The power system's stability restriction is expected to prohibit some experimental conditions and events from occurring directly in the power system. Power systems have been designed using transient analysis, steady-state analysis, expert systems, power system software simulation, and physical systems. As a result, a real-time digital simulator (RTDS) was created to model real-world power systems. DTT handled the above-mentioned fault analysis simulation admirably. The computation of power flow, occurrence of three-phase short-circuit, controlling of equipment, and optimal scheduling operations will be analyzed by applying DTT. The power system modeling method creates a relatively simple operational environment. It will also make causality or the working mechanism quite obvious.

The obtained data is required by the physical model of the power system to determine the essential indicators for the low-dimensional transformation. This physical model has the problem of having to solve sophisticated system software, maintain correctness, operate at high speeds, and handle error in a sub-physical model's transmission mechanism. In engineering applications, evaluating a sub-physical model may lead to an incorrect conclusion. To develop a complicated power system network, a high-dimensional data space model is required.

The classifications for the DTT that has been offered for defining the power systems are dependent on the methodology they support. Model-based approaches, data-driven approaches, and hybrid approaches are the three main techniques/ approaches adopted in DTT.

3.4.1   Model-based approach

White box modeling functions are used to create it. The traditional power system network, which uses Twin Technology to provide an application-specific model, supports automated simulation and feeds the digital twin's fundamental engine. Due to the size of the model, the digital twin technique has computational complexity and simulation execution time. The digital twin's intricacy is determined by the type of application employed.

The dimensionality of the dynamic models root mean square and electromagnetic transient is high, but the dimensionality of the load and quasi-stationary models is low. For detecting and fixing short-term voltage instability problems, dynamic models are faster than real-time digital twins of power systems. Power firm's models accurately portray fault induced dynamic voltage recovery (FIDVR) event propagation and mitigation strategy because to the increased information. Using the Python Application Programming Interface (API) for Power Factory software, ultra-fast simulations create a virtual twin that is faster than real-time. A model-based digital twin for problem identification in distributed solar systems is built using limited Field Programmable Gate Array (FPGA) components.

3.4.2   Data-driven approach

In the power network digital twin concept, black box simulation models can be used with a data-driven approach. The basic engine in twin technologies is reliant on statistic and machine learning algorithms. Machine learning methods' rise in popularity facilitates the establishment of a large number of new apps. By using random matrix method and deep learning, the digital twin analyzes the actual power flow in the power system. Extracted data and information retrieval for the temporal-spatial dataset were performed by supposing situational awareness.

3.4.3   Combination of both

In this method, a combination of both frameworks was utilized using the grey box model. The constantly updated grid topological model makes use of a digital twin framework that is developed using the inter PSS software. The machine learning-based fast dynamic security assessments are also being used as the decision support system.

Figure 3.5 shows a Simulation diagram of a wind power generating unit by applying DTT. The data required for the wind power plant such as wind speed, blade position, type of generator used are fed as input using DTT in a virtual mode only. Therefore, a huge power generation in a virtual model has been obtained using DTT. Changes in the parameter have also been done as per requirements.

Solar power generation has also been modeled using DTT as shown in Figure 3.6. In this energy conversion, solar panels, AC to DC converters, electric motors are

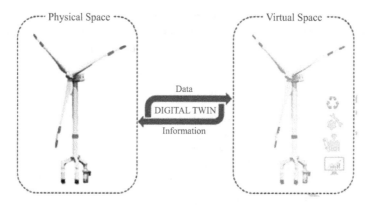

Figure 3.5   Model of wind power generating unit using DTT

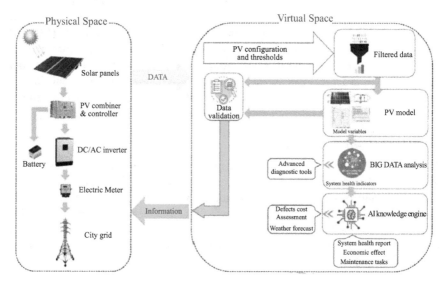

Figure 3.6   Modeling of solar power plant using DTT

modeled using DTT in a virtual space. In physical mode, this solar power plant occupies more space. The load flow, fault analysis has been carried over using simulation tools. By using DTT, the above said analysis can be done without any time delay. Therefore, the installation and erection have also been done within the time.

3.5   Integration of power system with DTT

DTT is improving the transformation and reliability of an interconnected system. Take, as example, a local system operator whom connects the electrical distribution network to the district heating network. Because of the coupled and integrated energy system, power-to-energy converters have become more common in residential, commercial, and industrial establishments. A digital twin can make a big difference in how a networked system operates and how reliable it is. The emergence of smart appliances (fridges, washing machines, etc.) with the viability of solar installations and other appliances), and the usage of electric heating are all changing gradually in the grid topology, and according to energy system operator (with boilers and heat pumps). In order to handle a significantly more complex area, the power system operator copes with the changing in network architecture. Since this digital twin is a virtual replica of the precise system. By assessing the influence of modern technology, the distribution network has already been tested and operated with it. The new technology's usage and capacity have been expanded as needed, among other things.

The primary use of DTT in energy system operators is to plan and predict distribution network maintenance. Based on a continuous quantity of information linked with previous measurements, the operator of a power system can assess network performance and take appropriate action. Physical models can be used to investigate relatively recent occurrences by looking ahead in time several hours to many days. To avoid any uncomfortable situations. It is critical to verify the network sooner, such as line failures in the electric network or leaking pipes in the combined heat and power network.

Owners of P2X devices in an interconnected system can use a digital twin to learn more about how the devices work and how to assess their health status. The modeling and simulation of the interconnected system improves the network's and equipment's' operational lifetime and is therefore. Two techniques could be used to convert into a single model a fully integrated energy system. The environment is designed utilizing domain-specific applications in the first method. The second method integrates all subsystems through using individual subsystems and co-simulation.

Digital twin developments will support domain-specific applications utilizing languages and techniques in building energy management (e.g. EnergyPlus). The complex interactions within as well as between energy pathways cannot be properly treated as a single digital model. Modeling languages, such as Modelica, present a number of issues in developing integrated energy system models. The following are the challenges:

1. Domain-specific model libraries that are well-developed and advanced.
2. Domain experience in simulating the individual system.
3. The capacity to meet context simulation requirements, for example. The Digital twin's full potential cannot be realized without existing approaches.

Co-simulation, often known as linked modeling, a computation technique that enables numerous designs (physical equation-based, data-driven, and so on) to be integrated collaboratively. For a power system operator, this is a significant advantage. Different divisions of a model also included the district heating network structure produced by that of the heating division and the electricity network model

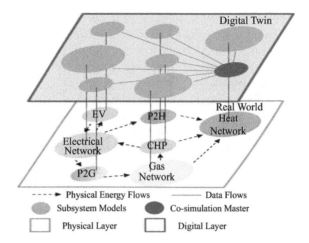

Figure 3.7   Integrated digital twin with electrical network

proposed by the electricity division. Without transforming from one or more sub-system types to a generic modeling tool, the above-mentioned systems can be properly integrated. The above-mentioned models might be integrated in one machine or to manage DTT, it is distributed among many devices.

The co-simulation approach has been used in a master algorithm that also regulates the interchange of data between the different subsystems as well as the simulation's temporal variation. To synchronize the development in distributing subsystems modeling techniques, standard protocols such as distributed co-simulation protocol (DCP) can be implemented. A co-simulation approach integrating Inter technologies (information or structural) attempted to exploit the faster-than-real-time environment. Simulated aptitudes of current manipulative environments. With the aid of online twins, integrated approach operators are expected to design, monitor, and manage densely interconnected power sources in such a new way. A digital representation of an integrated energy system that is involved to other external surroundings can be seen in Figure 3.7.

3.6   Future scope of DTT in power systems

The role of DTT applications in power systems is increasing in the fields relating to future power systems networks. DTT provides a correct, reliable, and supporting tool for stakeholders to take correct decisions in all levels implemented on control room advisory, education and training, post-mortem analysis of grid, long-term decision support, asset management, field operation support through augmented reality, col-laborative decision-making among stakeholders, and model-predictive operations.

Consider an example of an electric car manufacturer who has to replace the engine part of an electric vehicle by accumulating huge amount of data on the cars while in use. The information needed to read the pivot-table and also extent for further logging. From the driver profile and the car's geographical location, the received data can always be examined and evaluated. The perspectives on the selection processes for an electric car, having produced valuable and acceptable outcomes. An electric car is one such example of data that strengthens the plethora of angles from fresh angle potential and provides new insight. When a battery management system exhibits unusual behavior or malfunctions, an electric car manufacturer might send notifications to the local garage or the end-user.

The usage and consumption patterns of an electric utility can be learned through the combination of logging and reporting. By accumulating the vast amounts of data using AI, which can be accomplished in electric utilities through controlling residential boilers and heaters to ensure sufficient backup power or consistent operation, is now termed simply demand response.

To conclude, predictive maintenance is done at the customer end earlier to any foreseeable breakage failure that might have been predicted using those possible methods. Just before consumer is even aware that almost everything misleading has happened, the successful outcome can be evaluated and action taken.

Control room advisory: The power supply ensures the reliability, decisions making, and judgment of grid operators. The experienced grid operators will be able to make quick decisions on time with reference to past scenarios. The grid operators can able to handle new challenging situations by themselves due to an increase in penetration of diversified energy sources and demand responses. The above-mentioned drawbacks are overcome by taking the timely actions.

Education and training: It is the important application of DTT. The education and training have to be given to building to set up two teams the red team and the blue team. The exercises have been given to the trainees for improving the virtual: natural and linear abnormalities, as well as attacks on power systems.

Post-mortem analysis: Engineers in power sector look to develop a series of events in post mortem analysis. An unfortunate breakdown in a power grid may lead to a rise in the toughness of the system for upcoming activities. Because it simulates the forking of different pathways. The DTT smoothens the situation from dangerous events and also protects the power system network under causality.

Long-term decision support: Stakeholders require accurate and comprehensive models in making decisions for a period of long term. The feasibility and reliability of alternatives can be evaluated due to DTT and it helps in tough times.

Asset management: The more precise variants are used to perform maintenance on power line carriers, circuit breakers, and other substation equipment. Such models have been compromised by the virtual model.

Support for field operations using virtual reality: The maintenance personnel can be augmented by automated systems which have awareness to virtual environments. The safety of technicians and the security of the network both can be strengthened by examining decisions in real time before putting them into action.

Stakeholder collaboration in decision-making: Infrastructure expansion and developmental decision-making frequently requires the alignment and participation of stakeholders. DTT's constructive options are provided on both back-end and front-end systems.

Predictive operations based on assumptions: Distribution is regulated by processors with on-load tap changing transformers. grid voltages optimally. To decrease congestion, intelligent rooftop photovoltaic DC to AC converter can utilize a digital twin. Complex challenges in distribution grid cannot be controlled and coordinated by embedding with conventional linear controller. Therefore, adequate solution could be provided by data center.

3.7 Conclusion

In power systems, controllers not only have their twin but every component in the power system also has the twin. Such as electric vehicles, converters, heat pumps, PV inverters and windmills will have their twin-component to represent them in digital form. The digital twins will optimize the work of components. Thus, it makes the work simple and reduces the complexity.

An embedded system with intelligent components is expected for a self-organizing, stable, and progressive power system to function. Big data methods and analytical technologies should be tightly linked to DT technology development and use in the power business. The interconnection of these technologies has the potential to lessen PSDT's reliance. The research of the data-driven model will be strengthened to a greater extent by the physical entity of the power system. By using DTT to the power sector, the connected problems of uncertainty network parameters and measuring error may be tackled more effectively.

References

[1] J. Wu, Y. Yang, X. Cheng, *et al.*, "The development of digital twin technology review," in *2020 Chinese Automation Congress (CAC)*, 2020, pp. 4901–4906.

[2] X. He, Q. Ai, R.C. Qiu, *et al.*, "Preliminary exploration on digital twin for power systems: challenges, framework, and applications," *arXiv*:1909.06977 [eess, stat]. 2019; arXiv: 1909.06977.

[3] P. Palensky, M. Cvetkovic, D. Gusain, and A. Joseph, "REVIEW: Digital twins and their use in future power systems," *Electric Sustainable Energy*, Sep. 2021.

[4] H. Jianping, "The application of digital twin on power industry," *Earth and Environmental Science*, vol. 647, p. 012015, 2021, doi:10.1088/1755-1315/647/1/012015.

[5] H.M. Moghadam, H. Foroozan, M. Gheisarnejad, and M.-H. Khooban, "A survey on new trends of digital twin technology for power systems," *Journal of Intelligent & Fuzzy Systems*, vol. 3, pp. 1–21, 2021, DOI:10.3233/JIFS-201885

[6] H. Pan, Z. Dou, Y. Cai, W. Li, X. Lei, and D. Han, "Digital twin and its application in power system," in *2020 The 5th International Conference on Power and Renewable Energy*.

[7]   S. Ferguson, Apollo 13: The First Digital Twin, 2020.

[8]   M. Shafto, M. Conroy, R. Doyle, *et al.*, "Modeling, simulation, information technology and processing roadmap," *National Aeronautics and Space Administration*, 2012.

[9]   M. Grieves, Origins of the Digital Twin Concept, vol. 8, 2016.

[10] C. Brosinsky, D. Westermann, and R. Krebs, "Recent and prospective developments in power system control centers: adapting the digital twin technology for application in power system control centers," in *2018 IEEE International Energy Conference (ENERGYCON)*, 2018, pp. 1–6.

[11] A. Rasheed, O. San, and T. Kvamsdal, "Digital twin: values, challenges and enablers from a modeling perspective," *IEEE Access*, vol. 8, pp. 21980–22012, 2020.

[12] B. Lheureux, W.R. Schulte, and Velosa A, "Why and how to design digital twins," *Gartner Tech Rep.* 2018; G00324934.

[13] T. Liu, H. Yu, H. Yin, *et al.*, "Research and application of digital twin technology in power grid development business," in *2021 6th Asia Conference on Power and Electrical Engineering (ACPEE)*, 2021, pp. 383–387.

[14] M. Zhou, J. Yan, and D. Feng, "Digital twin framework and its application to power grid online analysis," *CSEE Journal of Power and Energy Systems*, vol. 5, no. 3, pp. 391–398, 2019.

[15] P. Schavemaker and L. van der Sluis, Electrical Power System Essentials, 2008.

[16] X. He, Q. Ai, R.C. Qiu, *et al.*, Preliminary exploration on digital twin for power systems: challenges, framework, and applications, arXiv:1909.06977 [eess, stat]. 2019; arXiv: 1909.06977.

[17] J.H. Chow and J.J. Sanchez-Gasca, *Power System Modeling, Computation, and Control*, New York, NY: John Wiley & Sons, 2020.

[18] A. Agouzoul, M. Tabaa, B. Chegari, *et al.*, "Towards a digital twin model for building energy management: case of Morocco," *Procedia Computer Science*, vol. 184, pp. 404–410, 2021.

[19] P. Palensky, A. van der Meer, C. Lopez, *et al.*, "Applied cosimulation of intelligent power systems: implementing hybrid simulators for complex power systems," *IEEE Industrial Electronics Magazine*, vol. 11, no. 2, pp. 6–21, 2017.

[20] Y. Fathy, M. Jaber, and Z. Nadeem, "Digital twin-driven decision making and planning for energy consumption," *Journal of Sensor and Actuator Networks*, vol. 10, no. 2, p. 37, 2021.

[21] Z. Jiang, H. Lv, Y. Li, *et al.*, "A novel application architecture of digital twin in smart grid," *Journal of Ambient Intelligence and Humanized Computing*, vol. 13, pp. 3819–3835, 2021.

[22] I. Bishop and C. Stock, "Using collaborative virtual environments to plan wind energy installations," *Renewable Energy*, vol. 35, no. 10, pp. 2348–2355, 2010.

Chapter 4

Digital twins in e-health: adoption of technology and challenges in the management of clinical systems

S.S. Saranya[1], N. Kanimozhi[2] and C. Santhosh[1]

Over a past decade, a development of Artificial Intelligent (AI) in medical discipline has been utilized to predict and prescribe drugs on day basis. It has large influences on predicting and diagnosing ailments totally based on the information that have been accrued through an embedded sensor. The sensor collects excessive dimensional facts which have a descriptive clarification on every symptom and diagnostics. It has been stated that more than 75% of clinical executives count on to make investments in digital twin (DT) technological know-how over previous few years. As DT is the replication of any physical/virtual objects like people, manner, and equipment which help to put together a digital transformation of scientific files that are gathered. Due to developments in big data analytics and AI in analyzing records that have been accumulated over a length of time for prediction, DT science is being developed and commercialized aviation and manufacturing processes. Rather than making an attempt to acquire a best duplicate of the human mind, AI structures take advantage of strategies emulating human reasoning as information to grant each helping equipment and higher services. Super intelligence of AI not only performs all physical and manpower-related task but also handles prediction and discovering novel applications and remedies to medical problems as business perspectives. DT is defined as virtual object or computer entity or model that simulates or twinning any real-world things like human or objects. Every DT is linked with a unique digital key that normalizes a bijective relationship with its original. The DT has been used to surveillance the functionalities of physical entities uninterruptedly and make a decision over a problem. This paper portraits digital recreation of healthcare systems like lab, hospital ecosystems, and psychology of a human being and how far it is useful in medical science which in flips hikes revenue and enterprise market of healthcare industry along with a study that focuses on DT applications in medical industries and healthcare applications. Finally, the research has serious diversion into various challenges in medical digitalized system and DT technology.

[1]Department of Computer Science and Engineering, Kongu Engineering College, India
[2]Department of Computer Technology, Kongu Engineering College, India

4.1   Introduction

To formulate conception into best practice, digital twin (DT) technology has been applied to an industry as a simulator for precision decision concerning the future. In healthcare or medical industry, decision making and prediction plays a major role as it promotes resource allocations and planning of new practices and methodologies on medication. Integrating DT technology with medical practices and services facilitates efficient and robust provisions to the aged people. The accuracy and integrity of medical services is being ensured by DT technology to propagate faster and sensible help whenever indeed. But it is a massive deal to reap person health and wellbeing super-vision of an elderly man or woman via a digital international to offer a clever hospital treatment on critical phase. A system of artificial intelligence (AI) does all kinds of physical work that has been done by human as a replication of individual mind, rather than creating a replica, emulation process has evolved for human reasoning to attain advanced services. The novelty in DT technology compared with different fitness care providers like hospital, laboratory, and clinical executives is discovered as its diagnose fitness associated statistics of an individual person for monitoring and making authentic decisions. The health aspects of each human being may vary each other based on the circumferences and environment which has been captured and passed to the fitness tracking structures through a wearable sensors to cloud surroundings. Later amassed statistics have processed the usage of huge facts on analytics and IoT technologies.

   In digital era [1], AI caries theory and implementation part of a computer systems that is capable of imitating and simulating human brain and intelligence adhere with their behaviors. As DT technology endorses machine or virtual systems to behave like a human being rather appropriate human, it performs tasks perfectly with a human intelligences. The intelligences like speech recognition, making accurate, and sensible decisions toward future accomplishments. Consequently, AI algorithms were devel-oped for discovering biological relations with more novelty. A study of human organs and its functioning uncovers hidden patterns and pharmacological information needed for treatments that were gathered by huge volume of high dimensional big data. To remove redundant information, big data analytics techniques have been proposed. Finally, DT technology plays a vital role in healthcare applications and services which have a tremendous growth in enabling healthcare sectors along with other leading technologies like IoT, AI, machine learning, and big data analytics.

4.2   Digital twin

The essential concept behind DT is defined as the digital transformation of constructing substantial structure into a digital real entity as lookalike authentic object. Figure 4.1 represents the digital twin. It has been considered as core and simulation strategy which integrates essential multidisciplinary technologies to map physical objects lifecycle process in virtual space. DT technology concept is used in Apollo NASA's program to replicate two spacecraft for a mission. While one spacecraft is launched, the another win simulates the model of space ground to reflect the status of a vehicle. The vehicle which

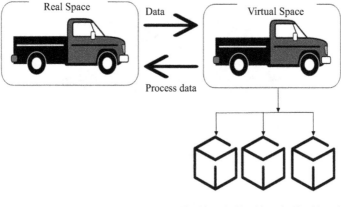

Figure 4.1   Representation of digital twin. Result of Grieves' model

is already on mission accurately predicts the working condition of a real machine. The tremendous efforts have been taken in support cosmonaut in geostationary orbit to formulate accurate pronouncement in emergency situations. There is a variety of applications in medical care, whereas persistent syndrome like diabetes, low blood pressure, hypertension, respiratory diseases, and stroke has features like high prevalence, durations, and hard to restore to health. Especially, a disease like cancer affects our immune system which provides resistance to infection and toxins.

Comparatively, elder people forget health-related information about them due to memory loss and may have a weak body condition. They ought to be looked after most of the time than youngster. Due to low visiting rate of elder person to clinic centers or hospital, the type of disease cannot be predicted and not identified earlier that leads to low diagnostic accurateness. Hence, elder people never get timely information concerning their medical situation of their body. The DT periodically obtains status of physical twin changes over a time during its lifecycle process which describes the status of equivalence surroundings of physical entity. So they can get a periodic consultation and supervision on time. In addition, diversification of medical facilities like hospitals, medical centers, and medical laboratories increases the waiting time of consultation and payment to medications. Figure 4.2 represents the prototype of the various medical services.

The DT has the following unique features:

(a)   Real-time mapping and reflection of real objects.
(b)   Union and interface.
(c)   Virtual and iteration model.

The conventional model promotes health services and remedies based on the report that has been provided by the patients. Most recent applications like Digital Twin HealthCare Services (DTHCSs) perform authentic and real-time monitoring through the DT which has been created as like physical objects. The medical recommendations have been send to the caretakers or family members on time and scheduled basis.

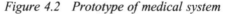

Figure 4.2   Prototype of medical system

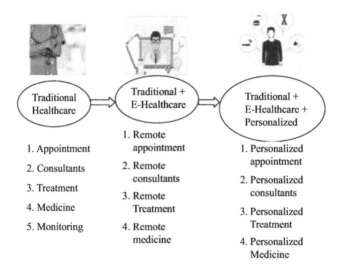

Figure 4.3   Evolutions of personalized healthcare services

The DT is mainly used in designing of product, product management, product service management, and equipment life prediction. The DT plays a vital role in industry and this concept can be applied to the healthcare also. In assisting the healthcare staff, DT helps to give treatment and test medicines for virtual patients to reduce the threat and operational cost. The doctors no need to have a physical contact with the patients which need the healthcare to treat them. Doctor can analyze the symptom and based on that treatment to the patients is being given by this DT model without meeting the patients in physical mode. The healthcare service can be provided as private hospital, pharmacy, and other parties for medical service, clinic, and community hospitals. By these ways, everyone get the medical services. Figure 4.3 represents the difference ways to get medical services.

4.3 Evolution of healthcare services

In healthcare, the interaction becomes very complicated with patients, healthcare organization, and business organization. Due to ambiguity property of current medical systems, it is very complicated to focus on the prototype of medical system with actual situation.

To deal with these types of healthcare systems, new production and simulation need to be constructed. Particularly, this simulation deals with reduced cost and high bendy of research in healthcare. By means of this cloud computing behavior, it makes the simulation to overcome the problem in disease diagnosis, diseases treatment, and medical pathway for each patient, and distribution of resources in this computing environment. Also, this simulation provides maximum efficiency in medical services. It also provides high accuracy and quality to provide service based on this DT model.

Figure 4.3 explains how the personalized healthcare evolutes, first it starts as traditional healthcare where the patients should check the appointment. Next, patient's directed to the doctor for consultants. Next, according to the patient's condition, doctors start the treatment to each patient. Doctors carry out all the required treatment and prescribe medicine to each one. At last, patient's condition is monitored regularly. Then next it moves to e-healthcare where each steps are done on online mode. Patients can get appointment from anywhere, doctors guide then remotely.

4.4 Elderly medical services and demands

In recent years, elderly people require suitable and precise medical services that are combined with the leading computer technologies like networking and digitalization with intelligence. With various IoT sensors, the real-time data has been collected and sent to the cloud on scheduled basis. The data stored in the cloud has to consider as big data. The smart healthcare information collected by the sensors must contain patient name, medical report, and patients' past history. The Internet end result of those evolutions is that the brand new scientific carrier mode is moving to an individual and non-stop healthcare carrier mode, and greater intelligent scientific structures and systems are being constructed to realize customized smart healthcare.

The intelligent health systems nowadays focus on the following aspects:

1. **Medium of platform for communication:** The hierarchical platform has to be considered for sharing information among the participating nodes. Most probably, distributed platform can be adopted for centralized processing systems to reach and share information related to healthcare easily and rapidly.
2. **Healthcare technologies and improvements:** Advancement in medical business rapidly increasing its features in cloud environment, through cloud based medical services that help to reduce overall establishment cost and increase in resources utilization of resources.

3. **Interoperability:** As elderly people deprived in maintaining and reproducing the information about their health status, IoT wearable devices attached to them for tracking and monitoring real-time information and has been transferred to cloud environment through Internet by enabling interoperability among all the devices. The interoperability plays a vital role between communication devices and alerting devices to alert intended people notice. The conventional healthcare services never provide continuous monitoring services about old person. The conversation between health firms and patients no longer extended throughout the life cycle.

4.5   Cloud computing

The healthcare centers are going ahead to progress from the conventional to the smart healthcare system. Due to the growth of many technologies like Internet of Things, cloud computing, big data, and AI. This technology provides the pathway and prediction method for many healthcare centers all over the places. These can be used in healthcare. This DT can be applied to any practice of the healthcare. By joining this DT with medical applications, it provides many pathways in research and medical services can also be increased with high precision. There are some challenges in the healthcare such as the maintenance of health record which is the vital one for each patients, difficulty in management over the cycle of patients, and how to convert the real healthcare into the virtualized platform. The cloud-based platform can be used to make the digital twin. The cloud computing is the delivery of services such as database, storage, and networking. The on-demand service of cloud makes it more scalable and high virtualization. Figure 4.5 represents the cloud computing architecture. The cloud-based frame work can be used to reduce the space between the real healthcare and virtualized one. Nowaday's

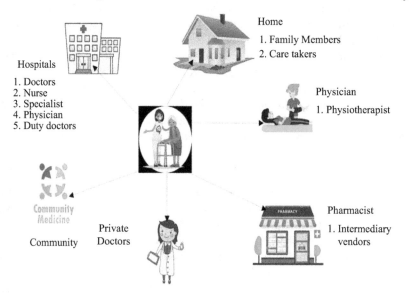

Figure 4.4   Elderly health/medical services and demands

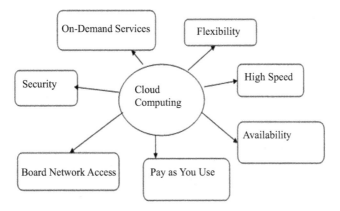

Figure 4.5   Features of cloud computing

cloud and healthcare framework are developed and used by many of the healthcare. The cloud healthcare and e-health differ in many aspects like access to healthcare date and chance for new industry model. The cloud computing features are listed in in Figure 4.5.

Currently, many research applications are based on the following topics of healthcare system:

- The cloud computing makes the changes in the medical business model as cloud services in imaging, cloud-based medical services that decrease the production rate and increase the consumption fee.
- The integration in healthcare devices, monitoring, and altering in removable device are attained by the IoT and Internet that is in cellular phone.

A problem that rises during healthcare services are as follows:

1. The unbroken private healthcare administration system is not provided by the current system.
2. There is no implementation between the mixture of information system and healthcare.
3. There is no interface between patients and healthcare.
   ✓ To address the above problem, the interaction between real healthcare and virtualized healthcare need to be resolved.
   ✓ Hence, the concept called digital can be implemented.

4.6   Cloud computing DT in healthcare

The DT can be used in enormous ways in healthcare like diagnosing patient's diseases, treatment decision support system, and patient monitoring in which the patient's symptom can be detected before getting sick, operation risk assessment, and medical devices. The DT mechanism has four parts; first the DT model is created by analyzing the physical entity by using advanced tools and techniques. Second, the connection is maintained between the virtual entity and the physical entity by using IoT devices.

Third, the model is valuated with stimulation. Fourth, the model is optimized according to the need conditions. Thus, the data from this model is feed to the physical system to get the excepted result. Without this DT, the medical staffs will depend only on their basic domain knowledge, basic treatment, and they have to wait for the result of the treatment. The DT makes it easier to personalize the treatment according to each individual based on their genetic feature, body condition, and other feature.

4.6.1   Use cases

4.6.1.1   Customized drug

The research centers located in different location implement digital technologies to customize the drugs for individual based on the diseases affected on them. Customization of the drugs are done based on their age, lifestyle, and genetic.

4.6.1.2   Industries

Industries use DT technology to increase the ongoing training, operations, training the new product or equipment before delivering to the world which becomes very difficult to fix the problem after it.

4.6.1.3   Water supply

Water supply organization uses DT technology mainly to check the nonstop water supply and to train for any emergency satiations. By means of this, DT can identify the current water system and breakdown before taking place. The real-time example is water supply through the city.

4.6.1.4   Manufacturing units

The DT is used to increase the production process. The monitoring of the strength of equipment and product is done better by DT. Detection of abnormality in the product is done in a suitable manner. The real-time examples are pharmacy and goods manufacturing.

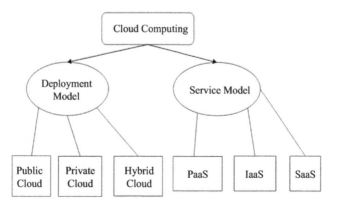

Figure 4.6   Elderly health/medical services and demands cloud computing

4.7   Digital healthcare modeling process

In medical field, interaction among patients and health providers like doctors, pediatrician, and clinical support becomes tedious process to track and monitor periodically. At present, medical and healthcare services have been promoted through simulation, education, and medical training to capture the health-related information about concern patients, which need to be processed by healthcare providers after a sequence of storing procedure followed in cloud environment. The simulation of surgery, equipment design, training, and treatment for critical disease has been done in various methodologies for improving the flexibility in medical system that also reduces cost associated with the treatment. It helps to recreate healthcare simulation by incorporating resource allocation, virtual simulation, decision making, intelligent systems, etc.

The real-time data and history of patients can be easily monitored through real-time sensors of healthcare devices [2]. The DT medical care system mainly focuses on virtual and real-time physical objects followed by real-time healthcare data that has been gathered from real sensors that are associated with physical objects. This simulation promotes healthcare and clinical services through virtual mode and services on timely manner. The real-time objects may be medical devices, patients, wearable sensors associated with medical objects or machines, activities of elderly patients. The virtual objects may be digital and wearable devices or simulation objects. The healthcare data has been captured from wearable devices, simulation data from digital devices, chronological and past health data from various healthcare service providers like hospitals, clinic and care takers at home. A digital twin technology combines substantial and virtual objects in real world that facilitates the visual representation on smart devices like mobile phones, laptops, and personal computers with higher configurations to enhance the visual quality of data which is projected on device screen. In medical healthcare simulation, the person who desires to be monitored should connect with few wearable sensors or medical devices termed as monitoring equipment or devices.

The information which is collected from these devices must be sent to doctors, healthcare takers, or pediatricians through wireless sensor technologies like Bluetooth, WiFi, and radio frequency. The wireless technologies play a prominent role in predetermining status of the patient who is under the control. The data is collected from these wearable devices known as Figure 4.7 represents DHR architecture. The information will be accessible to all administrative body/people like doctors, hospital, pharmaceutical stores, or private clinics. The information automatically set to be allocated in cloud environments for better and faster access to owner/patients who are authoritative about their health records rather than care takers or others. The instrumental or electronic devices can send alarm signal when an anomalous or irregular activity has found out to protect patients health status.

The modeling process has the following categories:

(a)   **Data modeling:** The information about patient like Name, Age, Gender, Medical History, and genital background.

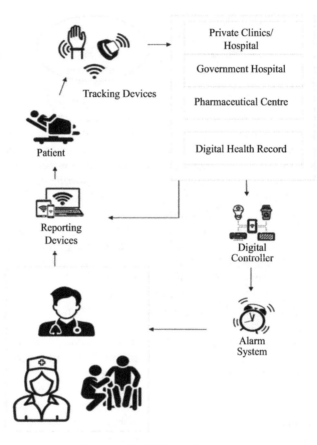

Figure 4.7   DHR architecture

(b) **Sensor modeling:** The information about type of sensor, indexing para-
     meters, alarm system, etc.
(c) **Activity modeling:** The behavioral information about elderly person like
     medication.
(d) **Constraint modeling:** The information of constraints, association of rules
     and past medical constraints.
(e) **Rule modeling:** The information that is comparable and associated with each
     other like rise of blood pressure level due to stress and heavy workload.
     Example, people who have a hectic work schedule and work stress may have
     a rise in blood pressure in turn rise in blood glucose level also.

4.8   Cloud-based healthcare facility platform

Due to demand, monitoring real-time information of patients, elderly people, crisis
notification, disease identification, reminder of medical scenarios, pathways of medical
plan need an optimal remedy and solution based on status of patients health condition

as well as environmental changes in patients surroundings. The model has to be selected for various services that have been provided to both virtual and physical objects. The reports or information extracted from the wearable sensors or medical supporting devices must sent to virtual design for evaluation and verification then transferred to real-world objects known as physical people for implementation. Information can be gathered from various sources like real-time, third party and health reports produced by hospitals. The data related to real-time objects are health reports, medication bills, images of damaged parts, medical diagnosis, etc. The data are related to blood pressure level, blood glucose, heart beat rate, visual eye sight range, body fat level etc. The third party data are termed to be a health insurance report and health diagnosis final consultation. The physical and virtual information combined together through neural networks algorithms to form a data fusion. The resultant fused data stored in database with unified data structure approaches. The data structure must be common and well defined in the database so that the retrieval process can be done without any inconveniences. Finally data send back to the physical and virtual objects for optimization and implementation of necessary precaution techniques to stabilize the health status of patients. The services provided by the cloud environment have been categorized into two ways. First, it may be a free cost service cloud platform termed to be community cloud environment; second, it can be charged by the service providers like private cloud environments for each service that is mapped to the applications and time utilization period. The application that has to be operated needs to decide which type of cloud supporting platform required for further services based on the cost effectiveness and duration of monitoring process.

The functionality and data processing in cloud-based digital healthcare service platform are as follows. Figure 4.8 depicts the functionality and data processing in cloud-based healthcare platform.

- Collection and transmission of data from various sources like physical and virtual model.

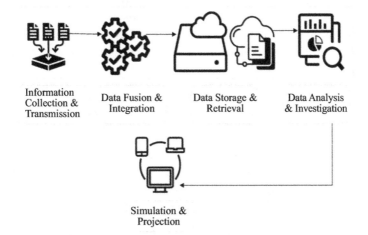

| Information Collection & Transmission | Data Fusion & Integration | Data Storage & Retrieval | Data Analysis & Investigation |

Simulation & Projection

Figure 4.8   Functionality and data processing in cloud-based healthcare platform

- Data fusion and mining using neural networking algorithms.
- Data integration.
- Data storage like database.
- Data analysis and investigation.
- Data comparison with simulation.
- Data projection on smart devices like personal computers, laptops, and monitors.

4.9   Applications of DT technology

4.9.1   Cardiovascular application

The normal and abnormal activities of an elderly/normal people are being monitored periodically in real time. If any deviations in normal behavior or symptoms of abnormal activities, the preventive steps can be taken and healthcare service providers plan medical supports immediately.

4.9.2   Cadaver high temperature

The physiological meters and measures like temperature of a human body and hotness in skin tissues monitored through activities and body sensors. The increase in body temperature may be consequences of stress and medical conditions. The medical conditions can be interpreted as heart attacks, stroke, and shock due to mishandling of devices or electrical machines. The indication in increase of body temperature may alert the caregivers of a patient to predict and prevent them from severe medical complications.

4.9.3   Diabetes meters

The diabetic patients have to be monitored continuously for avoiding severe complications like glaucoma, blindness, nerves-related diseases in eyes, kidney and liver malfunction, heart attacks, and blood pressure levels. The diabetic patient must undergone medical test periodically with no delay in reports and medications.

4.9.4   Stress monitoring

Due to high workload, people who are working as employee in an organization suffer a lot for protecting themselves from stress. Stress may lead severe nervous related problems, anxiety, and depression. They never trust anyone and level of dissatisfaction on work they possess. The untrustworthiness causes various depression-related consequences like addiction to smoking and drugs. Finally they may be addicted to alcoholism. The technologies like smart watches, health bands support human by continuously monitoring and projecting reports on screen immediately. The security and privacy of the information has to be maintained with their biometric impressions.

4.10 Benefits of DT technology

4.10.1 Remote monitoring

It is very difficult to get the physical view of larger system. By using DT, the system can be accessed from anywhere; the user can control, monitor, and manage the system from anywhere.

4.10.2 Group cooperation

The methodological team members can access the system information as 24*7 and process automated completely which makes technical team to focus more on increasing team collaboration, team activity, and efficiency.

4.10.3 Analytical maintenance

As DT with Internet of Things generate a large amount of data in real time, company analyzes the generated data to find out any problems within the system. This facility allows the company to more correctly maintain analytical schedule, thus improving the production rate and reducing the costs.

4.10.4 Transparency

This DT makes it possible to provide transparency and improve the transparency between connected systems and other machinery operations.

4.10.5 Future prediction

The DT facilitates to use different technologies which allow predicting the business future in addition to examine the impact of issues that to deal with.

4.10.6 Information

The DT can also be used as a communication technologies and documentation device to recognize and explain the performance of one or more larger systems.

4.10.7 Big data analytics and processing

In modern world, Internet of Thing and cloud computing-based healthcare systems are capable of analyzing, manipulating numerous quantities of data that are scattered and distributed in nature. It requires Internet of Thing devices and sensors that have to be connected with a number of networking nodes for data transmission.

4.10.8 Cost effectiveness

To increase efficiency digital healthcare system integrate primary technologies like IoT for data collection using sensors, AI for decision making, big data analytics for analyzing and manipulating over collected information, and cloud computing as storage environment to sustaining the information in cloud storages. The usage of this healthcare system reduces the wastages, room, and maintenance services paid at hospital because patients can stay at home. Without any deviation, they can pay as they use and would like to use. It can be scaled up and scaled down easily.

4.11   DT challenges in healthcare

There are some key challenges in implementing the DT.

4.11.1   Cost effectiveness

The DT is not used widely in healthcare because to implement this, DT in health-care, the units such as labs, pharmacy, hospitals should increase their impact toward experimental procedure, digital replication, and improve all other medical process. Even though it all satisfied in healthcare the implementation cost remain expensive, it cannot be used and accessed by many peoples. Hence, this would be used by the authorities who are very rich in financial status and this will create the difference in the medical field.

4.11.2   Data collection

The AIs in DT can learn from the huge data set collected from various medical related companies. The quality of the medical data plays a vital role in developing the model. If the quality is not good, then the representation of those data become challenging. That will affect the consistency of created model in treatment procedure.

4.11.3   Data protection

The healthcare DT needs high levels of information from the various medical organizations and business companies. This information includes details related to physical activity, lifestyle, and all day to day activities which should be kept at high privacy.

4.11.4   Team collaboration

The increased productivity and functioning efficiency achieved because of high team collaborations in which the technicians can access the system at any time.

4.11.5   Monitoring

It is very difficult to have a real and in intensity monitor on the very large system. But this digital can be accessed from anywhere and can be used for many where remotely.

4.11.6   Software maintenance and assurance

The software development and maintenance plays prominent role in cloud-based medical health monitoring systems. The latest technologies like wireless sensor networks, smart devices, monitoring and controllers and data transmission technologies like Bluetooth, WiFi, etc. need to be integrated properly. The data structures and protocols that have been followed and supported by each digital software and hardware must be colliding for higher degree of integrity, reliability, and confidentiality.

4.11.7 Regulatory complications

The regulatory bodies like drug association (DA) have to approve all medical technological devices and medicines. The agencies must approve the medicines and medical supporting and monitoring devices after being documented and submitted to approval process. The information stored and gathered by these medical devices may lead to strangers or unethical people who can manipulate and provide erroneous treatments to patients.

4.11.8 Security and privacy-related issues

As information stored in cloud can be attacked and penetrated by unauthorized person called as attacker that has potential ability to destruct the entire monitoring system. They may possibly spoil the life time of the patient and terminate their life by providing irrelevant information. The sensors' controls can be taken by the attacker to produce incorrect information about the health conditions of a patient who is under the surveillance. If the attacker penetrate healthcare monitoring systems to manipulate and steal health-related records of a patients to threaten and blackmailing for monetary reasons. It leads to unethical behavior of a human being and severe consequences to the patient's health.

4.11.9 Targets of attackers

The attacker/unauthorized person can modify the health-related information like medical images, medical reports, and medical screening test reports about patients intentionally by prescribing higher dosage medicines without the knowledge of patients.

4.11.9.1 Patient

Inadvertent sharing of personal information occurs in a variety of ways, including conversations between patients, test results processed by a lab technician can be revealed, information which left on a desktop in a medical centre, so that a stranger can see it.

4.11.9.2 Information

The confidential and sensitive reports like medical/insurance, claim bills, test plan, surgery deadlines, and Master checkups reports. The confidentiality may be lost due to blackmailing or threatening the patients by keeping their medical records.

4.11.9.3 Gadgets and medical devices

The devices that are associated with patients can be implanted or wearable. The devices can be hacked by the attacker by enabling Denial of Service attack mode. So that devices never respond to patients and denied the work which is indented for.

4.11.9.4   Organization

The attacker hacks the communication network links between organization and medical equipment that transfer health-related information of a patient's status. If the entire network has been hacked completely, the hacker can take a control over a network for unauthorized access.

4.11.9.5   Cloud environments

The protocol of cloud environment and devices may vary each other. Interoperability issues rise while transferring information from medical devices to cloud storage.

4.12   Conclusion

In recent years, technologies like Internet of Things, cloud computing, AI, ML algorithms along with Internet facilities are widely used in digital healthcare services. Most researches concentrate on platform and environment rather than real-time monitoring and reporting about crisis to elderly people for precautions. DT technology integrated with IoT-based cloud environment offers an efficient path to resolve restricted access to information, communication, and convergence. It can support IoT-cloud healthcare services for the elderly person. The main contribution of this chapter is as follows: DTHCSs was proposed in order to unravel predicament of existent control and precision of crisis forewarning for elderly. Second, digital healthcare service platforms were developed and various benefits and challenges have been discussed in terms of security and privacy.

References

[1]   Y. Liu, L. Zhang, Y. Yang, *et al.*, A novel cloud-based framework for the elderly healthcare services using digital twin. *IEEE Access* 7, 49088–49101, 2019.

[2]   J. Jimenez, H. Jahankhani, and S. Kendzierskyj. Healthcare in the cyberspace: medical cyber-physical system and digital twin challenges. 2020. DOI:https://doi.org/10.1007/978-3-030-18732-3_6.

[3]   I. Lee, O. Sokolsky, S. Chen, *et al.* Challenges and research directions in medical cyber–physical systems. *Proceedings of IEEE* 100(1), 75–90, 2012.

[4]   T. Soyata, R. Muraleedharan, C. Funai, M. Kwon, and W. Heinzelman. Cloud-vision: realtime face recognition using a mobile-cloudlet-cloud acceleration architecture. In: *2012 IEEE Symposium on Computers and Communications (ISCC)*, pp. 000059–000066, New York, NY: IEEE, 2012.

[5]   G. Nalinipriya and R.A. Kumar. Extensive medical data storage with prominent symmetric algorithms on cloud-a protected framework. In: *2013 IEEE International Conference on Smart Structures and Systems (ICSSS)*, pp. 171–177, New York, NY: IEEE, 2013.

[6]   K. Bruynseels, F. Santoni de Sio, and J. van den Hoven. Digital twins in healthcare: ethical implications of an emerging engineering paradigm. *Frontiers in Genetics* 9, 31 2018.

[7]   Y. Ma, Y. Wang, J. Yang, Y. Miao, and W. Li. Big health application system based on health Internet of Things and big data. *IEEE Access* 5, 78857897, 2017.

[8]   World Health Organization, *Preventing Chronic Diseases: A Vital Investment*, vol. 126, no. 2, Geneva, Switzerland: World Health Organization, 2008, p. 95.

[9]   B. Jin, T.H. Thu, E. Baek, *et al.* Walking-age analyzer for healthcare applications, *IEEE Journal of Biomedical and Health Informatics* 18(3), 10341042, 2014.

[10] B. Li, L. Zhang, and W. Shilong. Cloud manufacturing: a new service oriented networked manufacturing model. *Computer Integrated Manufacturing Systems* 16(1), 1–7, 2010.

[11] L. Guo, F. Chen, L. Chen, and X. Tang. The building of cloud computing environment for e-health. In *Proc. IEEE Int. Conf. E-Health Network., Digit. Ecosystem. Technology*, April 2010, pp. 89–92.

[12] P. Van Gorp and M. Comuzzi. Lifelong personal health data and application software via virtual machines in the cloud. *IEEE Journal of Biomedical and Health Informatics* 18(1), 36–45, 2014.

[13] A. Bahga and V.K. Madisetti. A cloud-based approach for interoperable electronic health records (EHRs). *IEEE Journal of Biomedical and Health Informatics* 17(5), 894–906, 2013.

[14] C. He, X. Fan, and Y. Li. Toward ubiquitous healthcare services with a novel efficient cloud platform. *IEEE Transactions on Biomedical Engineering* 60(1), 230–234, 2013.

[15] M. Pasha and S.M.W. Shah. Framework for E-health systems in IoT-based environments. *Wireless Communications and Mobile Computing* 2018, 1–12, 2018.

[16] A.M. Rahmani, T.N. Gia, B. Negash, *et al.* Exploiting smart e-Health gateways at the edge of healthcare Internet-of-Things: a fog computing approach. *Future Generation Computer Systems* 78, 641–658, 2018.

[17] Y.H. Robinson, X.A. Presskila, and T.S. Lawrence. Utilization of Internet of Things in healthcare information system. In Balas, V., Solanki, V., Kumar, R. (eds.) (Eds), Internet of Things and big data applications. *Intelligent Systems Reference Library*, vol. 180, Cham, Switzerland: Springer, 2020, pp. 35–46.

[18] M.S. Islam, F. Humaira, and F.N. Nur. Healthcare applications in IoT. *Global Journal of Medical Research: (B) Pharma, Drug Discovery, Toxicology & Medicine* 20, 1–3, 2020.

[19] A. Abbas and S.U. Khan. A review on the state-of-the-art privacy preserving approaches in the e-health clouds. *IEEE Journal of Biomedical and Health Informatics* 18(4), 1431–1441, 2014.

[20] S. Majumder, T. Mondal, and M.J. Deen. Wearable sensors for remote health monitoring. *Sensors* 17(1), 130, 2017.

[21]   R.G. Sargent. Verification and validation of simulation models. In: *Proc. IEEE Winter Simul. Conf.*, Baltimore, MD, December 2010, pp. 166–183.

[22]   E. AbuKhousa, N. Mohamed, and J. Al-Jaroodi. e-Health cloud: opportunities and challenges. *Future Internet* 4(3), 621–645, 2012.

[23]   S.S. Ahamad and A.S.K. Pathan. A formally verified authentication protocol in secure framework for mobile healthcare during COVID-19-like pandemic. *Connection Science* 33(3), 532–554, 2021. https://doi.org/10.1080/09540091. 2020.1854180

[24]   R. Barricelli, E. Casiraghi, and D. Fogli. A survey on digital twin: definitions, characteristics, applications, and design implications. *IEEE Access* 7, 167653–16765371, 2019.

[25]   R. Liu, F. Wang, B. Yang, and S.J. Qin. Multiscale kernel based residual convolutional neural network for motor fault diagnosis under nonstationary conditions. *IEEE Transactions on Industrial Informatics* 16, 3797–3806, 2020.

[26]   W. Raghupathi and V. Raghupathi. Big data analytics in healthcare: promise and potential. *Health Information Science and Systems* 2, 3, 2014.

[27]   Elisa NegriLuca FumagalliMarco Macch A Review of the Roles of Digital Twin in CPS-Based Production Systems 2351-9789 © 2017.

[28]   M. Garetti, M. Macchi, A. Pozzetti, L. Fumagalli, and E. Negri. Synchropush: a new production control paradigm. In: *21st Summer Sch. Fr. Turco* 2016, 2016, pp. 150–155

[29]   S. Hagemann and R. Stark. Automated body-in-white production system design: data-based generation of production system configurations. IEEE ICKEA, 2018.

[30]   T.Y. Melesse, V. Di Pasquale, and S. Riemma. Digital twin models in industrial operations: a systematic literature review. In: *International Conference on Industry 4.0 and Smart Manufacturing (ISM 2019)*.

[31]   Y. Liao, F. Deschamps, E.D. Loures, and L.F. Ramos. Past, present and future of Industry 4.0 a systematic literature review and research agenda proposal. *International Journal of Production Research* 55, 3609–3629, 2017.

[32]   B. Ashtari Talkhestani, N. Jazdi, W. Schlögl, and M. Weyrich. A concept in synchronization of a virtual production system with real factory based on anchor-point method. *Procedia CIRP* 67, 13–17, 2017.

[33]   E.A. Lee. Cyber physical systems: design challenges. In: *International Symposium on Object/Component/Service-Oriented Real-Time Distributed Computing (ISORC)*, 2008, pp. 364–369.

[34]   F. Biesinger, D. Meike, B. Kraß, and M. Weyrich. Open access a digital twin for production planning based on cyber-physical systems: a case study for a cyber-physical system-based creation of a digital twin. *Procedia CIRP* 79, 355–360, 2019.

[35]   M. Weyrich, M. Klein, J. P. Schmidt, *et al.* Evaluation model for assessment of cyber-physical production systems. In: S. Jeschke, C. Brecher, H. Song, and D. Rawat (Eds.), *Industrial Internet of Things: Cyber manufacturing Systems*, Cham: Springer International Publishing, 2017, pp. 169–199.

[36] F. Biesinger, D. Meike, B. Kraß, and M. Weyrich. Methode zum automatischen Abgleich eines Digitalen Zwillings von Automatisierungskomponenten im Feld und deren digitalen Planungsständen, in Automation 2018, 03–04.07.2018.

[37] F. Biesinger, D. Meike, B. Kraß, and M. Weyrich. A Case Study for a Digital Twin of Body-in-White Production Systems General Concept for Automated Updating of Planning Projects in the Digital Factory, *2018 IEEE 23rd International Conference on Emerging Technologies and Factory Automation (ETFA)*, Turin, Italy, 2018, pp. 19-26, doi: https://doi.org/10.1109/ETFA.2018.8502467.

[38] Conference on Emerging Technologies and Factory Automation (ETFA), Turin, Sept. 2018.

[39] T. Bauernhansl, M. ten Hompel, and B. Vogel-Heuser. Industrie 4.0 in Produktion, Automatisierung und Logistik. Springer Fachmedien Wiesbaden, Wiesbaden, 2014, p. 639.

[40] E. Westkämper, D. Spath, C. Constantinescu, and J. Lentes. Digitale Produktion, Berlin, Heidelberg: Springer Berlin Heidelberg, 2013.

[41] M. Weyrich, J.P. Schmidt, and C. Ebert. Machine-to-machine communication. *Software Technology, IEEE* 31(4), 19–23, 2014.

[42] S. Hagemann and R. Stark. Automated body-in-white production system design: data-based generation of production system configurations. IEEE ICKEA 2018.

[43] E. Geisberger and M. Broy. Agenda CPS – Integrierte Forschungsagenda Cyber-Physical-Systems, Deutsche Akademie der Technikwissenschaften acatech, 2012.

[44] J. Ma, Z. Mo, and D. Gal. The route to improve the effectiveness of negative PSAs. *Journal of Business Research*, 123, 669–682, 2021.

[45] R.A. Rosalia, K. Wahba, and N. Milevska-Kostov. How digital transformation can help achieve value-based healthcare: Balkans as a case in point. *The Lancet Regional Health – Europe* 4, Article 100100, 2021.

[46] M. Parviainen, J. Tihinen, and S. Kääriäinen. Teppola tackling the digitalization challenge: How to benefit from digitalization in practice. *International Journal of Information Systems and Project Management* 5(1), 63–77, 2017.

[47] I. Rubbio, M. Bruccoleri, A. Pietrosi, and B. Ragonese Digital health technology enhances resilient behaviour: evidence from the ward. *International Journal of Operations and Production Management* 39(4), 594–627, 2019.

[48] D.R.A. Schallmo and C.A. Williams. Digital transformation now! – guiding the successful digitalization of your business model. Cham: Springer Briefs in Business, 2018.

[49] K. Yousaf, Z. Mehmood, I.A. Awan, *et al.* A comprehensive study of mobile-health based assistive technology for the healthcare of dementia and Alzheimer's disease (AD). *Healthcare Management Science* 23, 287–309, 2020.

[50] T. Chakravorty, K. Jha, and S. Barthwal. Digital technologies as enablers of care-quality and performance: a conceptual review of hospital supply chain network IUP. *Journal of Supply Chain Management* 15(3), 7–25, 2018.

[51] M.N. Kavitha, S.S. Saranya, K. Dhanush Adithyan, K. Soundharapandi, and K.S. Vignesh. A novel approach for driver drowsiness detection using deep learning. In: *Proceedings of the 4th National Conference on Current and Emerging Process Technologies e-CONCEPT-2021 AIP Conf. Proc.* 2387, 2021, 140027-1–140027-6.

[52] N. Kanimozhi, N.V. Keerthana, G.S. Pavithra, G. Ranjitha, and S. Yuvarani. CRIME type and occurrence prediction using machine learning algorithm. In: *Proceedings of the International Conference on Artificial Intelligence and Smart Systems (ICAIS-2021)* IEEE Xplore, March 2021.

[53] S.S. Saranya, C. Santhosh, and M. VijayaKumar. Blockchain endorsement technology – a review of future smart paradigms. *International Journal of Aquatic Science* 12(3), 975, 2021.

[54] S.S. Saranya, N. Kanimozhi, M.N. Kavitha, K.S. Atchayaprakassh, and K.K. Ragul. Authentic news prediction in machine learning using passive aggressive algorithm. In: *Second International Conference on Artificial Intelligence and Smart Energy (ICAIS)*, IEEE Xplore, 2022, pp. 372–376.

[55] M.N. Kavitha, N. Kanimozhi, and S.S. Saranya. Face mask detection using deep learning. In: *Second International Conference on Artificial Intelligence and Smart Energy (ICAIS)*, IEEE Xplore, 2022, pp. 319–324.

[56] M.N. Kavitha, V. Vennila, G. Padmapriya, and A. Rajiv Kannan. Prevention of Sql injection attack using unsupervised machine learning approach. *International Journal of Aquatic Science* 12(3), 1413–1424, 2021.

[57] K. Sathya, J. Premalatha, and V. Rajasekar. A modernistic approach for chaotic based pseudo random number generator secured with gene dominance. *Sādhanā* 46, 8, 2021. https://doi.org/10.1007/s12046-020-01537-5.

Chapter 5

Digital twin and big data in healthcare systems

*P. Nancy[1], K. Jayashree[2], V. Sudha[3], R. Akiladevi[4]
and Prithi Samuel[5]*

Digital twin (DT) emphasizes the visual of biological systems based on in silico computational methods that include data both from the individual as well as the community. By augmenting medical care with digital surveillance and advanced simulation of the human body, the usage of DT in medical field is transforming clinical operations and healthcare administrators. Investigators can use these technologies to learn more about diseases, new medications, and medical gadgets. In the future, this could potentially be used to assist clinicians in maximizing the effectiveness of physician therapeutic approaches. Nevertheless, in the medium run, DTs will aid the healthcare system in bringing life-saving breakthroughs to the marketplace more quickly, at cheaper prices, also with enhanced patient safety. In the medical field, DT can be used to maintain medical devices and enhance their effectiveness. By translating a significant volume of patient records into valuable information, DT and Artificial Intelligence (AI) technologies are furthermore utilized to elevate the life-cycle of healthcare. The supreme goal of digital twinning in medicine is to assist organizations with patient management and coordination. Increasing services, patient desire, deteriorated technology, a lack of beds, enhanced waiting period, and lines plagued Mater remote clinics in Dublin (intended for radiology and cardiology). These issues showed that the existing framework needed to be improved in order to meet rising demand.

5.1 Introduction

Digital twin (DT) technology is among the most essential Industry 4.0 technology accessible today. DT gives users a look at all aspects of a specific industry. Various viewpoints could then be used to think strategically, and dynamic measurements

[1]Department of Computing Technologies, SRM Institute of Science and Technology, India
[2]Department of Artificial Intelligence and Data Science, Panimalar Engineering College, India
[3]Department of CSE, Kumaraguru College of Technology, India
[4]Department of CSE, Rajalakshmi Engineering College, India
[5]Department of Computational Intelligence, SRM Institute of Science and Technology, India

can be used to optimize the decision-making system. Throughout other words, digital tools for investigating, researching, and assessing resources, operations, and organizations are provided by digital twins. This talent allows users to see exactly what has been happening right now as well as what may occur in the future. A DT uses virtual and wearable technology, along with 3D graphics and statistical modeling, to construct a virtual representation of a system, structure, product, commodity, and perhaps other physical thing. This DT is an exact replica of the modern environment. Through real-time upgrades, its identical clone state is brought up to date. It is a versatile device that may be employed in a range of situations, such as device surveillance and in use across the course of development. Professionals in applied mathematics or predictive analysis investigate the physical phenomena and transactional processes of a physical object or person in order to create a computer simulation that replicates the original. A DT is made up of three major components: data from the past, data in the present, and future data.

5.1.1   Working of DT technology

Developers of DTs focus on ensuring that the virtual computer framework can collect information from sensors that collect statistics beginning the real-world edition. This allows the digital copy to simulate and replicate what is actually occurring with the original version in a real-time basis, allowing for observations into effectiveness and possible complications. A DT can be as challenging or as simplistic as you need it to be, with different volumes of information evaluating how accurately the framework replicates the physical version in the real world.

DTs are often used in different areas of the economy for a variety of applications and purposes. Some prominent examples include manufacturing industry where manufacturing can be made more constructive and optimized, with shorter throughput times, automotive industry where collection and analysis of operational information from vehicles were done in order to evaluate their activity in real time and notify upgrades. Aside from manufacturing and automotive industry, digital twins are used in retail to model and improve customer satisfaction, regardless of whether of a shopping center or individual stores. The medical industry has benefited from DT in areas such as organ transplantation, surgical mentoring, and procedure de-risking. Frameworks have also been developed to prototype the flow of people through hospitals in order to monitor where infectious diseases may arise who might be at risk due to interaction. It also extends its usage in managing disasters. Rising temperatures has had an influence on people all over the world in recent days, and besides, DT can help address it by notifying the development of intelligent facilities, backup plans, and climate science supervision. A DT can also assist cities in becoming financially sound, ecofriendly, and socially responsible. The challenges making drug discovery flawed, delayed, uncertain, and even scary include

- Lack of precise description of reality
- Lack of employing the required number of patients on time
- Lack of treating every patient with the trial's new drug
- Experimental drugs are as not safe as they should be

DT addresses the above challenges by providing the following features.

Protection: Because DTs can recreate a wide range of patient attributes, they can provide a representative picture of a drug's influence on a larger number of people.

Speed: Artificial intelligence can help to systemize research strategy by improving visibility into patient accessibility for a variety of specific criteria.

Predictability: With DTs forecasting patient response, no alternative therapies or illegal substances will be required. As a result, every patient in a trial can be assured of receiving the new treatment.

Safety: By decreasing the number of patients who require genuine screening, DTs can help to reduce the risk of earlier start of drugs.

5.2   Need for DT and big data in healthcare

For healthcare professionals and patients, real-time screening, successful therapy regimens, and preventative treatment of people are the processes that take a long time. The adoption of the DT idea and big data has eased patient monitoring and assessment, allowing for more successful results. Aside from critical patient screening, the DT can be useful for constructive monitoring systems of diagnostic instruments and preventative analysis of smart objects to diagnose complications or performance difficulties before they occur, such as diagnostic device/equipment condition monitoring during downtime. This can help to maintain consistency of treatment while also economizing, effort, and time and energy.

A modeling of the consequences before developing a development kit or real healthcare gadget is another feature that might be beneficial. This means less money spent on design and technology, as well as fewer prototypes and production time. The DT is a first stage forward into an extremely developed digital revolution with exceptional economies that will improve the planet for humanity. The essentials to an effective implementation of the digital twinning are optimization, forecasting, and simulation.

Medical methodological approaches could be revolutionized thanks to DT technology. Capable of answering intelligent questions, obtaining better responses, and drawing valuable intelligence using the technologies without endangering the healthcare of real-life people. Employing DTs, of necessity, involves a data-driven approach. More data allows for more DTs, which leads to more breakthroughs and better therapy. The best way to overcome the destiny of healthcare is data. Further with the introduction of "big" health data – health records, computerized medical imaging, and genomic decoding are all possibilities for digital twinning.

DTs make it feasible to aggregate groups of similar patients which would otherwise be impractical or ridiculously expensive to put together in everyday life. The software also eliminates the hazards and concerns that come with using genuine patients. DT technology in the medical industry, when applied correctly, allows practitioners to discover optimal medicines, enhance outcomes for patients, and increase efficiencies, resulting in healthcare cost savings.

5.3   DT and big data benefits for healthcare

Many sectors including smart cities, healthcare, aerospace, and manufacturing have all embraced DT technology. These are areas with a lot of potential. Together with data from IoT, DT application in healthcare can now perform a significant part in the growth of the medical and health sector. DT solutions can enable health organizations and practitioners in determining the best path to enhance and simplify operations, improve patient perspective, minimize the cost, and increase care quality. DT generates a working prototype of spaces and processes in which the cost and quality utilization specifications are investigated. Furthermore, the DT application in healthcare can be enhanced with emerging technologies such as real-time locating systems, which provide an influential source of data as well as appears to be a means to test modification in setup, procedure, and so on. DTs solutions enable to determine the outcome before the medication is chosen by simulating an intrusive clinical assessment. It enables tremendous activities from the selection of a medical device to the identification of surgical parameters.

5.3.1   Monitoring of patients

DT technologies assists practitioners in monitoring patients who are located remotely. It employs adaptable insights and computational methods to produce accurate results while continuously revamping data gathering and preservation capabilities. Smart wearables help in monitoring patients. Tiny and much more convenient wearables with sensors can be used to serve factual data from the cloud-based digital twin. Novel models can be developed that sense ailments at initial stages, providing physician and users the capacity to detect the patient before becoming ill, with enough knowledge of disease advancement and enhanced patient data collection. Furthermore, it will be also possible to check whether or not the treatment is effective while it is being administered.

5.3.2   Individualized medical care

DT model could be functional to hospitals and administrators allowing nurses and doctors to get a thorough, meaningful analysis of patient insight and outsight thereby recommending a proper workflow schedule. This aids in reducing patient wait times while verifying appointments and keeping accurate portfolio techniques and preservation. The technology also uses Artificial Intelligence to help doctors make more accurate diagnoses of how different medicines affect patients' bodies. It can also be used to determine signs and symptoms by analyzing microbiology data in order to track any specific infection.

5.3.3   Patient individuality and freedom

DT can also offer patients and healthy individuals more control over treatment decisions such as decision in going to a physician and when, how to take therapies, what to discuss with the physician and other interested parties, and how to react appropriately to screening and medical advice. Indeed, as more information becomes readily accessible and observable to both the patient and the specialist, the relationship between the two changes, allowing both the professional and the patient to make better decisions about next steps. However, the use of DTs is predicted to boost independence in the particular instance of avoidance, for decision-making that were previously in the hands of medical professionals.

The use of DTs in medical technologies provides significant benefits such as distant accessibility of patients, their internal organ systems, and mechanisms, as well as knowledge of the behavior of physical devices used on them. In order to forecast the future, it uses a set of inputs obtained from patient characteristics to run a prediction algorithm. The DT of a patient eventually enables data gathering at the best quality exactness of single cells direct interaction in the body's numerous organs. This DT, combined with genomics information, biomedical time series data, and healthcare data, can generate a new data model for each individual.

5.4 Applications of DT in healthcare

DT is a technology integrating many core applications. It finds many applications in various fields. Among those, it plays a prominent role in healthcare applications. Few of the applications in healthcare are diagnosis of diseases, patient monitoring, complicated surgeries, designing medical devices, drug development, and many more which is depicted in Figure 5.1. The interior functioning of the central

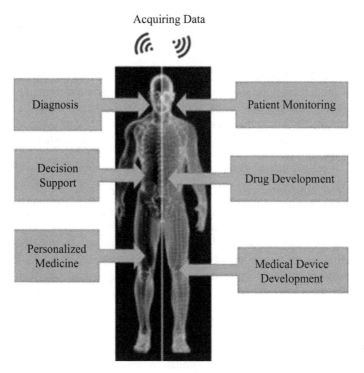

Figure 5.1   Applications of DT in healthcare

nervous system might also be observed using this digital twin approach. Some of the technology's uses are explored in this section.

5.4.1   Diagnosis and decision support

Usually, to diagnose disease for a patient with various parameters from health records, scan and medical reports will be considered. The disease and the consequence of the same varies from patient to patient. Hence, with the help of these parameters, a functional model could be designed and from this simulation, the exact disease could be diagnosed.

5.4.2   Patient monitoring

Diagnosis of disease at the early stage can help us to recover from the same at the earliest. For example, many of their lives could be saved in a pandemic situation such as COVID-19 if it was possible for us to predict the existence of the virus in the human body in an early stage. This is possible with the help of wearable devices. These devices are tiny and smart which can collect the patient's information continuously. The collected information can be passed to the DT to construct the model. This construction helps us to study patient details continuously and helps in predicting the diseases. Thus, it helps us to monitor a patient's health. Reference [12] combined data-driven technologies for instance machine learning and DT as a remarkable technique for not only continually tracking patients' physical disability but also digitally evaluating the implementation and development of medical therapies. They expanded into deeper depth regarding the organization's corporate atmosphere for DTs in the context of continuous supervision and tailored digital information diagnostics procedures. Reference [21] developed a special DT model solely on medical data and genetic traits which might help professionals safeguard patients more effectively. Medical technology, as is well known, necessitates the acquisition and management of huge amounts of data. Björnsson *et al.* [13] devised a method grounded on the DT to tackle the challenges of excess data.

5.4.3   Drug and medical device development

Not only DT technology helps to diagnose disease but can also be used for identifying new drugs. Usually, to find medicine for the health issues of a human being, various possible medicines we apply to the digital twin and select the best. Along with this, this invention can also be used for inventing new drugs [27]. That is, small parameters in the existing drugs can be varied to find one that suits the current disease.

5.4.4   Personalized medicine

In general, medicines prescribed for a patient depend upon the disease diagnosed for them and the patients that have similar records. Though medicines are prescribed based on previous similar predictions, for 28–75% [3] patients, these medicines do not work successfully. Hence, medicines must be suggested based upon the individual patient records. With the help of a digital twin, this is achievable. Making use of this technology, a personalized model for the patient could be designed and medicines could be prescribed based upon it. This seeks to address the problem through delivering medical and disorder therapies, as well as preventive and therapy interventions. It is targeted at precise customization since it is adapted to the qualities that distinguish each patient distinct, such as the surroundings, genetic composition, and behavioral circumstances. DTs are a reasonable, complementary technique for implementing customized treatment since they may mimic individual individuals with varying physiological features and mechanical differences. The DT of a patient can help personalize therapy protocols for a specific person without having to rely for screening results. For example, scientists at Oklahoma State University constructed a DT of the cardiovascular system to recreate aerosol nanoparticle motions in lung cancer treatment. The flow of the above process is shown in Figure 5.2. The human in A is affected with disease, say elbow pain. The DT of the human in A is designed. Many such twins are designed.

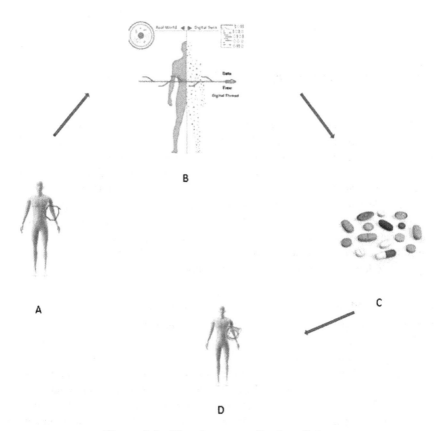

Figure 5.2 Flow in personalized medicines

To each of these designed twins, various possible medicines are applied and from it the medicine that suits best is selected.

Thus, DT could help us to simulate a model that aids doctors in diagnosing the details about the disease they have very quickly and economically.

5.4.5   Medical imaging and wearables

The application of the digital twin can be further improvised by using medical imaging and wearables. These things can help us to capture the real state of a human that in turn aids in building a clearer digital twin. Medical imaging services are in high demand these days. As a result of the enormous demand, diagnostic and interventional imaging has become a logistical issue for providers all over the globe. How could organizations make the most of their available area, technology, and personnel to give patients with the highest care? In this case, the value of a solid, slightly elevated modeling is obvious. Because all of the data is sent into the system, technologies maintain a record of the physician from verification through report delivery. DT presents a patient-centered pipeline by constructing a strong model of a treatment center in which the service organization may identify and eventually open guiding principles in order to maximize productivity, patient satisfaction, and quality care.

5.5   Enabling technologies for DT and data analytics in healthcare

Healthcare analytics has the ability to lower treatment costs, forecast epidemic outbreaks, prevent preventable diseases, and increase overall quality of life. Demand analytics has been strengthened by the introduction of technologies such as AI, IoT, and other sensor-based devices. Automotive, healthcare, aerospace, defense, and manufacturing are some of the end-users. The enabling technologies have a wide variety of applications in the healthcare domain and offer absolute results for exact diagnosis as well as following the treatment methods appropriate for the patient, which is one of the utmost significant principles of medicine. It is the future of personalized healthcare, in which each individual receives the appropriate level of care at the appropriate time.

5.5.1   Technologies for DT in healthcare

Sensor technologies and wireless network advancements have accelerated Internet of Things (IoT) applications and contributed to the real implementation of DT technology. Because of the IoT, DT can collect considerably more real-world and real-time data from a variety of sources, allowing them to develop and preserve more systematic simulations of physical items, their operation, and changes over time. [8]. The IoT objective is to make our daily lives easier as well as improve the effectiveness and production of trades and workers [7]. With the development of digital communication, substantial intelligence, and cognitive systems, the future seems bright and the notion of DT has steadily gained widespread responsiveness in recent years and it has been applied for various applications. [1].

DT modeling and simulation, data fusion, interface, and service are the four phases of the development process for DTs. For the realization of DTs, modeling and simulation are essential. Because DT models contain a great quantity of data, they should have a high data fusion capability. For the digital model to perform properly, multiple building blocks of DTs collaborate with one another. DT provides a variety of services, including health management, status monitoring, prognostics, and decision-making [5].

The incorporation and analysis of enormous dimensions of data is required for personalized medicine [13]. All have suggested a solution to this problem based on the creation of DT. The architecture might find the optimum medication for the surgeon's complaints among drugs used in the treatment depending on the good information computational resources of digital twins. A DT approach for systemic health monitoring was presented by [4]. The DT model comprises three chief modules such as physical system and data acquisition, the model's real-time upgrading technique depends on multivariate Probabilistic models. The DT model, which is based on a non-parameter Bayesian network, is initially built to represent the wellbeing status development method and the spread of uncertainty in epistemology. The modified Gaussian particle filter is then used as an interpretation technique to upgrade the states of the system and variables on a continuous basis. Lastly, Dirichlet process mixture model is provided as a method for estimating hidden variables and detecting the nonparametric Bayesian network's self-learning.

Fuller *et al.* (2021) discussed the functional domains and enabling technologies of a DT are (1) application domain, (2) middleware domain, (3) networking domain, and (4) object domain. The application domain is divided into three levels, the first is the model architecture and visualization layer, which is required for producing high-fidelity prototypes of physical entities. The layer is supported by tools like Simulink and Twin Builder, and allows for the visualization and architecture modeling of DT. The second tier is programming and APIs, that are being used to assist in the modelling of such DT architecture, enabling the third stage, pre-processing and collections, to take place. This third layer is required to verify that the data is appropriately captured. The middleware domain comprises two layers such as storage technology and data processing. The first layer enables data storage through MongoDB, On-demand libraries, and MySQL facilities. Data processing layer is necessary for transferring data from Middleware to the Networking domain. The network domain is divided into two tiers, the first being the technology and communication layer, that guarantees that collected data is transferred across sectors. The wireless transmission layer is the second tier in the virtual network, and it is responsible for ensuring that transmission of data within a DT design maintains the standard as well as delivering information to the next domain. The commercial and industrial applications and sensor technologies are excellent opportunities levels in the object space. Both of these are essential to ensure that the necessary infrastructure for DT analytics is in place, and to enable collection of data more convenient employing sensing devices.

Reference [2] has created a DT model that consists of a customizable AI-assisted framework that could be utilized to model the living organism as a whole and anticipate the progression of pathophysiology illnesses. The first module uses a graphical neural net to anticipate therapeutically suitable outcomes, while the second uses a feedforward neural network to show that inter monodromy is possible. Liu *et al.* [24] suggested a cloud medical system approach that relies on digital twin healthcare (CloudDTH). The platform is a cloud platform that is novel, extensive, and extendable for monitoring, diagnosing, and forecasting elements of an organization's effectiveness. The primary key requirements used in the development of that kind of system can be divided into six categories such as Healthcare Resource Access, Healthcare Data Management and Analysis, Healthcare Data Security, DTH Model Management, Healthcare Service Management and Healthcare Information Fusion and Sharing.

Orcaja has discussed technologies behind DT such as statistical and mechanistic modeling. All mathematical approaches for inferring relationships from data, such as Bayesian and frequentist inference, as well as artificial learning methods, are included in statistical modeling. Inductive reasoning is used in statistical models. These techniques are increasingly being employed in patient monitoring, diagnosis, and therapeutic decision-making. Deductive reasoning is used in mechanistic models. They deliver a structure for combining and augmenting experimental and clinical data, as well as finding mechanisms and predicting outcomes in previously unknown settings. Surgical simulation, medical device optimization, medication development, and regulatory decision-making are all areas where these technologies are increasingly applied.

5.5.2   Technologies for data analytics in healthcare

Big data in healthcare allows for strategic planning, electronic medical records, real-time alerting, predictive analytics in healthcare, telemedicine, and to prevent unnecessary emergency room visits [22,25]. Big data solutions are used in the healthcare industry today. This can be a major stepping stone in personalized healthcare, population health, setting healthcare guidelines, prediction of viral diseases at an earlier stage and finding evidence-based medicine. The predictive analytics of big data can provide early detection of diseases. Pattern detection through wearable sensors for elderly people can be helpful in avoiding fatal attacks. The data from the healthcare centers such as private clinics and government hospitals have valuable data like the identity of the patient with the disease and the treatment procedure and other clinical entries. These data can be used to draft public policy as they provide summarized data of a particular region which can be made as the base for the same. Analytic solutions can mine data to predict the future trends. The custom of enumerated investigation and numerical study by surgeons can custom diagnosis [9]. In healthcare, streaming data analytics is demarcated as the methodical use of uninterrupted waveform and related medical record information developed over practical diagnostic restraints such as empirical, qualitative, environmental, intellectual, and prognostic data to initiate decision making for patient care [23]. The overall prevalence of cross-field estimations in nutrition massive data is an indication of big data's ability to integrate data from various healthcare data sources, like those of integrating epigenetics and cognitive ability data in central nervous system research, and to relate sensation and prognostics to therapeutic interventions and coordinate care at various levels of therapeutic assessment [26].

The authors have suggested an inclusive framework for Big Data Analytics (BDA)'s application in healthcare. The six components that are in the framework include medical records, sensor data, ethical aspects, technology integration, hospital management, and customized care [20]. In medical applications, business intelligence is a proficient means of combining, identifying, and analyzing vast amounts of complex data including genomic data, empirical studies, health information systems data, and online social networks. BDA is able to entangle numerous domains, including computational biology, diagnostic imaging, sensory intelligence, healthcare analytics, medical technology, and quantitative bioengineering, respect to the implementation of such different data [15]. Reference [10] described the BDA of four different types. They are predictive, perspective, diagnostics, and descriptive.

Predictive: In this process, the previously found data is checked for patterns with possible solutions that were used and their effect on the trend. This information is used to predict the future trends and possible solutions needed for the patterns.

Perspective: In this process, the outcome is a list of possibilities of what may happen if a particular solution is followed. It recommends the steps to be taken for a result that is predicted. It handles the multiple solutions and its most likely outcomes.

Diagnostic: In this process, the answers to how, what and why regarding the past information is extracted. It helps to identify the root cause of certain events that were impacted directly or indirectly.

Descriptive: Here the data from the events in real-time is operated upon to plan needs and near future possibilities. It is among the analytics that turns large amounts of information into little volume of information and has been used by numerous businesses to establish rates. Alexandru *et al.* [19] have discussed that in precision medicine, phenotype, and infection type pose a significant problem. Whenever a differential diagnosis of the same or comparable illnesses can be separated into suitable categories, more effective individualized therapy can be provided. Sub-categorization is also an effective instrument for therapeutic interventions, since it allows for better medical diagnoses for therapeutic strategies by categorizing individuals based on substantial phenotypic differences.

Kumar and Singh [16] examined Map Reduce, Mahout, Hive, HBase, Oozie, Avro, Zookeeper, Yarn, Sqoop, and Flume, among other technologies in the Hadoop Cluster framework. Patient screening in remote places has been done by [11,17] with an emphasis on cardiac disease patients. Those who collect information with data and transmit it to the cloud, in which big data analytics are implemented, the information is recorded in S3 cloud services, and the data can be analyzed with MAHOUT, that also delivers Map reduce for improving the data collected and machine learning techniques for analyzing the data to determine the symptoms of the condition.

5.6   Research challenges of DT and big data in healthcare

Because each individual's personal DT must be developed, which is costly, a reasonable compensation system must be developed to reimburse/pay for the creation of such virtual objects. For constructing and constantly improving digital twin prototypes, a huge volume of data must be stored and analyzed on a constant schedule, which would be a time-consuming procedure.

Healthcare organizations' data handling capabilities must also be enhanced in order to handle such massive data collections. To promote patient safety, DTs necessitate complicated data processing, technologies, and information architecture, necessitating substantial training. Entities must evaluate their authentication methods because analytical data is exposed. Individual data must be protected by stringent restrictions and norms.

5.6.1   Problem complexities and challenges

There have been certain major concerns and problems that would need to be researched and solved progressively, and they are all vital for the research's future in this area.

5.6.1.1   Ethical issues

The ethical difficulties posed by the sharing of data describing/produced by multiple perspectives, its collaborators and consumers, twinned hospitals, health practitioners, and healthcare workers should be addressed by programmers. This necessitates that developers and users treat data in accordance with privacy policies and regulatory limitations that must still be established. This is particularly important when it comes to personal medical records.

Availability of high samples with high attribute values and plenty of variance, particularly in medicine, will be critical for effectively training intelligent algorithms. Records from research trials, as well as statistics from relationships with healthcare facilities and clients, might be combined to create such datasets. Effective rules should ensure that these kinds of documents are rendered private and only utilized with the approval of the clients.

5.6.1.2   Privacy and security

Because of the widespread use of network technologies, any digital twin environment must be built with a strong focus on security against threats from hackers. Hacking of confidential, sensitive, or essential information might jeopardize several of the resources engaged in the twinned external surroundings. Privacy and security must be prioritized when using DT technology in the medical and healthcare industries. There is no standard for digital twins because the innovation is still in its initial stages of a project. With the advancements in virtualization and connectivity, a vast amount of personal data is being stored in the server. As a result, privacy and security must be considered, particularly in smart healthcare. As a result, cryptographic protocols and security mechanisms will become major elements of digital twins.

5.6.1.3   Development cost

The fundamental development platform, including the equipment of industrial machines and its virtualized interface, must all be reconsidered and reconfigured when creating a digital twin system. This entails high expenditures and may limit the use of DT technology to major corporations with sufficient money and personnel management. Fortunately, a significant amount of research is being done, and experimental DTs have indeed been established in the medical fields, with some of them being presented or offered as public archives for purposes of research. Without accessible libraries, the importance of developing and using DTs may be limited to a small number of companies.

5.6.1.4   Equal wealth distribution

The establishment of decentralized DT systems necessitates the provision of continuous and pervasive connectivity, sensors, and understanding exactly across all people concerned. When it comes to under development countries (UDC), this capability is lacking. As a result, the development of DT technology in business may expand the social inequalities, metropolitan and remote areas. In the situation of DTs of internal tissue, clinicians and investigators must be trained how to utilize them properly in order to encourage their attention in using them. As a result, a standardized structure for specialist education and skill building is critical to ensuring the development of medical DTs.

5.6.2   Research challenges for DT in healthcare

As described below, there are a variety of obstacles to overcome when addressing open research issues for DT.

5.6.2.1   Multidisciplinary

The diverse frameworks utilized for development and deployment pose a substantial challenge. These contribute to a variety of several diverse disciplines of descriptive research design in collaboration, that can promote innovations but also be a burden because aims in numerous domains guide the research in different ways, leading to decreased outcomes.

5.6.2.2   Consistency

An even more challenge confronting DT is the absence of uniformity, and evident across several new and developing innovations. As a consequence, there are differences among initiatives in the DT. The range of interpretations encountered is a major contributor; this, combined with the lack of regulation, is a problem, impeding the advancement of the DT technology.

5.6.2.3   Innovations at a global level

Numerous opportunities, as well as obstacles, arise with the significant improvements in DTs and their accompanying technologies. Future-oriented and unsustainable ambitions delay the design and implementation of recently adopted technology and viewpoints. With the advent of industrial revolution 4.0 and the massive development of digitalization, distinct technologies are developing at varying rates. Unfortunately, the rapid expansion creates a slew of connections and information exchange issues. Enhanced performance or intelligent devices, for instance, might not have been interoperable with the DT. This varying pace of development can introduce new surveillance issues in terms of revealing security flaws.

5.6.3   Useful information

A high-quality, unhindered, and substantial amount of information is necessary for DTs. The Internet of Things seems to have the capability to boost massive amounts of data. The accuracy of the data will have an effect on the effectiveness of DTs, particularly in the areas of business intelligence and computing. As a result, it is essential to guarantee that the DT technology's data frame is functional and of excellent quality. For the performance and reliability of specific operations, there is almost no standard DT paradigm because the technology is in its early years of development. It might be easier for individuals who want to use a DT paradigm to cope with particular situations if there could be a common strategy.

5.7   Future research directions

In recent decades, there has been a transition in the expansion of DT utilization, aided by a rise in the number of academic studies and industry representatives spending extensively in the development of DT technology. Without the growth of AI and machine learning, Internet of things, and automation, which has become crucial facilitators for DTs, there would be no DTs which is conceivable. A majority of reports addressing the need for DTs for business intelligence of human users have drawn on common ideas in terms of health monitoring and reporting. It also emphasizes remote surgical improvements and the significance of cooperative sensing research, owing to the nature of confidential documents used in healthcare.

Customized and specificity therapies, "to strengthen physiologically precise digital recreations" of a nervous system or a cardiovascular system, specialized model for different circumstances such as brain pulmonary emboli, modeling techniques for operations or several intervention strategies using the "-omics": "genotyping, biomics, bioinformatics, or metabolic engineering, and also physiological markers, psychographic, and personality data over time" are known to be influenced by the transition to DTs in universal healthcare.

The need for DTs in the healthcare system has provoked arguments about its moral and environmental implications, as well as major expectations for improved diagnosis and management. To begin with, digital twins acquire the majority of the socio-ethical security and privacy issues and uniqueness that have previously been related with personalized healthcare analytics. It is uncertain how that DT will aggravate or solve these issues in the long run. Notwithstanding, as a technical concoction, it is reasonable to assume that a digital doppelganger will elicit more, but instead of very few, points of discussion. As a result, the time has come to conduct a socio-ethical assessment of the need for DT in healthcare systems.

5.8 Conclusion

The concept of building a digital clone of a tangible commodity to monitor, evaluate, and forecast outcomes appears potential for the healthcare business, that is moving toward value-based care with measurable results. Efficient algorithms are used to generate digital copies of people, healthcare facilities, and medical devices, which could be crucial in solving concerns such as personalizing healthcare provision, maintenance and support of health centers, and rising research and development expenses. Drug development trials of animals and humans are projected to be replaced by DTs of living creatures in the future. Organizations should use the DT approach more frequently to save production costs, enhance quality of life for patients, and deliver innovative therapies to the marketplace. Even though data validation and a scarcity of trained personnel to enhance and supervise massively complicated methodologies for DTs are significant concerns that could stymie their improvements in healthcare, regulatory requirements such as the General Data Protection Regulation and training and skill development programs will ensure a proper transition for digital twins in the healthcare industry.

References

[1] C. Yi, B. Starly, P. Cohen, and Y. S. Lee, Sensor data and information fusion to construct digital-twins virtual machine tools for cyber-physical manufacturing. *Proc. Manuf.* 10, 1031–1042, 2017.

[2] P. Barbiero, R. Viñas Torné, and P. Lió, Graph representation forecasting of patient's medical conditions: toward a digital twin. *Front. Genet.* 12, 652907, 2021. doi:10.3389/fgene.2021.652907.

[3] B. Björnsson, C. Borrebaeck, N. Elander, *et al.*, Swedish Digital Twin Consortium Genome Medicine. Digital twins to personalize medicine. *Genome Med.* 12, 4, 2020.

[4] S. Yue, J. Yu, D. Tanga, X. Liang, and J. Dai, A digital twin approach based on nonparametric Bayesian network for health monitoring. *J. Manuf. Syst.* 58, 293–304, 2020.

[5] D. Yang, H.R. Karimi, O. Kaynak, and S. Yin, Developments of digital twin technologies in industrial, smart city and healthcare sectors: a survey. *Complex Eng. Syst.* 1, 3, 2021. https://dx.doi.org/10.20517/ces.2021.06.

[6] A. Fuller, Z. Fan, C. Day, and C. Barlow, Digital twin: enabling technologies, challenges and open research, *IEEE Access* 8, 10895, 2020. DOI:10.1109/ACCESS.2020.2998358.

[7] K. Jayashree and R. Babu, Privacy in the Internet of Things, in *The Internet of Things in the Modern Business Environment*, Hershey, PA: IGI Global, 2017. DOI: 10.4018/978-1-5225-2104-4.ch005.

[8] M.N.K. Boulos and P. Zhang, Digital twins: from personalised medicine to precision public health. *J. Pers. Med.* 11, 745, 2021. https://doi.org/10.3390/jpm11080745.

[9]   S. Borikar, M. Bhagchandani, R. Kochar, K. Pardeshi, and M. Gahirwal, A survey on applications of big data analytics in healthcare. *Int. J. Soft Comput. Eng.* 5(5), 36–39, 2015.

[10]   P. Chunarkar-Patil and A. Bhosale, *Big data analytics. Open Access J. Sci.* 2(5), 326–335, 2018.

[11]   T. Anitha, P.L. Charlyn, S. Sridhar, and S. Prithi, Cardio-vascular disease classification using stacked segmentation model and convolutional neural networks. *J. Cardiovasc. Dis. Res.* 11(3), 149–154, 2020.

[12]   L.F. Rivera, M. Jiménez, P. Angara, N.M. Villegas, G. Tamura, and H.A. Müller, Towards continuous monitoring in personalized healthcare through digital twins, in: *Proceedings of the 29th Annual International Conference on Computer Science and Software Engineering*, 2019, pp. 329–335.

[13]   B. Björnsson, C. Borrebaeck, N. Elander, *et al.*, Digital twins to personalize medicine. *Genome Med.* 12, 4, 2020. https://doi.org/10.1186/s13073-019-0701-3.

[14]   A. Bende and S. Gochhait, Leveraging digital twin technology in the healthcare industry – a machine learning based approach. *Eur. J. Mol. Clin. Med.* 7(6), 2547–2557, 2020.

[15]   B. Ristevski and M. Chen, Big data analytics in medicine and healthcare. *J. Integr. Bioinform.* 15(3), 20170030, 2018.

[16]   S. Kumar and M. Singh, Big data analytics for healthcare industry: impact, applications, and tools. *Big Data Min. Anal.* 2(1), 48–57, 2019. DOI: 10.26599/BDMA.2018.9020031.

[17]   S. Smys and J.S. Raj, Internet of Things and big data analytics for healthcare with cloud computing. *J. Inf. Technol. Digital World* 01(1), 9–18, 2019. https://doi.org/10.36548/jitdw.2019.1.002.

[18]   E.M. Orcaja, 6 Digital Twin Applications in Healthcare – The Revolution of the Next Decade Article, 2021.

[19]   A.G. Alexandru, I.M. Radu, and M. Biizon, Big data in healthcare – opportunities and challenges. *Inform. Econ.* 22(2), 43–54, 2018. DOI:10.12948/issn14531305/22.2.2018.05.

[20]   S. Khanra, A. Dhir, A.K.M. Najmul Islam, and M. Mäntymäki, Big data analytics in healthcare: a systematic literature review. *Enterprise Inf. Syst.* 14(7), 878–912, 2020. DOI:10.1080/17517575.2020.1812005.

[21]   G. Fagherazzi, Deep digital phenotyping and digital twins for precision health: time to dig deeper. *J. Med. Internet Res.* 22, e16770, 2020.

[22]   G. SwarnaLatha and G. Sridevi, Application of big data analytics: an innovation in healthcare. *Int. J. Comput. Intell. Res.* 14(1), 15–27, 2018.

[23]   A. Belle, R Thiagarajan, S.M.R. Soroushmehr, *et al.*, Big data analytics in healthcare. *BioMed Res. Int.*, 370194, 16, 2015. http://dx.doi.org/10.1155/2015/370194.

[24]   Y. Liu, L. Zhang, Y. Yang, *et al.* A novel cloud-based framework for the elderly healthcare services using digital twin. *IEEE Access* 7, 49088–49101, 2019. DOI:10.1109/ACCESS.2019.2909828.

[25]   S. Prithi, T. Poongodi, D. Sumathi, and P. Suresh, Real time health mon-itoring using IoT sensors, in: *Electronic Devices, Circuits and Systems for Biomedical Applications*, New York, NY: Elsevier, 2021.

[26]   M. Ienca, A. Ferretti, S. Hurst, M. Puhan, C. Lovis, and E. Vayena, Considerations for ethics review of big data health research: a scoping review. *PLoS One* 13(10), e0204937, 2018. https:doi.org/10.1371/journal.pone.0204937.

[27]   F. Pappalardo, G. Russo, F.M. Tshinanu, and M. Viceconti, In silico clinical trials: concepts and early adoptions. *Brief Bioinform.* 20(5), 1699–1708, 2019.

Chapter 6

Digital twin data visualization techniques

C.N. Vanitha[1], S. Malathy[1] and S.A. Krishna[2]

6.1   Introduction – twin digital

A graphical interface of a physical thing is referred as a "Digital Twin" (DT) or activity that acts as its real-time digital equivalent. A DT is a computer simulation of real things, such as a jet power train, wind turbines, and skyscrapers. Twin technologies can be used to reproduce activities in order to collect data and forecast how they will behave, in addition to real assets.

The virtual process twin's [1] absolute lowest layout and specification is depending on the virtual threads for precision, and the "twin" is also reliant on the virtual threads for correctness. Engineering change orders (ECOs) are used to make adjustments to a product's design (ECO). When an ECO is applied to a basic item, it creates a new DT and also a new edition of the product's virtual threads.

A DT [1] is a software which it uses traditional data to develop models which forecast that a product/service would develop in the future. To improve the output, these applications can use IoT (Industry 4.0), AI, and data analytics. Thanks to advances in machine learning and features like large datasets, such innovation becomes essential for modern architecture to stimulate growth and enhance effectiveness. In brief, having one can help improve strategic technological trends, prevent costly breakdowns in physical objects, and test processes and services utilizing superior analytical, monitoring, and predictive capabilities shown in Figure 6.1.

6.2   Invention of DT

DTs were first mentioned in David Gelernter's book "Mirror Worlds," in 1991, later employed in manufacturing by Florida Institute of Technology's Michael Grieves. By 2002, Grieves had gone to the University of Michigan, and he publicly revealed the notion of the DT at a Society of Manufacturing Engineers convention in Troy, Michigan. Actually, NASA was the first to adopt digital twin idea, and in a

[1]Department of Computer Science Engineering, Kongu Engineering College, India
[2]Department of Mechatronics Engineering, Kongu Engineering College, India

Figure 6.1   Digital twin

2010 Report on the Roadmap, NASA's John Vickers gave the concept its name. The concept was used to test space rockets and spacecraft using digital models.

When the DT was named one of top ten recent technologies by Gartner in 2017, it gained even more attention. Since then, the principle has been used to an ever-increasing variety of uses.

6.2.1   Function of DT technology

Specialists in maths or information science examine the science and data records of a physical entity or process before developing a computer simulation that replicates the actual [2]. The architects of twin digital make certain devices that collect information from the physical version can provide input to the virtualization model. This allows the digital copy to replicate and emulate what is going on with the earlier design in real time, allowing data on performance and potential issues to be collected.

The quantity of data used determines how closely the model resembles the real-world version, thus a DT can be as complicated or as simple as you need it to be. The twins could be used in combination with sample that provide information about the product as it is being made, or it can be used as a concept on its own to model what will happen when the actual model is produced.

6.2.2   What problems has it solved?

It has been utilized to tackle a wide range of problems since it may be applied in a variety of areas, from transportation to medical and electrical production. Among the issues are stress monitoring and resistance to corrosion for offshore wind farms, as well as advances in racing car efficiency. Hospital modeling, for example, has been used to identify current processes and staff in order to improve operations. A DT can be used to replicate an issue, allowing a solution to be designed and evaluated in a computer instead of in the actual world.

6.3 DT types

DTs work in a similar bottom-up way, where the lowest level is the simplest and yields limited information, with each additional level [3] providing more sophisticated and more diverse types of information. This concept is at the core of an emerging hierarchy of the DT, which includes shown in Figure 6.2.

• Parts twinning
• Product twinning
• System twinning
• Process twinning

6.3.1 Parts twinning

The foundation of digital twinning is the need for robust parts twinning. At this level, designers can grasp the biological, chemical, and electric aspects of a part thanks to virtual simulations of individual parts. Many computer-aided design (CAD) systems, for example, now include the capacity to perform a number of durability studies, such as dynamic stress and thermal stress. Electronic circuit simulation software, for example, tells us how electronic components will react as various electrical signals are injected into a circuit. It requires a mathematical model of sufficient complexity to be able to best predict real-world behavior under a variety of scenarios.

6.3.2 Product twinning

Individual item twinning provides helpful information, but replicating the interoperable components as they interact allows for product twinning. Understanding how components interact with one another and with their surroundings enables for component part optimizing, enhancing operating characteristics while minimizing things like MTBF and MTTR [4].

6.3.3 System twinning

System twinning takes things a step further, which allows engineers to manage and maintain whole fleets of diverse items that work together to attain a system-level goal.

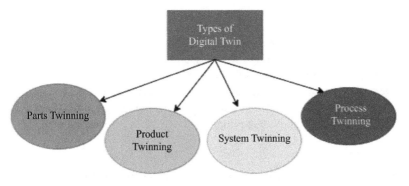

Figure 6.2   DT types

Think of an energy grid that can spin up or spin down electrical generation by monitoring the demand. Consider how this idea could be used to a wide range of system families. Groups that design and operate communications infrastructure, traffic control systems, or advanced manufacturing networks will have unrivalled capacity to monitor and explore with their processes in order to attain unprecedented efficiency and effectiveness [5].

6.3.4   Process twinning

DT is not just for physical items; it may also be used to duplicate tasks and procedures. Process twin allows for the improvement of tasks in the refinement of raw material and the manufacturing of final goods [6]. Even processes with humans in the loop would benefit from DT modeling, since it would allow managers to modify inputs and see how outputs are affected without risking upsetting processes, which can cause operations to grind to a halt. Superior corporate management will be able to monitor important business metrics in a far more information approach than previous feasible thanks to process twin.

6.4   When to use

The numerous occasions when the method can be employed can be split down into three basic sorts of DT:

- DT prototype: Performed prior to the production of a specific object.
- DT instance: Performed after one product is created to conduct testing in different application areas.
- DT aggregate: This program collects DTI data in order to predict a product's capability, perform prognostics, and test operating parameters.

Only a few of the applications for these umbrella types include logistic planning, product creation and re-design, safety analysis and monitoring, and necessary for the identification. A DT can be used to save time/money while testing a product or a service, whether it's for creation, execution, observation, or research.

6.5   Design DT

- DTs are used for a variety of uses, including testing a prototype or design, determining and monitoring lifecycles, and assessing how a product or process will perform under various situations.
- Data is gathered and computer models are created to test a DT design. This could include an actual connection for sending or receiving feedback and information between both the digital system and a physical object [7].

6.5.1   Digital data

In order to produce a virtual model that can reflect the qualities or phases of an actual item or technique, a DT requires data about the thing or process. This data could be related to the lifecycle of a product and could include design specifications, manufacturing procedures, or engineering data. It may also contain details regarding the manufacturing process, such as infrastructure, material, components, procedures, and quality assurance. Actual input, research, and maintenance records are all examples of data that can be linked to operations. Business information and end-of-life procedures are two other types of data that can be employed in DT design.

6.5.2 Models

Once the data is collected, it may be utilized to build computerized predictive methods that can predict behaviour, forecast operational implications, and detect operational repercussions. Actions can be prescribed using architectural simulation, mathematics, biochemistry, economics, deep learning, intelligent systems, business rules, and outcomes. To improve human understanding of the data, these models can be exhibited using 3D visualizations and interactive 3d modeling [8].

6.5.3 Linking

DT discoveries can be integrated to provide insight, such as placing hardware twin findings into a production line double, which could then inform a production line DT. Intelligent manufacturing solutions for correct functioning advancements and enhancements could be enabled by utilizing linked DTs in this approach.

6.5.4 Examples

Manufacturing, maintenance, and failure prevention/lifecycle monitoring are all examples of DTs used in industry and beyond. Automotive, where satellite tracking detectors send information from automobiles to the DT curriculum, production, where DTs recreate processes in order to improve efficiency, and health, where sensing can instruct a twin to monitor and anticipate a patient's well-being, are some of the applications.

The production of digital companions for physical things using 3D modeling is another example of DTs. It can be used to see how a physical object is doing right now, allowing tangible objects to be projected into the digital realm. When detectors capture data from a linked device, for examples, the information could be utilized to continuously create a "digital twin" duplicate of the equipment's status.

The thought of a digital model is commonly referred to as a "electronic shadowing." The digital representation is supposed to be an exact and real-time representation of the real object's characteristics and aspects, such as shape, location, motion, condition, and mobility. A DT can also be utilized to optimize asset performance and utilization through monitoring, diagnostics, and prognostics. Sensor data, historical information, human mind, fleets, and simulator learning can all be used to improve prognostics in this market.

DTs of automated cars and their detector suites integrated in a simulated reality of roads and surroundings were also reported to be responsible to address the automotive firm's massive project, checking, and verification difficulties, particularly when the linked methods are primarily based on AI methods that require massive train and test data sets.

6.5.5 How has it impacted the industry?

The digital twin develops a simulation model that can update alongside or in place of a physical counterpart by combining AI, ML, and data analysis with data. This method can be used to evaluate an entirely computerized development cycle, from design to deployment to decommissioning. A DT helps industry foresee disruption; respond to changes, test design updates, and much more by modeling real wealth, systems, and processes to deliver continuous data.

The DT is critical to the advancement of Industrial revolution 4.0 since it allows for robots, data management, and the integration of manufacturing methods, as well as the reduced risk of initial deployment. Employees in the industry can monitor processes in real time, detecting possible breakdowns early and enabling for real-time optimization and evaluation with minimal lost output.

6.5.6 DT usage

DTs are utilized for a range of purposes and applications in a variety of sectors. Some well-known examples are as follows.

6.5.6.1 Manufacturing

Twins can improve productivity and streamline processes while reducing throughput times. Twin in production is a virtual combination of physical item as created, produced, and managed, complemented by real-time process data and analytics based on accurate configuration of the actual product, production processes, or equipment [9].

6.5.6.2 Automotive

DTs are also used in the auto motor industry to gather and analyze management information from vehicles so that they can be monitored in real time and product improvements can be made. The vehicle sector has profited from DT technology [10]. Focusing on auto-mobile business, DTs are deployed by utilizing current data to streamline procedures and lower marginal costs. Designers of automobiles and mobile devices are now using software-based digital capabilities to augment the existing physical materiality.

6.5.6.3 Retail

Apart from industrialization, new devices are used in retail to simulate and improve user experiences, whether at the levels of a shopping area or for individual businesses [11].

6.5.6.4 Healthcare

Organ transplantation, surgical training, and operation de-risking have all benefited from the use of twins in the medical industry. Systems have been developed to predict the patient population through clinics and to track where diseases might be hiding and who might be at risk owing to contact. DT technologies have an impact on the healthcare industry, which is well-known. For item or device forecasting, the DT concept was initially presented and applied in the healthcare business. When it comes to medicine, a more information strategy is the way to go, a DT can improve clinical health, sport, and learning.

It is now possible to construct customized models for patients that are constantly adjustable depending on recorded health and lifestyle variables thanks to technological advancements. The ability to adapt healthcare to anticipate unique patient responses is the most significant benefit of the DT for the healthcare business. DTs will not only improve the precision with which a patient's health is defined, but they will also alter the image of a healthy patient. There are certain disadvantages to the rise of the DT in medicine. Because the technology may not be available to everyone, the DT has the potential to exacerbate inequality by increasing the richest and poorest persons.

6.5.6.5   Management of natural disasters

People all over the world have been affected by global climate change in recent years, but adopting a DT to construct better infrastructure, emergency plans, and global warming monitoring can help combat it.

6.5.6.6   Smart cities

The use of DTs can also help cities become more financially, ecologically, and sustainably [12]. Virtual models can assist planners in making better decisions and finding answers to the many complex issues that modern cities face. Real-time data from digital twins, for example, can inform real-time reactions to situations, allowing investments like healthcare facilities to react to crises in real time.

6.6   DT technology's characteristics

Some characteristics distinguish digital technologies from other types of technology. Connectivity, homogenization, reprogram ability and smartness, modularity, and the ability to leave digital traces are all characteristics of DTs [13].

6.6.1   Connectivity

The connectedness of the DT technology is one of its most distinguishing features. The technology allows the physical component to communicate with its digital counterpart. Sensors on the physical object create this connectedness by collecting data, integrating and communicating it via various integration technologies. It also makes it possible for businesses, goods, and customers to be more connected. It is an example servitization, which is a result of technology's interconnectedness. Through services, it adds value to their core corporate offers.

DT's combines IoT, AI, and ML. Software analysis of DT is combined with spatial network graphs which allows for the creation of live digital simulation that update and develop in the same way that their physical equivalents do. Data integration trains and modifies itself from a multitude of different in order to represent its relatively close state and operational conditions. This educational model teaches itself by analyzing sensor data that reflects a variety of aspects of its working environment. In addition, a digital twin's digital model includes historical data from previous machine operation.

6.6.2   Homogenization

DTs are a type of digital innovation that really is both the outcome of and a facilitator of data uniformity. The uniformity of data and the separation of data from its own embodiment have enabled the creation of digital twins. DTs, on the other side, allow an increasing quantity of data about physical objects to be kept physically and separated from the object.

Information can be transported, saved, and processed more efficiently and cost-effectively as it becomes increasingly digital. As a consequence, building DTs would have potentially lower costs, and evaluating, predicting, and resolving issues on virtual models is far cheaper than checking on mathematical model and awaiting for goods to fail before acting.

6.6.3   Reprogrammable

Another essential feature of DT technology is its abilities to be reprogrammed. A DT allows remote modifications to be made using the digital component of the twin. It allows you to reprogram a physical product in a certain way. Using detectors on the physical thing, AI-based technologies, and predictive analytics, DTs can automatically adjust to keep the physical item updated and functioning as well as possible. This reprogrammable nature has resulted in the emergence of features. Using an engine as an example, DTs can collect data on its operation and, replace the engine, if necessary, producing in a greater version of the device.

6.6.4   Digital traces

Another distinguishing feature of DT technologies is that they leave digital traces. When a machine malfunctions, for example, engineers can utilize these traces to read the DT's trace and figure out where the issue started. These diagnoses may be used by the machine's manufacturer in the future to enhance the design of the equipment so that similar faults occur less frequently.

6.6.5   Modularity

In the manufacturing industry, modularity is especially crucial. It's the process of designing and customizing products and production units. Manufacturers acquire the capacity to alter models and machinery by incorporating modularity into their manufacturing models. Manufacturers can require DT system to keep track of the machinery they use and discover areas where they might improve. When these machines are made flexible using data integration technologies, businesses may determine which aspects are causing the device to perform badly and swap them with good fitting parts to optimize the production process.

6.7 Twin data to data

The expansion of new technological advancement, the digital economy will continue to prosper on a global scale (e.g., IoT, Cloud, data science, and AI). As an innovative manner to merge traditional enterprise with the digitalization, the DT is attracting interest from a variety of industries, including aircraft, automobile, transportation, electricity cities, and smart energy city. Focusing on the area of intelligent production, DT is broadly used in store coordination and monitoring, quick setup of production plants, product management, sensors were placed, scheduling, robot procedure enhancement, product quality management, industrial machinery preservation, and human-robot interaction [14]. The design and validation of digital models, the creation and control of smart applications, real-time device monitoring of physical items, malware communication and merging, cross data association and integration, and so on are all examples of practical DT applications.

Due to the introduction of new data technology in recent years, a high quantity of information can be gathered in real time by sensing, Internet of Things, portable devices, and wearable technology, and analyzed through an interconnected computer system (e.g., Cloud technology, edge computing, and grid computing).

6.7.1 Requirements for obtaining complete data

To enhance the precision, reliability, and flexibility of DT-based solutions, extensive data is essential (e.g., quality control, process improvement, and efficiency prediction). Data on both usual and ill conditions, data on common and extraordinary events, data on certain and uncertain situations, and so on are all included in comprehensive data. DT technologies that rely on partial data face a number of difficulties. Other research relies on data from DT models, which might be difficult to recreate because too fast interruptions and moment data with significant uncertainty. Extensive data from the actual and virtual worlds should be used to power a successful DT solution.

6.7.2 Requirements on knowledge mining

Data mining is necessary to extract information from raw data in order to create insightful virtual models that can mimic the internal operations and laws of a physical institution. Deep data mining for new knowledge (e.g., actual entities, model complexity, and data management) continues to be a difficult task. On the one hand, not all information is likewise beneficial for extracting knowledge and information, particularly when it comes to irrelevant, aberrant, and redundant data. However, fully analyzing the underlying linkages behind the data (e.g., causal, comparable, and complimentary correlations) in order to support in-depth knowledge mining is difficult.

6.7.3 Data fusion in real time

Because DT-associated information originates from a variety of sources, there are data noise, inconsistency, and dispute (e.g., physical thing, a digital model, and a resource). Sensor failure, environmental instability, and human intervention can all change the information entropy of data collected from a physical object (a measure of the amount of informational ambiguity). Due to low model effectiveness, data reliability would be affected if virtual models replicated data that differed from physical reality. Furthermore, neither the data that was obtained nor the information that was generated are sufficient for the generation of global perspectives. As a result, data fusion is required, which involves synthesizing and combining data from several sources. This allows data to be evaluated, corrected, and supplemented by one another, resulting in more precise and consistent data extraction.

6.7.4   Data interaction in real time

Actual data exchange is required for active cooperation. Virtual models can be constantly updated utilizing actual information from sensor entities, and virtual model simulation information can be returned to the real entity to match its behavior with a simulated strategy. For early detection, information from DT-based goods must be sent to the actual thing, operation, and control and actual information from the physical object can be used to develop and change the services in order to create different realities. Service data can be used to validate digital objects and increase accuracy because network services must be validated before execution.

6.7.5   Optimization in phases

Adaptive management is a cyclic process in which new information is constantly combined with older information to generate new information. Adaptive improvement is required to enhance virtual systems and methods. In reality, iterative improvement faces two challenges. To begin with, the loss of control and stability makes efficient information merging very hard. Further, even if an additional step can be maintained, information growth is sometimes not guaranteed, because image fusion can occasionally result in data lost.

6.7.6   On-demand data usage

Because DT users have a variety of positions and tasks, they have a diverse set of data requirements. Area operator, for example, want on-site data sets (such as assembly sequence, service phases, and controlling order); specialists, process information (information about the current condition, devices quality attributes, and diagnostics information); and top executives, marketplace information (e.g., materials required, competitive analysis, and brand benchmarks). In light of considerable user disparities in terms of market value, skill, level of knowledge, and so on, it is difficult to execute standard information processing (e.g., search, match, combine, activation, and visualization). To tackle this problem, data supply must be contained as on-demand service.

6.7.7   Data composed of DTs

Real object information, digital design information, customer information, fusion information, connections information, and specialized knowledge are the six sections of the DTD. Figure 6.3 depicts how these elements interact to generate a DTD.

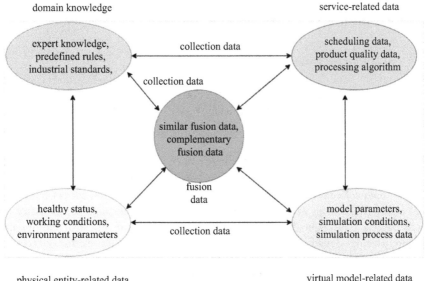

domain knowledge

service-related data

physical entity-related data

virtual model-related data

Figure 6.3   Data composed of DTs

A physical entity is an object with specified functions, behaviors, and structures that exists in the physical world [15]. Real object data can be used to represent
the static properties of a physical entity (e.g., size, position, attribute, and capacity)
as well as its dynamic state (e.g., health status, sudden disturbance, and working
circumstances). The construction of a DTD is based on real object data.

In terms of geometric qualities, physical parameters, dynamic behavior, operation and maintenance standards, and so on, real models represent and characterize a
physical thing in digital world. Real design data includes things like components of
the model and the data from simulations (e.g., circumstances, information generated
during the process, and outcomes). Because real design is fundamentally constructed
on a real thing, virtual model-related data is inextricably linked to physical entity
related data. Application and functional services are the two types of DT services.

Based on physical object data and real design data, application services are provided to effectively resolve issues in a particular application situation, including such
machinery prediction, scheduling, and products quality control. As a result, performance, scheduling, and quality data are the most common types of provider data.

Functional services, on the other hand, are provided to aid DT's routine operations by implementing critical functions such as business solutions, data analysis, and
data connectivity. Related data includes, for example, model configuration information, algorithmic configuration files, and services encapsulating data.

Connection data is information generated from and transmitted between real
object data, digital design data, customer information, fusion information, and domain
knowledge. In contrast to raw data from the five categories, network data is frequently

compressed via information processing. Fusion data, as opposed to single-source data, can merge data from many perspectives, resulting in additional knowledge.

6.8   Data principles for DTs

Data principles focus on broad data collection, expertise extraction, proper information fusion, data communication, adaptive enhancement, information equality, and data usage (see Figure 6.4).

6.8.1   Principle of complementary

The DTD notion is a complimentary concept that matches to the need for significant data collection. It emphasizes the process of information collect both from real and digital worlds at the same time, which complements and compensates for each other's flaws. On the one side, data associated with physical entities can precisely depict dynamic changes in real life, such as ambiguities, fuzzy sets, and complex, which are hard to emulate. Virtual models, on either side, can simulate a broad range of uncommon data sources, unimaginable data, and inter coupling data that cannot be gathered directly from the physical universe at a low cost.

6.8.2   The principle of standardization

DTD derived from a variety of representations, things, situations, and scenes must be turned as much as feasible into standardized data with a common structure, format, type, encapsulation, interface, and so on. To help discover variations between the standard version and the data, a template would be created that explains the data in terms of many elements. The standardization principle is intended to ensure that DTD satisfies the data universal applicability requirement by enabling direct interactions between the different application components, data integration and repurpose in a wide range of application situations, and information sharing and integration along a variety of application situations.

6.8.3   The principle of timeliness

In order to enable real-time data interaction, the time-related concept highlights the significance of trying to transfer and making adjustments connected to an external

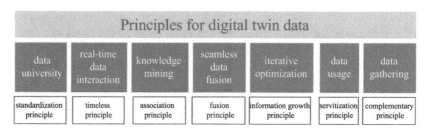

Figure 6.4   Data principles for DTs

between any two parts of a DTD (i.e., real object data, digital design data, customer data, fusion data, and domain expertise) in a timely basis. The link data should be effectively reduced for data transfer in order to reach this aim. Moreover, if the link data among two elements is incorrect (i.e., the difference exceeds a certain threshold), an immediate improvement is achieved to detect and restore consistency.

6.8.4   The association principle

The information extraction demand conforms to the association principle. It focuses on extracting a variety of association links between different portions of the DTD, such as causal, related, and complimentary relationships between real object data, digital design data, customer data, and domain expertise. The discovered associations can reveal useful information including actual entity behavior patterns, digital simulation model methods, and behavior-performance maps between different components of DT. On the basis of given data, basic information can be determined.

6.8.5   Fusion principle

The necessity for smooth data fusion refers to the fusion concept. Its main goal is to create data fusion by combining data from numerous sources with varying relationships. It is feasible to lessen the ambiguity, unpredictability, and fuzzy sets of actual object data or improve the stability of digital design data by combining equivalent data from physical and virtual realities that can be confirmed by each other. Furthermore, more extensive data can be generated by combining complimentary data from several sources, resulting in richer knowledge.

6.8.6   Information growth principle

The iterative optimization requirement conforms to the information growth concept. As data accumulates, iterative data aggregation between new and old data should be used to modify the DTD. To guide future data fusions, the principles of extracting information must be extracted via multiple fusions. The actually reduce in knowledge amount after each fusion can be examined to decide whether or not it should accept the combination, ensuring long-term data growth.

6.8.7   The principle of servitization

The servitization concept implies confining DTD-related resources (information, statistical, data production technology, and presentation approaches) in services that are available on demand that can be thought of as black boxes in converting inputs into useful outputs, production, management, and method. When a user submits a data request that is divided into sub-demands, the having consistent are identified, matched, and connected to provide the information. The goal of this method is to lower the expectations that on-demand data services have on users' items of value.

6.9   DTD methodology

The structure of DTD consists of collection, storing, contact, connection, fusion, adaptation, and automation. To attain data completeness, the complementary notion states that information from both the physical and digital worlds must be obtained together. According to the standards development concept, information in various forms, structures, protective coatings, and interactions should be turned into specified dimensions for storage. Real-time communication is accomplished via the timeliness concept, which entails timely transfer and modification of link data [16]. The data development principle is utilized to understand the continuing data growth. To enable on-demand data usage by multiple consumers, information materials are bundled into services is based on the service marketing principle. Figure 6.5 shows the process.

6.9.1   Information gathering for the DT

The collection of real data layer, digital productions data, customer details, and expertise is referred to as DTD gathering. DTD's basis is made up of these four sets of variables, from which fusion and connection data can be formed. Fixed information (e.g., object property, achievement, and functional areas) can be collected using an off-line measurement equipment and sample selection testing processes (e.g., object property, environmental variables, and sudden disruptions) can be gathered in instantaneously using detectors, embedded devices, radio frequency identification (RFID), and other methods.

Digital design data is frequently generated during the design, simulation, and testing of those geometrical, mechanical, behavior, and rules systems. On the basis of application and functional services, service-related data is generated. Such information

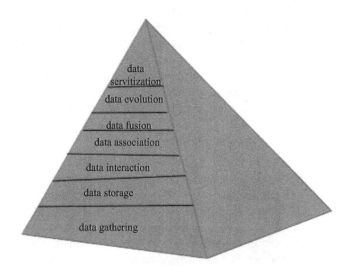

Figure 6.5   Methodology of DTD

can be retrieved at any time during the construction, operation, or maintenance of a service. Specialists, crowd sourcing information, information sources, historical information, and other domain specific sources are frequently employed.

6.9.2 Data storage of DTs

Data linked to physical entities, virtual models, and services collected from diverse application elements, scenarios, and events must be collected and saved for share, reusing, and exchange. Data must initially be represented in a standard fashion, which contains data style, organization, encapsulating, sample rate, previous data accumulating, interfaces communication system, and so on. When particular constraints are not satisfied, it signifies the application criteria are not up to par. For the qualifying ones, information from multiple circumstances (e.g., designing, manufacturing, and service) with variable forms, structure, and encapsulations is translated using a standard template. A single connection and communications method is used to send data from many devices (e.g., a robotic and a cutting tools).

6.9.3 DT data interaction

To facilitate real-time interactions, connectivity between different areas of the DTD should be developed. To begin, acceptable data must be chosen that contains valuable information from various parts of the DTD in order to facilitate message flow between any two components. For example, between both real object and virtual design data, the real states gathered from sensors, which would represent the equipment's actual productions, and the designed to simulate states produced by digital objects, which demonstrate the predicted states, can be provisionally chosen for message passing. Moreover, in the interests of data transmission, cleaning methods, dimensional reduction techniques, and compression techniques are employed to eliminate information noise, duplication, and redundancies [17].

6.9.4 Association of DT data

To promote deep learning, connection linkages between DTDs are mined. To begin, information from the specific object, positions, and services is highly processed to remove undesirable and irrelevant information using data filtration, data processing, and feature extraction. The second stage involves synchronizing time and space. Data must be synchronized in time and converted to the same spatial coordinate system, the least-square method, for examples, can be utilized. The data is then mined for relationships using Pearson correlation analysis, K-means, and other techniques (e.g., causation, similarity, and complementation). To enable future data fusion, two types of data linkages, called comparable and complementary relations, are particularly important.

6.9.5 Fusion of data from DTs

The majority of information fusion research focuses on fusing information from physical universe (e.g., manually generated sensors values), with very few attempts to fuse data from the real and virtual universes. On the other side, DTD fusion comprises the comprehensive combining of real object data, virtual design data, customer data, and domain specific. The aspects of DTD fusion listed below are included. Data's uncertainty, unpredictability, and fuzzy set can all be reduced. If the digital model and customer data differs from actuality, techniques like Bayesian classification and artificial neural networks can be utilized to combine the data that are similar actual object data to improve accuracy and reliability. Information variety for complimentary inter input from multiple areas of DTD can be promoted using methods such as learning algorithms and the weighted average methodology.

6.9.6   Data evolution in the DT

DTD development is a continuous process where new data is introduced, analyzed, and then merged with existing information. This technique is depicted using the data exchange networks created on top of the massive system. When fresh information is added to the network, pre-processing stage new data, attempting to align new information with historical information, attempting to extract organization connections from connected data using data mining technique, and then combining new information with similar or related relations for data adjustment and complement create new organization connections among both new and historical information.

An automated fusion system could guide this technique by reducing the requirement for physical labor. After each fusion, the network architecture can be examined in terms of distribution, connection similarity, cluster coefficients, and other characteristics. Specific DTD development principles, such as data transfer standards and relationships between network design and information sharing, can be extracted based on evaluation outcomes over time. Following that, the guidelines can be used to direct the collection of additional data connections in terms of fusion data analysis, techniques, and processes, assuring repeated development and data development.

6.9.7   Data servitization for the DT

The following features of DTD servitization strive to provide clients with on-demand data access. To begin, different digital materials are enclosed into facilities, which have features (e.g., information searching, preparation, and configuration management), inputs (e.g., data type, density, and component), outputs (e.g., processed data and graphic chart), reliability (e.g., date, price, and durability), and states (e.g. working and unemployed). In response to a customer need, appropriate solutions for extracting data, analysis, and visualizations, among other aspects, can be provided (e.g. search of device status information, part leftover life information, and maintenance recommendation information). Different products can then be combined to produce an integrated solution is based on relevant constraints (such as time and cost). Virtual reality (VR) and augmented reality (AR) can be utilized in addition to normal imaging device to explain the mappings relationships among real objects and model showing in DTD representation (i.e., a specific DTD service in its various forms). Eventually, the connected systems deliver the desired results to users.

6.9.8 DT data's key enabler technologies

Figure 6.6 shows the main contributing technologies for DTD, which are founded on the technological solutions for DT shop-floor (DTS) in specific and DT in general. The following are some of the most important technologies [18].

1. Unique data, severe data, inter coupled data, and other types of data are collected using DTD. Because it is difficult to measure such data directly, simulation-based data generation is necessary. A multitude of technologies can help in data generation. Multi-dimensional modeling technologies can be used to generate data on design, mechanics, behavior, and rules for a range of virtual models. In the situation of insufficient modeling data, domain adaptation technologies can be used to allow modeling with a small data set. To boost data creation efficiency, large simulations technologies (e.g., metamodel 49) can be utilized; however the quality of simulated data must be validated.

2. DTD storage is used to store data that has a variety of forms, formats, types, encapsulations, and interfaces. Unified data model-based technology can be applied database schema and inter-operability; general information functionalities such as adding, removing, changing, and confirming can be performed using data base management system innovation. The data physical planning system can adapt to the ever-changing DTD; data management software can link disparate information silos within the DTD; and different data security mechanisms are all examples of related technologies.

3. In terms of data interactions, data collection technologies is expected to gather network data from numerous portions of the DTD using a variety of ways,

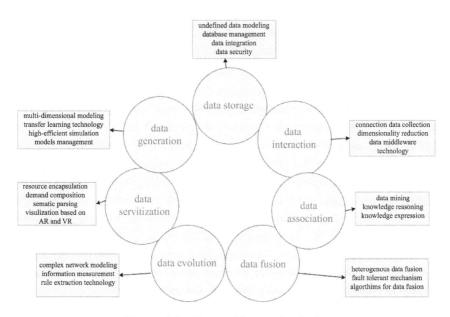

Figure 6.6 Key enabling technologies

including sensing devices crawling. Using dimensionality reduction technology, the unwanted data can be deleted. Data middleware technology completes data format, interface, and communication protocol conversions while ensuring synchronous data delivery. In addition, data consistency evaluation technologies can help with data alignment, data distance computation, and consistency threshold setting.

4. Geographic information alignments, data gathering, information thinking, information retrieval, and other technology are all related to data connection. DTD is synchronized in time and shares the very same reference frame in space thanks to geographic information synchronization technology. Various methods (such as correlation analysis and K-means) can identify DTD groupings and association linkages. Information reasoning technologies can be used to derive new information from existing data or derived associations and groups. To visually portray knowledge, knowledge carriers, and knowledge exchanges, conceptual modeling technologies (e.g., a knowledge graph) can be employed.

5. Data fusion encompasses detection methods, granular modification, heterogeneous information fusion, failure technologies, and other similar technologies.

Before fusion, aberrant data can be removed using anomaly detection technology. Using granularity transformation technology, data with different levels of granularity (e.g., sparse information and dense information, actual data and extraction of features, conceptual symbols and physical data) can be turned to same level. Data with varied features, such as kinds, dimensions, and sample frequencies, can be converged using multisource heterogeneous combining data technology. To improve the data energy's robustness, failure technology can be used.

Demand decomposing technologies can break down a complex consumer demand into specific sub, making it easier to locate a specific provider. In the midst of conflicting goals, a inter-optimal solution can be used to combine multiple services. Timing, price, and accuracy, for example. VR and AR technology visualization techniques can be utilized to more intuitively depict links between information, virtual models, and physical things.

6.9.9   Advantages of DT

In real time, the industry can track a constant stream of consumption and performance data. Industry can create digital threads by combining end-to-end asset or product life cycle data.

- New products as service business model are supported by industries [19].
- It propels advancements in manufacturing, research and development, supply chain management, customer service, and logistics.
- Medical innovation is accelerated by the use of digital twins. Tumor research and treatment development benefit from the use of DTs.
- These tools aid clinicians in precisely optimizing the effectiveness of patient specific treatment strategies.

- This technology has the potential to bring life-saving innovations to market more quickly, save medical costs, and improve patient safety.
- One can examine prospective changes in operational strategy, capacity, personnel, and care delivery models by creating a virtual model of a hospital.

6.9.10   Disadvantages of DT

- The success of technology is determined by its ability to connect to the Internet [20].
- The safety of the public is in jeopardy.
- The concept of DTs is based on 3D CAD models rather than 2D drawings.
- Across whole supply chains, DTs will be necessary.
- Globalization and new production techniques are among the issues at hand.
- As the physical product matures, managing all of these design data for the DT across partners and suppliers will be a difficulty.

6.10   Conclusion

The use of data is a primary motivator for DT. Real object data, virtual design data, customer data, domain expertise, fusion information, and connections data are all explored in this research. With the introduction of DT, information gathering, processing, fusion, interactivity, iterative optimization, universal, as well as on utilization all become increasingly significant. Seven key principles are offered to help organize and handle DTDs that are generated by these requirements. Using these notions as a guide, related approaches for DTD collecting, storing, communication, connection, fusion, development, and innovation are provided. Finally, the important enabling technologies are explored.

References

[1]   A. Rasheed, O. San, and T. Kvamsdal, "Digital twin: r31 values, challenges, and enablers from a modeling perspective," *IEEE Access*, 8, 21980–22012, 2020.

[2]   C. Day, C. Barlow, Z. Fan, and A. Fuller, "Digital twin: enabling technologies, challenges, and open research," *IEEE Access*, 8, 108952–108971, 2020, doi: 10.1109/ACCESS.2020.2998358.

[3]   M. Liu, S. Fang, H. Dong, and C. Xu, "Review of digital twin about concepts, technologies, and industrial applications," *Journal of Manufacturing Systems*, 58(Part B), 346–361, 2021, https://doi.org/10.1016/j.jmsy.2020.06.017, ISSN 0278-6125.

[4]   C. Sturm, M. Steck, F. Bremer, *et al.*, "Creation of digital twins-key characteristics of physical to virtual twinning in mechatronic product development," *Proceedings of the Design Society*, 1, 781–790, 2021, doi:10.1017/pds.2021.78.

[5]   C. Zhou, J. Xu, E. Miller-Hooks, *et al.*, "Analytics with digital-twinning: a DSS for maintaining a resilient port," *DSS*, 143, 113496, 2021, https://doi.org/10.1016/j.dss.2021.113496, ISSN 0167–9236.

[6]   H. Solman, J.K. Kirkegaard, M. Smits, B. Van Vliet, and S. Bush, "Digital twinning as an act of governance in the wind energy sector," *Environmental Science & Policy*, 127, 272–279, 2022, https://doi.org/10.1016/j.envsci.2021.10.027, ISSN 1462-9011.

[7]   V.V. Makarov, Y.B. Frolov, I.S. Parshina, and M.V. Ushakova, "The Design Concept of Digital Twin", *Twelfth International Conference on "Management of large-scale system development" (MLSD)*, doi:10.1109/MLSD.2019.8911091, pp. 1-4, 2019.

[8]   C. Cimino, E. Negri, and L. Fumagalli, "Review of digital twin applications in manufacturing," *Computers in Industry*, 113, 103130, 2019, https://doi.org/10.1016/j.compind.2019.103130, ISSN 0166-3615.

[9]   F. Biesinger, B. Kraß, and M. Weyrich, "A survey on the necessity for a digital twin of production in the automotive industry", in *2019 23rd Int. Confon Mechatronics Technology (ICMT)*, 2019, pp. 1–8, doi:10.1109/ICMECT.2019.8932144.

[10] Y. Liu, L. Zhang, Y. Yang, *et al.*, "A novel cloud-based framework for the elderly healthcare services using digital twin," *IEEE Access*, 7, 49088–49101, 2019, doi:10.1109/ACCESS.2019.2909828.

[11] S. Shirowzhan, T. Willie, and S.M.E. Samad, "Digital twin and CyberGIS for improving connectivity and measuring the impact of infrastructure construction planning in smart cities," *ISPRS International Journal of Geo-Information*, 4, 240, 2020, https://doi.org/10.3390/ijgi9040240.

[12] D. Jones, C. Snider, A. Nassehi, Y.Y. Jason, and B. Hicks, "Characterising the digital twin: a systematic literature review," *CIRP Journal of Manufacturing Science and Technology*, 29(Part A), 36–52, 2020, https://doi.org/10.1016/j.cirpj.2020.02.002, ISSN 1755-5817.

[13] C.N. Vanitha, S. Malathy, K. Anitha, and S. Suwathika, "Enhanced security using advanced encryption standards in face recognition," in *2021 2nd International Conference on Communication, Computing and Industry 4.0 (C2I4)*, 2021, IEEE Xplore, pp. 1–5, doi:10.1109/C2I454156.2021.9689403.

[14] C. Wu, Y. Zhou, M.V.P. Pessôa, Q. Peng, and R. Tan, "Conceptual digital twin modeling based on an integrated five-dimensional framework and TRIZ function model," *Journal of Manufacturing Systems*, 58(Part B), 79–93, 2021, https://doi.org/10.1016/j.jmsy.2020.07.006, ISSN 0278-6125.

[15] P. Aivaliotis, K. Georgoulias, Z. Arkouli, and S. Makris, "Methodology for enabling Digital Twin using advanced physics-based modelling in predictive maintenance," *Procedia CIRP*, 81, 417–422, 2019, https://doi.org/10.1016/j.procir.2019.03.072, ISSN 2212-8271.

[16] F. Xiang, Z. Zhang, S. Ke, and Y. Zuo, "A enhanced interaction framework based on VR, AR and MR in DT," *Procedia CIRP*, 83, 753–758, 2019, https://doi.org/10.1016/j.procir.2019.04.103, ISSN 2212-8271.

[17] F. Tao, T. Hu, N. Anwer, *et al.*, "Enabling technologies and tools for digital twin," *Journal of Manufacturing Systems*, 58(Part B), 3–21, 2021, ISSN 0278-6125, https://doi.org/10.1016/j.jmsy.2019.10.001.

[18] A. Liezina, K. Andriushchenko, O. Rozhko, O. Datsii, L. Mishchenko, and O. Cherniaieva, "Resource planning for risk diversification in the formation of a digital twin enterprise," *Accounting*, 6(7), 1337–1344, 2020.

[19] R. Pluhnau, S. Kunnen, D. Adamenko, A. Loibl, and A. Nagarajah, "Review and comparison of the methods of designing the digital twin," *Proc. CIRP*, 91, 27–32, 2020, ISSN 2212-8271, https://doi.org/10.1016/j.procir.2020.02.146.

[20] S. Malathy, C.N. Vanitha, M. Mohanasundari, and Hari V. Prasath, "Improved face recognition using convolutional neural network with unaided learning", in *2021 5th International Conference on Electronics, Communication and Aerospace Technology* (*ICECA*), 2021, IEEE Xplore, pp. 1–6, doi:10.1109/ICECA52323.2021.9676104.

Chapter 7

Healthcare cyberspace: medical cyber physical system in digital twin

Vani Rajasekar[1] and K. Sathya[1]

The current pandemic has necessitated the development of a powerful and intelligent healthcare system capable of effectively monitoring patients and managing the situation that occurs as a result of the disease's dissemination. Cyber–physical systems and digital twins (DTs) are widely utilized in industry today, and the healthcare industry is eager to adopt these technology solutions to improve their abilities and provide good quality outcomes. Indeed, the introduction of IoT-based Wireless Body Area Networks (WBAN) and healthcare platforms as resulted in the creation of novel approaches for patient monitoring and treatment. However, there are various performance and security issues that come with the use of new technology. However, there are varied performance and security challenges that come with the use of new technology. Given that WBAN can be worn or placed under the skin, the overall idea raises a number of cybersecurity concerns that would necessitate more examination. This chapter explores the importance of WBAN on the healthcare system. It also defines terms like medical cyber–physical systems and DTs, as well as technical enablers like cloud and IoT.

7.1 Introduction

A good healthcare infrastructure is a foundation for every smart city in the current epidemic. When a network can satisfy the price and quantity condition, efficient and appropriate patient monitoring, as well as regular supply of necessary drugs and treatments with medical equipment, is achievable. A prediction mechanism that analyzes the medical system and works effectively to handle the medical emergency makes such a circumstance possible [1]. Smart Healthcare Cyber Physical Systems (SHCPS) are the futuristic systems that will assist the medical community in efficiently dealing with pandemic situations. Patients' physiological realms, medical equipment, and hardware are all part of such systems, as are externally monitored and controlled medical interventions, which are linked to the

[1]Kongu Engineering College, India

cyber world via communications infrastructure for data transmission and exchange of information of physiological parameters, which is evaluated for feed forward control transmissions. By offering efficient and intelligent services, such systems increase the quality of clinical services. The design and implementation of medical cyber physical systems has raised some important topics of conversation, such as autonomy level, privacy, and consistency, all of which are critical for these systems. Production has entered the new era due to better in information systems, information systems (IS), and communication systems. The manufacturing industry is confronting global problems as a result of significant improvements in communications technology against a backdrop of digitalization.

Modern manufacturing approaches, such as the Internet Economy, Industry 4.0, and Asia's equivalent program, have been launched in this framework. These solutions all have the same goal in mind: smart manufacturing. Manufacturing is transitioning from experience and understanding smart manufacturing to information and knowledge-enabled industrial automation, with "smart" referring to increased data and usage. As a result, smart manufacturing is a modern edition of smart manufacturing that emphasizes the use of modern data and communications technologies as well as big data analysis. Smart manufacturing is a future outcome of production wherein real-time data transmitted and evaluation from all over the product life cycle, combined with design modeling and optimization; create intellectual ability that has a positive impact on all areas of manufacturing. Cyber–physical interaction is both a requirement and a core component of smart manufacturing. Cyber physical systems (CPS) is multifaceted and complex systems that bridge the gap between the virtual and real worlds. CPS provides real-time monitoring, knowledge reinforcement, dynamic control, and other functions through the cooperation and communication of computation, communications, and control, sometimes referred as the "3C." Another notion connected with cyber–physical

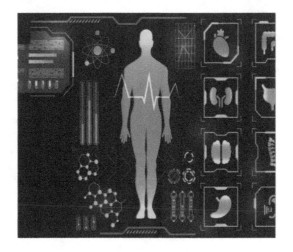

Figure 7.1   DT in healthcare

interaction is the DT. A DT generates high-fidelity digital representations of physical items in digital environment to imitate and offer feedback on their behaviour in the real world [2,3]. A DT is a dual directional dynamical mapping method that breaks down obstacles in the life cycle of the products and gives items a comprehensive digital footprint. The structure of DT in healthcare is shown in Figure 7.1.

7.2 Cyber physical systems

CPS originated from the widespread use of embedded systems, and their origins may be tracked all the way back to 2006. Helen Gill of the National Science Foundation (NSF) created the terminology "cyber–physical system" to characterize increasingly complicated system which could not be adequately described using traditional IT terms. CPS was successfully identified as a highest priority problem in the United States for scientific investment. CPS is depicted as the basis and cornerstone of Industry 4.0 in Germany. There is little uncertainty that CPS will have a significant economic impact and will radically alter current industrial operations [4]. CPS is characterized as seamless integration and bi-directional to satisfy the primary goal of preserving coherence between as-planned simulations and as-builts in the construction realm.

CPS is more fundamental than embedded systems, the Internet of Things, sensors, and other innovations because they do not directly mention implementation methodologies or specific applications. Because cross-over consequences might bring unforeseen vulnerabilities, neither cyber nor physical security paradigms can safeguard CPS. Physical assaults can harm or undermine the device's information management system, while cyber-attacks can cause physical problems. Because CPSs are used in so many essential applications, any form of attack can have disastrous real-world effects. Because a CPS is by definition strongly tied to its physical surroundings, it is substantially less predictable than even cloud technology. Because of the unpredictability of this physical environment, problems such as intermittent power supply and uncertain load conditions arise. CPS has applications in medical devices and systems, traffic monitoring, safety engineering, and infrastructure control, to name a few. The cyber-augmented system (CAS) is a system that can handle complicated system and network behaviors. The agricultural ecosystem is a complicated subject that can benefit greatly from CPS in order to address modern difficulties and challenges. Within the CPS paradigm, multi-sensor collaboration is employed to optimize the amount of pesticide needed for precise spraying [5]. In addition, a three-layer CPS framework has been established: the physical layer, the network layer, and the decision layer. CPSs are systems that combine computer, networking, and mechanical methods. These systems build huge networks that interact with one another and use actuators and sensors to control and maintain complicated physiological processes, resulting in intricate feedback loops between both the physical and cyber worlds. CPSs create totally new markets and opportunities for growth in a variety of industries, bringing development in terms of societal and economic benefits. Healthcare, logistics, precision farming, energy efficiency, pollution monitoring, avionics, key infra-structure control, high degree of confidence healthcare devices and systems, traffic management and monitoring, vehicle manufacturing systems, control systems, distributed robotic systems, industrial production, and urban planning engineering are just a few of the fields where CPSs are being used. Any one of these application areas has a massive beneficial economic impact.

7.3   Digital twin

Manufacturers, smart cities, commerce, automobile, oil and gas, aeronautics, geology, and healthcare are just a few of the industries that have used digital twin technology. These fields have a lot of potential. DT application in healthcare will now play an essential part in the improvement of the health and medical industry, in addition to data from IoT. The emergence of DT models – mimicking the merger of transformative technologies like IoT, Cloud, AI, and XR has been sparked by the advent of digital transformation capabilities [6–8]. A digital depiction of property resources, operational processes, persons, or locations is known as DT. It aids firms in improving their performance by displaying the visualization of complicated assets and processes. Between the physical object and its effectiveness, DT can operate bi-directional automated data flow. To create visual representations, cap-ture, store, analyze the data, as well as provide useful insight, the DT uses four technologies. Remote accessibility of assets, systems, and operations, as well as knowing the behavior of physical devices, is all major advantages of DTs. It per-forms a prediction algorithm using asset behavior information to forecast the future. Furthermore, these insights assist in good decision and automating the decision-making procedure, hence increasing productivity and profitability. It also does risk analysis on various what-if situations and assists firms in increasing operational efficiency. In contrast to digital simulation, which is static and does not change in real time, DT is dynamical and receives real-time changes from a phy-sical asset, structure, or process. As a result, it generates more accurate results for business decisions.

7.4   DT in healthcare

The DT application in healthcare can evolve with new technologies such as real time locating systems, which provide a rich data source and a way to evaluate layout, procedure, and other improvements [9]. The process involved in digital twin is shown in Figure 7.2.

7.4.1   Patient monitoring using DT

The patient's DT is intended to collect statistical information from the individual regarding various vitals, medical conditions, drug and treatment responses, and the environment. The data of each patient is saved in the public cloud and transmitted

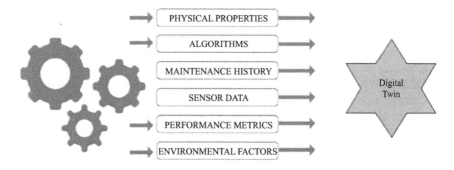

Figure 7.2   Processes in DT

into the DT platform via Azure or AWS. Each patient's historical and real-time data aids the machine learning (ML) system in predicting future health issues [10–12]. The model alerts the patient for prescriptions, dietary habit modifications, and medical consultation based on the patient's environment, daily eating patterns, and blood sugar data. As a result, DT uses AI-powered models to generate more tailored and better treatment plans based on a substantial amount of rich information from disparate IoMT devices. Using insights from previous data, each person's specific DT can assist determine the best therapy, forecast the result of a certain operation, and manage their chronic disease. Consider the case of a heart failure patient who requires cardiac resynchronization therapy (CRT) via pacemaker implantation. Few people do not react to the therapy due to the varying heart features.

Furthermore, in order to avoid future risks, the placement of the proper patients must be accurate. A DT of the patient's heart is built using MRI, ECG, and blood pressure information, and it aids cardiologists in defining the position of leads and digitally testing with insertion before interventional surgery. Another instance is cancer treatment recommended approach using the proper therapy. The doctor can use the patient's camera images, genetic data, and test results to determine the best treatment option, which could be surgery, radiation treatment, or hormonal treatment. To control chronic disease in a huge population, DT analyzes behavioral and physiological data to detect chronic illness at an early point. The virtual twins of patients created by fast stream technologies assist clinicians in virtually monitoring patients. With continual updating of data gathering capabilities and curation, it leverages adaptable algorithms and techniques to produce accurate results. Smart wearable can be used to keep track of patients. Sensors will be utilized to transfer actual information from our digital counterpart in the cloud into smaller and much more comfortable devices. With sufficient knowledge about illness development and ongoing patient data collecting via health trackers, fast stream can create models that recognize symptoms early on, allowing doctors and users to diagnose patients before they become ill. Furthermore, we will be able to assess whether the medicine is beneficial during treatment.

7.4.2   Operational efficiency in hospital using DT

Initially, a DT could only represent a single item or component, but as Artificial Intelligence (AI) technology has advanced, DTs may now symbolize an entire complicated system, process, or location. The use of a DT to represent multiple hospital business operations aids in the optimization and improvement of the overall ecosystem. It simulates a variety of aspects of a hospital, including the mobility of doctors, patients, and technology, as well as real-time tracking monitoring systems, assets, and people [13]. The AI model is used to simulate increased efficiency by using actual information from all hospital pieces of data. The model algorithm can combine the results of imaging and non-imaging laboratory diagnostics and give them to the physician in a way that will assist him in making a better decision. After evaluating their processes and operations, we developed a virtual twin model for one of our companies' radiology departments. By eliminating long wait times, managing complex emergency workers, optimum utilization of lab and hospital instruments, staffing requirements, and managing device downtime, this simulation optimizes the process and enhances the patient outcomes. AI helps doctors make a more definitive diagnosis of how different medicines affect each patient's body.

7.4.3   Medical equipment and DT

Fast stream technologies have developed a virtual twin that contains thousands of medications and can identify the optimal one or ones for a given situation. However, this does not have to be limited to currently available medications. Fast stream can generate a digital ensemble of real patients with varied phenotypes who share complaints and test new prospective medications and see which one has the best chance of success and the best dosage. In the DT application in healthcare, improving the first shoot will reduce the number of clinical studies required. In medical teaching and diagnostics, a DT is a patient's model generated prior actual surgery and simulated surgery conducted on it by a multidisciplinary team to avoid human anatomy harm. This real-time model also enables residents to do surgery simulations on patients, allowing them to better comprehend the physiological and anatomical variances between each patient. Cardio insight mapping technology from Medtronic, which gathers and integrates patients electrical properties data with heart-torse anatomic data to generate a 3D map of heart's electrical activity, is one example of diagnosis employing DT paradigm. The FDA has also given their approval to this diagnostic procedure. Medical imaging services are in high demand these days. As a result of the enormous demand, diagnostic medical imaging has become a logistical issue for suppliers all around the world. As all of the data is fed into the model, fast stream technologies keeps track of the patient from check-in to report delivery. Fast stream presents a patient-centered workflow by constructing a strong model of a care facility in which the provider organization may identify and open up best practices in order to increase efficiency, patient experience, and care quality.

7.4.4   DT in device development

To discover areas for improvement, foresee future issues, and optimize organizational strategies, DT technologies can be used to create a virtual twin of a hospital to assess strategic planning, capacity, personnel, and organization in several ways.

7.4.4.1 Resource optimization

Hospital management can predict bed deficits, optimize staff schedules, and aid operates rooms by using accurate and real data from hospital operations and the environmental elements to construct DTs. Such data improves resource consumption and optimizes the hospital's and staff's efficiency while lowering costs.

7.4.4.2 Risk management

DTs provide a secure environment in which to evaluate changes in network performance like as staffing levels, vacancy in operating rooms, device maintenance, and so on, allowing data-driven critical decisions to be implemented in a complex and delicate context.

7.4.4.3 Personalized diagnosis

Individuals can use digital twins to gather and use essential data like heart rate and oxygen levels at the individual basis, which helps them track chronic diseases and, as a result, their objectives and relationships with doctors by offering general information. As a result, such tailored data are used as the foundation for clinical trials and laboratory research [14]. Doctors do not develop remedies from huge samples since they focus on each person independently. Rather, they use personalized simulations to monitor every patient's responses to various treatments, which improve the overall medical plan's reliability. Despite the growing interest in personalized medicine and the rising level of effort put into it, there have been no DT implementations for real patients.

7.4.4.4 Drugs and drug development

To boost drug delivery effectiveness, scientists can use DT of pharmaceuticals and chemical products to change or rebuild drugs depending on the particle size and compositional features. A DT of medical equipment enables designers to evaluate the device's features or uses in a simulated environment before production, as well as make architectural or material changes and evaluate the successes or failures of the changes. This lowers the cost of failures while also improving the end product's quality and reliability.

7.5 Applications of DT in healthcare

The term "digital twin" defines a broad idea that includes a variety of devices and services. A DT is a virtual denotion of an actual or intangible thing. However, unless a DT captures a component of the entity's complicated multi-physics nature, these virtual duplicates are not a comprehensive depiction of the entity's comprehensive and multi nature. For instance, a DT of the heart can be used to establish a pacemaker because it replicates the electrical behavior of the organ [15]. For medication development, a digital duplicate of the chemical side of the hearth, or the mechanical reaction for surgical simulation. DTs will transfer the conventional treatment choice depends on the current state of the patient to an optimized status of the patients of the future, and it will be a key component of P4-Medicine such as predictive, preventive, personalized, and participatory medicine. Because each of us is so different in so many ways, most conventional therapies designed for the "average patient" are ineffective for the "actual patient." From ineffective medications and surgery unhappiness to device rejection or replacement, there are a variety of factors that might lead to device rejection or replacement. DTs will be a critical component in the transition from one-size-fits-all medicine to individualized medicine.

7.5.1   Patient monitoring using DT

During diagnosis, the patient's DT will be fed information from several healthcare sources of data such as imaging information, in-person measures, laboratory test results, and genetic information. The patient model will mimic the patient's health status based on available clinical data, with missing parameters inferred using statistical models. For example, the integration of cardiovascular scanning and computational techniques allows for non-invasive flow field characterization and diagnostic metric computation. The applications of DT is show in the Figure 7.3.

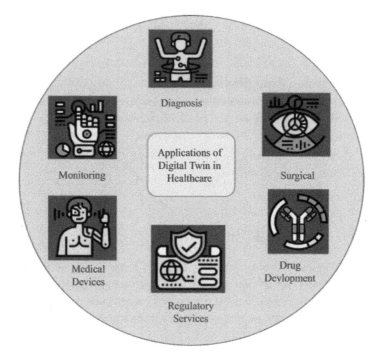

Figure 7.3   Applications of DT

7.5.2 Medical wearables

Smaller, more convenient wearable sensors will be employed to send real-time data into our cloud-based DT. With sufficient knowledge of disease development and constant patient data gathering via health trackers, biometric, behavioral, emotional, cognitive, and interpersonal data can be collected [16]. Medical documents, laboratory test results, pharmacy data, healthcare and medical management data, well-being device-generated data, and socioeconomic factors such as zip code, local weather, and buying patterns are just a few of the data sources that might feed our digital twin to customize our risk factors.

7.5.3 Medical tests and procedures

Surgery by nature is individualized. The procedure is adapted to the patient's needs from the current state to the optimum conclusion. To improve intervention success and lower patient risk, customization is essential. DTs will aid in this process by modeling an invasive tests and procedures which is used to forecast the outcome before the treatment is chosen.

7.5.4 Medical device optimization

The patient's DT captures the person's unique characteristics, and the healthcare device's DT records the device design. Both models can be used to see what occurs when a given device is implanted in a specific patient. This is the situation in groups where clinical research cannot be conducted without causing harm, such as individuals with uncommon disorders or children. DTs are also effective for optimization activities such as boosting the effectiveness of a gadget by performing hundreds of scenarios with varied environments and individuals. Furthermore, with the advent of 3D printing technology, individual DTs can contribute to the customization of medical equipment by allowing for the creation of one-of-a-kind designs for each patient.

7.5.5 Drug development

We can manage a DT digitally with thousands of medications in order to find the best one instead of ones for that particular scenario. This, however, does not have to be limited to currently available medications. We can establish digital cohorts of real patients with variety genotypes who share symptoms and test new possible medications to see which one has the best chance of success and the best dosage. The number of medical trials required will be reduced if the first shot is improved. In silico clinical trials will offer light on processes years to examine in vivo or estimate the level of uncommon cases that would require hundreds of patients to watch in a randomized clinical trial.

7.5.6 Regulatory services

Modeling and simulation have been included as forms of evidence in the legislative framework of biomedical devices by both the US Congress and the European Parliaments since 2016. Because of possibilities for cost savings in assessing medical devices, the FDA has determined to make digital information a valued regulatory tool [17]. Furthermore, several businesses have indicated that clinical trial costs may soon outstrip income, hastening the industry's migration to other credible and appropriate data sources for showing the safety and efficacy of medical devices and pharmaceuticals goods.

7.6   DT framework in healthcare

The proposed DT framework integrates connected devices, database management, and AI in three phases to construct a virtual duplicate of a patient, allowing healthcare providers to interact more effectively, and allowing patients with similar illnesses to cooperate. The patient's vital parameters are captured and transmitted in real time by the IoT sensing devices. The DT replica is located at the top of the network infrastructure and is sophisticated in terms of data management. The data will be cleaned, pre-processed, and converted before being used for analytics and the creation of various ML algorithms. This platform enables continuous health monitoring and early detection of anomalies. It will also allow healthcare practitioners to prescribe the best medicines, testing of which in controlled environment, and track outcomes. Furthermore, better lifestyles should be designed, and more efficient contact with patients should be provided, all of which would improve many aspects of the healthcare system. There are three phases available in this framework and it is shown in the Figure 7.4:

- Prediction phase
- Monitoring phase
- Correction phase

7.6.1   Prediction phase

The processing and forecasting step is what it sounds like. The patient information is recorded via IoT sensing devices in this phase, which is patient-centered. These sensors transmit real-time information on human body measurements that are critical for monitoring health and detecting irregularities. The information will be temporarily saved in a cloud server that is responsible for raw-data storage. This information will be used later in the training and predictions phase by a ML model [18]. The system will generate classifications and prediction models based on the raw data after purification, pre-processing, and representation, employing data ML algorithms technologies. The outputs of the classification model will be saved in the outcome repository, which is a scalable, secured, and irreversible cloud database. The patient and other framework phase components can access the outcome database for prolonged feedback, rectification, and model optimization.

7.6.2   Monitoring phase

The monitoring and repair part necessitates the involvement of patient-centered healthcare experts. The outcomes of the forecasting analytics from the result collection will be used by health experts who offer therapies and advice depends on

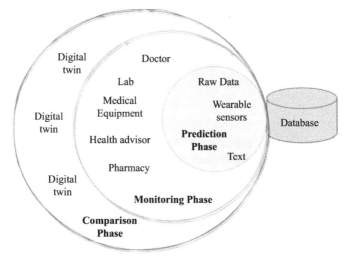

Figure 7.4   Various phases in DT framework

standardized experience and training. This would be in addition to the clinical diagnosis and tracking of the patient's health status in terms of improving his care. Continuously integrating real-time data into predictive models will aid in recognizing body measurements anomalies, proactively monitoring and identifying health risks before they develop, and prescribing the appropriate therapies and assist healthcare providers in creating a healthier lifestyle for the patient [19]. Professionals can rectify, validate, and provide informative comments in addition to having read permissions to the result information, allowing the model to be optimized.

7.6.3   Comparison phase

In the third stage, the comparative phase, individuals with comparable illnesses collaborate to use real-life circumstances, improve patients' DT, and so improve the overall framework. The model should be possible to consider findings of the patients currently available with those of other individuals by getting data and results from DTs for similar incidents. This technique will broaden the domain of prediction models by including real-world scenarios with much more predictable outcomes, hence improving model accuracy. It also allows healthcare providers to make more informed and precise decisions. Actions are based not only on real information tracking but also on the previous, present, and predicted future events of other patients, in order to duplicate, change, or avoid those events.

7.7   Cyber resilience in healthcare DT

A DT in healthcare is ideally a computerized clone of a person that uses a life-long data collection and AI-powered algorithms to forecast health as well as provide answers to a variety of clinical concerns. A DT in healthcare could be used to determine the outcome of treatments like lung cancer diagnosis. A DT framework for healthcare that uses a mix of separate process and agent-based methodologies to compensate for the intricacies of care delivery and also how patients move through a health service. A medical DT can monitor a patient's information, cross-reference them with registered trends in a healthcare system, and intelligently assess disease indicators. It uses data gathering and ML techniques to deliver reliable results, with data related to the collection capabilities that are constantly updated. Because its offerings provide lifetime development for hospitals and organizations, a healthcare DT can significantly save costs. It can help predict situations such as lung cancer, cardiac arrest, and respiratory failure, allowing hospitals and organizations to maintain better preventative maintenance while lowering healthcare costs. In the implementation and advancement of healthcare-related technologies, cyber resilience is a major challenge. The vast amount of patient data acquired, communicated, and analyzed, which is sent back and forth across the healthcare digital twin, can make it very difficult to manage the scope of these hospital processes. All through the DT procedure, hospitals and organizations must guarantee that client data is secure and trusted. On two conductive datasets with thousands and thousands of susceptible and non-vulnerable operations, a variety of tests are conducted to test the suggested approach [20].

By the use of encryption, strong authentication, and vulnerabilities detection technologies, cyber resilience should serve as an integrated enabler of development. Cyber resilience is built on technology, policy, and risk management to give healthcare personnel, customers, and patients the trust they need to engage with a hospital at digitized speed and scale. In the functioning of personalized medicine employing healthcare DTs, cyber resilience is a vital enabler of trustworthiness. To facilitate widespread use of healthcare digital twins, the appropriate cyber resilience techniques and policies must be implemented and maintained. In healthcare DTs and the Internet of Things, susceptibility detection is a critical tool for cyber resilience (IoT). Exploitable flaws in medicine-related IoT software can offer serious security risks to DT systems, increasing across the globe. In MIoT security, ML was used to detect application vulnerabilities as a supplement to existing static and dynamic methodologies. The capacity of ML algorithms to understand hidden susceptible code patterns has a high potential for identifying zero-day weaknesses and variations. The classic approach for predicting lung disease is based on clinical definition such as clinical manifestations, visible symptoms, and patients' undiscovered reasons. In addition, some studies recommend combining clinical symptoms with traditional diagnostic tests including an electrocardiogram, traditional D-dimer, spiral CT pulmonary, and pulmonary angiography to identify lung cancer with blood clot. In real-world situations, an intermediary interpretation is required, i.e., a doctor must swiftly create a precise link between the patient's health status and the actual situation. The tumor cell may spread through blood and lymphatic vessels as a result of the conventional pathologic diagnostic. Oncological surgeons are anticipated to benefit from ML in uncovering the complex links between data-driven medical evaluations and tailored treatment. Oncological physicians are anticipated to benefit from ML in uncovering the complex links between data-driven medical evaluations and tailored treatment.

7.8   Cyber physical system and DT

The principle of utilizing a digital version of a physical process to undertake real-time enhancement is made reference to as a DT. CPS is defined as a combination of computational and physiological changes, whereas DT is characterized as the idea of utilizing digital version of a traditional system to undertake real-time optimization. Both CPS and DTs in production have two categories such as the physical part and the cyber or digital part. These material assets carry out the production process. The cyber/digital component includes smart information maintenance, analytics, and computing problems, as well as a variety of ubiquitous services and apps. Programs and apps provide a wealth of features that enable manufacturing participants to increase productivity. The physical portion sensing and gathering information, and the cyber or digital part analyses and processes the information before making decisions, whereas the cyber or digital part analyses and processing data before making decisions.

7.8.1   Mapping in CPS and DTs

The goal of CPS is to extend the opportunities of physical processes by incorporating computing and communication into the physical methods. CPS provides real-time sensing, internal control responsibilities, and data management for complex systems through tight integration across the 3C. In comparison to DTs, CPS places a greater emphasis on the cyber world's superior communication and computation capabilities, which can improve the precision and accuracy of the physical world. Furthermore, whether it is a three tier, four tier, or five tier design, all of the CPS architecture described by researchers emphasize on management rather than replicated models. Feedback loops are critical in CPS, just as they are in DTs. The tasks of CPS are enabled by mutual mappings, real-time communication, and perfect integration of the computing and networking worlds. The computing system, on the other hand, may have an impact on multiple physical objects. A system, for example, could have several physical components. DTs have the goal of providing a complete functional and physical description of an element, product, or systems. The first and most crucial stage is to construct high-fidelity visual representations that accurately reflect the physical world's geometry, physical attributes, behaviors, and regulations. These virtual models are capable of simulating their spatiotemporal position, behaviors, functionalities, and more, in addition to being extremely stable with the original elements in terms of shape and framework. To put it another way, virtual models and actual entities have a strong resemblance, like twins, and behave similarly, like a mirror reflection. The hierarchical structure of CPs and DTs are represented as follows:

- Unit level
- System level
- System of system (SoS) level

7.8.2   Unit level

The lowest unit engaging in manufacturing activities, such as a compute node tool or robot arm, component or element with radio frequency identification

(RFID) systems and sensors, or even an environment conditions, is referred to as the unit level. The physical components of unit-level CPS and DTs are made up of these production elements. A mechanical device with sensors, motors, and embedded devices, for example, can be termed a CPS. A unit-level CPS allows more efficient and robust devices through data interchange and data management. CPS and DTs at the command level share the very same physical items, such as equipment, materials, and components. In the processes of cyber–physical interactions, unit-level of elements CPS and DTs can both develop alongside physical manufacturing, assembling, and interaction. A component DT, on the other hand, must be created by describing and modeling geometric structure, identification, and functionality data and also the wellbeing dependent on the operational status of unit-level material things. Furthermore, because a DT concentrates much on the building of components, such as geometric pattern, rule, behavior, and other constraints models, a DT can execute strong visual modeling.

7.8.3   System level

Several unit level CPS or DTs provide interconnectivity and compatibility over an industrial network, allowing a broader variety of data exchange and resource management. At this level, a framework CPS or DT is created by combining many components CPS or DTs. A framework CPS or DT is a development process that can be an assembly line, a shop floor, or may be example like factory. A framework CPS or DT can accomplish valuable assets of manufacturing resources and increase collaborative effectiveness among different resources by using a feedback circuit of sensing, evaluation, choice, and implementation. CPS and DTs both use the similar physical manufacturing system at the system level. A framework CPS's cyber components are similar to those of a component CPS. The digital components of a system-level DT, on the other hand, must be created by combining and collaborate many unit-level designs. In addition, a complex product might be regarded a system-level DT. An engines DT, for example, is used to check the operational state of an aircraft with huge parts and components, as well as to prognosis and diagnosis problems, while a wing DT is used to validate the flight orientation.

7.8.4   SoS level

By creating a smart platform called at the network level, cross-system connectivity, compatibility, and cooperative management across system-level CPS or DTs can be realized. Various system CPS or DTs form a SoS-level CPS or DT at this level, according to the platform as a service. An SoS-level CPS, as opposed to a framework CPS, concentrates on enterprise-wide connectivity and even cross-enterprise cooperation. Enterprise connection would enable a variety of collaborative applications, including commerce, supply-chain collaborative, and industrial collaboration. Personalized modifications, smart design, remote maintenance, and other benefits could be achieved through collaboration between manufacturing,

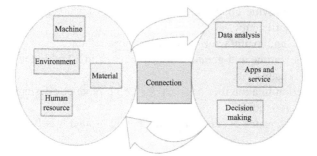

Figure 7.5 CPs and DTs mapping

configuration, and service businesses, for example. In the case of a DT, simulation and flawless data flow from one stage to next are critical all through product lifecycle.

7.9 Advantages of DT

DTs make it possible to combine groups of similar patients that would otherwise be impossible or prohibitively expensive to put together in real life. The technology also avoids the hazards and concerns that come with using real-life subjects. DT technology in the healthcare sector, when applied correctly, allows practitioners to discover optimal medicines, enhance patient outcomes, and maximize efficiency, resulting in hospital cost savings. As we try to overcome the effects of the pandemic, DTs provide such a safe and healthy environment for analyzing the effect of change. They will be crucial to many sectors. The pandemic has presented some new and distinct issues, and researchers have begun to use DTs to assist the millions of people who have been affected. For example, scientists are debating what many consider to be the next public health issue long-haul COVID-19. According to projections, one out of every 20 people infected with the virus will experience COVID-19 symptoms that last longer than eight weeks. Some people are still suffering from terrible effects months later. Many individuals are too unwell to tolerate experimental treatment regimens, and it is still unclear why some people heal fast while others suffer long-term effects. The various advantages of DT are as follows:

- You can use DTs to foresee potential issues in the future. This, among other things, eliminates product faults, and reduces production time.
- Real-time data is used to improve and optimize industrial operations.
- Reduce unscheduled downtime caused by possible faults.
- They prevent accidents because they enable for the simulation of a wide range of circumstances and scenarios.
- Servicing costs are reduced by conducting preventive maintenance procedures.

- Simulations provide opportunities for continual development by highlighting errors and inefficiency.
- Technology and manufacturing lines are more reliable.
- Reduced downtime and greater efficiency result in a higher OEE.
- Productivity gains.
- Risk reduction in a number of areas, including product offerings, marketplace credibility, and more.
- Reduce maintenance expenses by anticipating problems before they happen.

7.10 Summary

Manufacturing has entered the digital era due to better in information systems, information technology, and networking protocols. The manufacturing industry is confronting global problems as a result of significant improvements in digital technologies against a backdrop of digitization. Another concept related to cyber–physical assimilation is the DT. A DT creates high-fidelity virtual representations of physical items in digital universe to imitate and offer feedback on their behavior in the actual life. Smart manufacturing is becoming a must-have trend, and attaining cyber–physical connection and integration in the production process is a key requirement. CPS and DTs are the preferred methods for achieving this goal. These two techniques, however, are not similar.

References

[1] Liu, Y., Zhang, L., Yang, Y., *et al.* (2019). A novel cloud-based framework for the elderly healthcare services using digital twin. *IEEE Access*, 7, 49088–49101.

[2] Elayan, H., Aloqaily, M., and Guizani, M. (2021). Digital twin for intelligent context-aware IoT healthcare systems. *IEEE Internet of Things Journal*, 8, 16749–16757.

[3] Angulo, C., Ortega, J. A., and Gonzalez-Abril, L. (2019). Towards a healthcare digital twin 1. In *Artificial Intelligence Research and Development* (pp. 312–315). Amsterdam: IOS Press.

[4] Rajasekar, V., Premalatha, J., and Sathya, K. (2021). Cancelable Iris template for secure authentication based on random projection and double random phase encoding. *Peer-to-Peer Networking and Applications*, 14(2), 747–762.

[5] Zhang, J., Li, L., Lin, G., Fang, D., Tai, Y., and Huang, J. (2020). Cyber resilience in healthcare digital twin on lung cancer. *IEEE Access*, 8, 201900–201913.

[6] Yang, D., Karimi, H. R., Kaynak, O., and Yin, S. (2021). Developments of digital twin technologies in industrial, smart city and healthcare sectors: a survey. *Complex Engineering Systems*, 1(1), 3.

[7] Rajasekar, V., Premalatha, J., and Sathya, K. (2019). An efficient sign-cryption scheme for secure authentication using hyper elliptic curve cryptography and Keccak hashing. *International Journal of Recent Technology and Engineering*, 8(3), 1593–1598.

[8] Patrone, C., Galli, G., and Revetria, R. (2019). A state of the art of digital twin and simulation supported by data mining in the healthcare sector. In *Advancing Technology Industrialization Through Intelligent Software Methodologies, Tools and Techniques* (pp. 605–615). Amsterdam: IOS Press.

[9] Rajasekar, V., Sathya, K., and Premalatha, J. (2018, December). Energy efficient cluster formation in wireless sensor networks based on multi objective bat algorithm. In *2018 International Conference on Intelligent Computing and Communication for Smart World (I2C2SW)* (pp. 116–120). New York, NY: IEEE.

[10] Gochhait, S. and Bende, A. (2020). Leveraging digital twin technology in the healthcare industry – a machine learning based approach. *European Journal of Molecular & Clinical Medicine*, 7(6), 2547–2557.

[11] Rajasekar, V., Premalatha, J., and Saracevic, M. (2022). Cybersecurity in 5G and IoT networks. In *Secure Communication for 5G and IoT Networks* (pp. 29–46). Cham: Springer.

[12] Ayache, N. (2019, March). AI and healthcare: towards a digital twin? In *MCA 2019 – 5th International Symposium on Multidiscplinary Computational Anatomy*.

[13] Velliangiri, S., Manoharn, R., Ramachandran, S. *et al.* An efficient light-weight privacy preserving mechanism for industry 4.0 based on elliptic curve cryptography. *IEEE Transactions on Industrial Informatics*, 18, 6494–6502. doi:10.1109/TII.2021.3139609.

[14] Rajasekar, V., Venu, K., Jena, S. R., Varthini, R. J., and Ishwarya, S. (2021). Detection of cotton plant diseases using deep transfer learning. *Journal of Mobile Multimedia*, 18(2), 307–324.

[15] Erol, T., Mendi, A. F., and Doğan, D. (2020, October). The digital twin revolution in healthcare. In *2020 4th International Symposium on Multidisciplinary Studies and Innovative Technologies (ISMSIT)* (pp. 1–7). New York, NY: IEEE.

[16] Sathya, K., Premalatha, J., Rajasekar, V., Kumar M., M., Deepak, M., and Manoj, S. R. (2021, November). Modified linear congruential generator to secure random number generation. In *AIP Conference Proceedings* (Vol. 2387, No. 1, p. 140007). Baltimore, MD: AIP Publishing LLC.

[17] Rivera, L. F., Jiménez, M., Angara, P., Villegas, N. M., Tamura, G., and Müller, H. A. (2019, November). Towards continuous monitoring in personalized healthcare through digital twins. In *Proceedings of the 29th Annual International Conference on Computer Science and Software Engineering* (pp. 329–335).

[18] Krishnamoorthi, S., Jayapaul, P., and Rajasekar, V. (2021). A modernistic approach for chaotic based pseudo random number generator secured with gene dominance. *Sādhanā*, 46(1), 1–12.

[19] Popa, E. O., van Hilten, M., Oosterkamp, E., and Bogaardt, M. J. (2021). The use of digital twins in healthcare: socio-ethical benefits and socio-ethical risks. *Life Sciences, Society and Policy*, 17(1), 1–25.

[20] Rajasekar, V., Predić, B., Saracevic, M., *et al.* (2022). Enhanced multimodal biometric recognition approach for smart cities based on an optimized fuzzy genetic algorithm. *Scientific Reports*, 12(1), 1–11.

[21] Rajasekar, V., Premalatha, J., Sathya, K., and Saračević, M. (2021). Secure remote user authentication scheme on healthcare, IoT and cloud applications: a multilayer systematic survey. *Acta Polytechnica Hungarica*, 18(3), 87–106.

[22] V. S *et al.*, An efficient lightweight privacy preserving mechanism for industry 4.0 based on elliptic curve cryptography, in *IEEE Transactions on Industrial Informatics*, doi:10.1109/TII.2021.3139609.

[23] Velliangiri, S., Manoharan, R., Ramachandran, S., and Rajasekar, V. (2022). Blockchain based privacy preserving framework for emerging 6G wireless communications. *IEEE Transactions on Industrial Informatics*, 18(7), 4868–4874, doi:10.1109/TII.2021.3107556.

[24] Rajasekar, V., Jayapaul, P., Krishnamoorthi, S., *et al.* (2021). Enhanced WSN routing protocol for Internet of Things to process multimedia big data. *Wireless Personal Communications*, 126, 2081–2100, https://doi.org/10.1007/s11277-021-08760-1.

[25] Rajasekar, V., Premalatha, J., Rangaraaj, V., Rajaraman, B., and Prakash, A. O. S. "Efficient handwriting character recognition based on convolutional neural network," *2022 International Conference on Computer Communication and Informatics (ICCCI)*, 2022, pp. 1–5, doi:10.1109/ICCCI54379.2022.9741072.

Chapter 8

Cloud security-enabled digital twin in e-healthcare

Prithi Samuel[1], K. Jayashree[2] and R. Babu[1]

Digital twin (DT) is being used in commerce as precise model software through conception to practice as a result of the advancement of skills such as big data, cloud services and the Internet of Things. Furthermore, modelling is crucial in the health sector, particularly in research on healthcare process design, healthcare allocation of resources and medicinal activity forecasting, among other things. There would be a modern and improved technique to give more rapid and reliable operations by merging DTs and healthcare. Nevertheless, in the period of personalized medicine, how and where to accomplish personalized health monitoring all through the lifetime of older patients, as well as how to combine the healthcare material reality and the digital reality to actualize real smart medicine, remain two major obstacles. One of the main goals of precision medicine is to prevent disease from occurring through the use of inheritances, genomics and smart health monitoring surveillance systems. If the sickness cannot be avoided, it would be handled on an individualized or personalized basis, instead of as a group, as it has been in the past. Furthermore, medical technology using smart medicine in a data-driven service paradigm necessitates a wide range of information, including patient, healthcare, economic and fusion data. The innovative diagnostic provider mode is shifting to one of tailored and sustainable therapy as a result of global warming, and considerably more intelligent health devices and platforms are being created to accomplish secure data-driven smart healthcare employing DTs. The competence to explore, identify, comprehend and assess health information generated from electronic databases, as well as knowledge gained, to appropriately address or address health complications, is characterized as e-health. The Internet seems to have the ability to safeguard users from damage and allow people to actually engage in knowledgeable health-related decision making as a storehouse for health records and e-health analytics. Particularly

[1]Department of Computational Intelligence, School of Computing, SRM Institute of Science and Technology, India
[2]Department of Artificial Intelligence and Data Science, Panimalar Engineering College, India

essential, increased amounts of e-health interaction reduce the danger of receiving erroneous online information.

Numerous scientific approaches on privacy and security within Cloud-based e-health systems are addressed, with a focus on the prospects, advantages and difficulties of putting such methods in place. A potential strategic development is the integration of e-health systems with expert machines such as cloud technology to create smart aims and solutions.

8.1 Introduction

The digital twin (DT) paradigm is currently attractive with an interest of increasingly more researchers in diverse fields, particularly in manufacturing, enterprise, automotive, retail, smart cities, disaster management and smart health, which are extraordinarily evolved through the fast expansion of the Internet of Things (IoT), incessant developments in artificial intelligence (AI), big data handling methods and cloud computing. It is nowadays attaining more consideration in the healthcare industry in the method of well-being DT [1]. DT can mark manufacturing further productive and simplified whereas by decreasing throughput intervals. In automotive systems, DT is used to collect as well as analyse operating data from a means of transportation in directive to evaluate its standing in actual, and keep informed artefact developments. In the retail sector, to model and enhance the client circumstances. In smart cities, DT is used to aid cities further parsimoniously, ecologically as well as publicly workable. Simulated representations can monitor design choices, and provides elucidations towards several challenges met by modern municipalities.

In the healthcare background, DTs initially aimed at prognostic preservation of therapeutic procedures as well as for their enactment escalation. Models of DTs pertaining to health centre administration improvement are that established by means of GE Health Management. The aforementioned company has extensively concentrated on its prognostic analytical tool plus AI applications towards alerting about huge as well as several patient's information into applicable intellect. The ultimate purpose is to aid clinics as well as government associations in the administration and synchronization of medical service capability from a societal and populace perception [2].

Healthcare approach of DT emphasis by means of personal health management (PHM) and precision medicine (PM). PHM including patient recovery is moreover some of the recent research intrigue [3] incorporated machine learning (ML) and DT that dealt as a significant device to not simply record the fitness level of patients constantly, however, it besides estimates the use as well as the progress of therapeutic cures practically. The authors have also given details on the description of inner arrangements for DT to provision precision drug methods in the circumstance of incessant observing as well as custom-made data-driven therapeutics. PM is aimed at drug improvement, drug supervision and handling of infections. Corral *et al.* (2020) offered the primary phases of DT in cardiovascular medication as well as deliberated the complications and chances in the forthcoming. The authors emphasized the synergistic role of automatous as well as geometric prototypes in the cardiovascular study and understanding PM visualization. Subramanian (2020) suggested a DT archetypal to cure liver infection, grounded on enormous medical data. The authors' study exposed that the DT archetypal can correspondingly put into medication advance, supervision, and handling of further infections. Björnsson *et al.* (2020) suggested a structure towards addressing the problem of extra records created on the DT. The framework suggested finding the best medicinal drug for the affected person's disorder amongst several tablets cantered on the robust data handling abilities of DT.

The chapter is systematized as below. Section 8.1 gives an introduction to DT. Section 8.2 emphasises on e-healthcare and cloud security-enabled DT. Section 8.3 provides an overview of cloud healthcare service platforms and security and privacy requirements are also presented. Cloud-based challenges are deliberated in Section 8.5. The chapter is concluded in Section 8.6.

8.2 E-healthcare and cloud security-enabled digital twin

A range of different Information and Communication Technology (ICT) are carried out to enhance the effectiveness of all stages of healthcare. E-health is using ICT to increase the capacity to deal with patients to improve their health. Various advantages of E-health are cost saving and ease aimed at users, lessening of health amenity costs and enhancing health amenity acceptable, achieving remote or pilloried groups and amassed user as well as provider mechanism of the e-health intercession [4,5]. E-health involving of various ICT facilities such as telemedicine, mobile Health (m-health), Electronic Health Records (EHRs) and Health Information Systems (HIS) and is shown in Figure 8.1.

8.2.1 ICT facilities
The various ICT facilities available for incorporation with DT are given below.

8.2.1.1 M-health
It consists of the usage of cellular devices after gathering collective as well as affected person degree health information, offering healthcare facts to physicians, investigators, real-time intensive care of patient pulse, as well as the quickest endowment of attention [6].

8.2.1.2 Electronic health record (EHR)
It is an efficient gathering of electronic health particulars regarding each patient.

8.2.1.3 HIS
It denotes software elucidations for position arrangement, patient facts administration, work plan administration and further managerial responsibilities concerning healthiness.

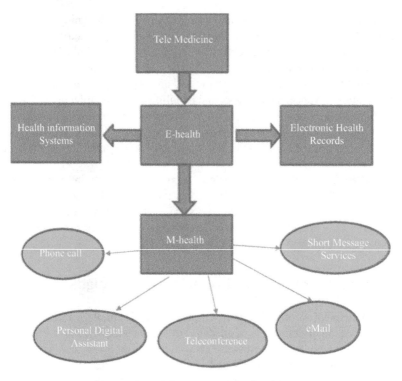

Figure 8.1   ICT use cases in healthcare

8.2.1.4   Medical Research using Grids (MRuG)

IT manners dominant workout as well as records control competencies to address massive volumes of dissimilar records.

8.2.1.5   Telemedicine

One more application geared towards this is telemedicine. Using the statistics this is usually remaining and being considered, it is able to agree for a real-time observing and estimation of the fitness repute of the affected person, which means that face-to-face communications among affected person and doctor can be decreased. [7]. Treatments can be accustomed by means of the acquaintance from the telemedicine methods, such that it provides further freedom to their life by not visiting the hospital every day.

8.2.2   *Cloud security-enabled digital twin*

With its properties of on-demand provision, enormous adaptability and automation, cloud computing (CC) technology is ideally suited for medical services. Cloud healthcare deals with current promises such as abundant access to therapeutic data, as well as chances aimed at novel commercial prototypes. A cloud-based perso-nalized health record (PHR) platform's philosophy of fitness elucidation influences virtualization tools to permit patients to create lifetime PHR registers and distribute them to the interested party. MyPHR machines are used for creating PHR. The major advantage of using CC in healthcare is that the gathered particulars from instruments can be sent to the cloud by means of a wireless network and the data are warehoused for further handling as well as investigation. This supports automatic real-time information gathering and decreases human record mistakes. Furthermore, the data are retrieved smoothly by means of more persons irrespective of their place.

8.3   Cloud healthcare service platform with digital twin

By utilizing statistical data of sensors and their execution records for incorporating DT into the healthcare framework, precise simulation model with multi-physics, multi-technological and multi-scale modelling techniques will be performed, allowing for legitimate health screening and timely forecasting of digital device malfunctions. A DT is an extensive clinical technology used by a medical interest to provide quick and accurate medical services. It is composed of three main parts: a physical object, a virtual object and healthcare data [8]. The operation mechanism of a DT includes four stages namely twin establishment, data connection, validation and model evolution, and are provided as feedback to the physical and amenity configurations to offer promising solutions for healthcare services as shown in Figure 8.2. DT can play awesome utility roles in healthcare: hospital management, design and personal healthcare using which troubles can be predicted earlier certainly reduces risks and save costs [9].

DT could be used to experience the entire capability of artificial intelligence (AI)-enabled healthcare by creating a DT of a person with an intention of personalized health prediction and tracking [10]. To enforce this, the following steps are useful.

1. Initially, smartwatch exercise records (daily sports), social media histories, telephone logs and so forth.
2. We may also require calculation techniques to utilize these resources to find records that could be accomplished through the usage of Cyber-Physical Systems.

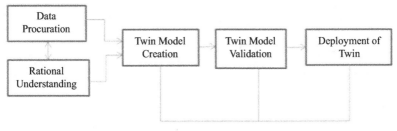

Feedback for learning and improvement

Figure 8.2   Development of digital twin

3. Integrate the heterogeneous information from numerous sources that are gained for predicting healthcare. Pre-processing is carried out to fit the system of regulations for prediction and data mining (DM) is used to achieve this goal.

4. With the pre-processed records, classifiers might be built with the aid of training classification algorithms with the support of machine learning (ML) technology.

5. Data mining and machine learning can be integrated to form AI within the DT healthcare framework.

6. Lastly, the preferred intellectual twin might be equipped with the competencies of healthcare monitoring.

ML has robust ties with IoT, allowing powerful evaluation, testing and prediction of multiple data streams. The availability of historical information enables ML fashions to examine the protection states where DTs require a glide of real-time information. In this ML context, the following modelling techniques have been used.

• **Behaviour and performance modelling:** This model encompasses supervised learning, unsupervised learning and reinforcement learning.

• **Location-based behavioural analysis:** The growing recognition of location-based offerings is supported by means of detecting technologies starting from location-based total recommendation structures or pattern mining from a very massive historical spatiotemporal dataset.

• **Temporal behavioural analysis of time series:** Seasonality and residue segmentation, intensity tactics, auto-regressive methodologies and the Box–Jenkins methodology are all part of this time-series data modelling strategy.

The DT is a tool that has been used in the health sector to improve, analyse and increase forecasts for patients, clinics and the pharmaceutical business, and it has been shown to be effective [11]. The uses of the DT in various fields are shown in Figure 8.3 and are discussed below.

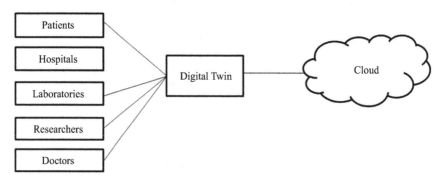

Figure 8.3 Cloud in DT-based healthcare

8.3.1 Wearable technologies

Fuelled by trends within the IoT, AI, service-oriented cloud computing, variety, velocity and voluminous big data, and virtual reality technologies, the DTs herald a tipping point in which the physical and virtual worlds can be controlled as one, and can have interaction with the virtual counterpart of physical things similar to the things themselves, even in 3D area around us.

In order to acquire a virtual photo of the employee within the warehouse, logistics organizations ought to gather and use the records without delay in a relevant manner. Recent development in remote sensing lets in especially gesture identification abilities via RF and mm-Wave radar, ambient light, image processing and wearable devices. In addition to the IoT, such technological traits in gesture monitoring and controlling can be vital in growing sturdier DT systems.

The analytics characteristic incorporated in wearable devices identifies itself as a crucial point for accumulating, aggregating and visualizing all critical information. The statistics are recorded without delay with the aid of the sensors incorporated into the pick-with the aid of-vision smart glasses and are continuously up to date [12].

8.3.2 Pharmaceutical industry

Organizations, physicians and researchers centred on longevity are searching at the nano level to know the progress of the ageing process and trying to come out with the proper drug treatments and remedies that could slow them down. Research is extensively done on improving medicinal drug production methods, customized medicine problems for individuals, computational biology and computational bio-remedy. A virtual dual is advised about how medicinal drugs can have an effect on the right areas, what eating regimen, workout and conduct are important to enhance first-class existence, and even how bones may be bolstered. Industries working in the area of cardiovascular, health device developers, medicine manufacturers and lots of organizations laboured collectively to innovatively develop the model. Incorporating computer and mobile-based simulation, medical doctors have the third eye to view the mobility of the heart tissue and to have a complete insight into the complicated shape within the heart with the advancement in practicing with the same organ version. It results in customized patient treatment with the aid of coming into specific crucial signs and symptoms of an individual and promotes clinical research in destiny medicinal remedies. Along with the supercomputer Watson, IBM targets to simulate biochemical methods inside the human by means of the usage of synthetic and automatic techniques to identify cancerous cells in fitness information based on patients' previous health records. Realistic predictions may be made by checking out situations along with changing the drug doses for the remedy of illnesses that include unique varieties of most cancers, heart diseases, liver sclerosis, tuberculosis and acute myocardial [13].

8.3.3 Digital patients

Patient's DT is designed to seize continuous statistics from the person about diverse vitals, medical circumstances, response to the drug, remedy and surrounding environment. Each affected person's statistics are saved in public cloud and fed to the DT platform. Historic and actual-time statistics of each patient enable ML set of rules to predict future health conditions. The pandemic has helped in the increase of virtual fitness services that help human beings examine and cope with easy clinical situations that uses AI. DTs permit series and utilization of essential facts at the character level which facilitates people to tune chronic situations and, therefore, their priorities and interactions with doctors via presenting primary data. Thus, such customized information serves as the premise of medical trials and study information at labs. A unique DT from every patient assists in figuring out the right remedy, predicting the final results of a specific procedure and managing the chronic disorder with them from historic data [14]. By leveraging the patient's MRI, ECG and blood pressure statistics, DT of the patient heart is created, and it enables cardiologists to define the location of leads and virtually examine the position before intervention surgical operation of a person affected person who needs a cardiac resynchronization therapy (CRT).

8.3.4   Hospital

A real-time DT in a clinic permits to unencumber the value of IoT – and all this data – to realize all desires of the quadruple intention of healthcare as gathered for future fitness.

DTs in hospitals additionally power packages on the level of clinical work-flows, operations and more. They provide a holistic view with several abilities incorporated and integrations are exactly what companies are after in the digital transformation of healthcare [1].

8.4   Security and privacy requirements for cloud security-enabled digital twin in e-healthcare

In this section, we will take a high-level look at the technological device requirements for security and privacy in a cloud security-based DT system, such as authentication, identification and authorizations.

8.4.1   Security requirements for cloud security-enabled digital twin in e-healthcare

In this section, a top-level view of technical device requirements associated with privacy and security in cloud security-enabled DT systems, including identification, authentications and authorizations.

The cloud security-enabled DT in e-health structures security must be capable of being acquainted with susceptibilities, privacy and security extortions, and proactively scheme the security architecture of DT in such a way that all the problems related to security are completely identified and addressed efficiently and effectively. Change in the format of storing medical records leads physicians to adhere to the improvement of infrastructures while preserving patient data with utmost care.

- **Access control:** Access control in DT is important to control and proscribe consumer access to privileged information by deciding on who can access which level of data and grant access only to them [15].
- **Anonymization:** Use of nameless authentication protocols to hold data securely and protect them [16].
- **Authentication:** Verifying and validating personal credentials.
- **Availability:** Availability is required to guarantee that the quality of service for the healthcare system offering is available to all the users without any intervention.
- **Confidentiality:** This security method is required to ensure that transfer of data between transmission and reception is protected from any deliberate or unprivileged user abuse, regardless of whether the broadcasts between various IoT devices, cloud computing or e-health structures [17].
- **Data integrity:** Data integrity is critically required to ensure that any sensitive data switched between a transmitter and receiver is not at all possible to tap or trace the information by any malicious or unauthorized persons [18]. This can be further avoided by performing an integrity test at every node that is part of the transformation between the sender and receiver.
- **Resistance attraction:** Keeping off or stopping assaults from unauthorized customers [19].

8.4.2 *Privacy requirements for cloud security-enabled digital twin in e-healthcare*

Privacy attention systems and privacy awareness measures offerings are required increasingly to agree with installed frameworks laws, rules, moral necessities and industry-specific operational requirements. The DT technique is distinctly designed and integrated to discourse IoT demanding situations and sizable difference from available preserving mechanisms via other design frameworks.

Data privacy and security is defined as the method by which patient health records are protected from unknown users or unintentional use, processing or revelation involving the number of strategies that includes cloud computing, statistics trade tracking, data anonymization and using massive facts evaluation to pick out suspicious movements. Privacy safety measures are extraordinarily numerous and ought to be tailor-made to particular needs such as non-stop monitoring, preventive care and AI-pushed diagnosis. Patient privacy ought to be actively taken into consideration at some point of the entire data lifecycle and must provide privilege on who can access sensitive information upon satisfying internal privacy policies.

Privacy, trust and security of cloud security-enabled DT in e-health structures may be bolstered via the combination of several factors.

- **Data lifecycle protection:** This factor involves processes which might be important to privacy from start to complete and it guarantees all records are maintained securely and then truncated securely on the last stage of the cycle [20].
- **Full functionality:** Full capability targets to incorporate all valid pursuits and targets in positive-sum, "win-win" patterns, thus creating change-offs among privacy and security protection useless without compromising the primary desires/reason of the goal structures [1].
- **Privacy protection in the workplace:** Big data communication chain makes it essential to develop location statistics for facts [1]. In order to preserve the announcement of location information associated with patients, effective privacy strategies are in strong need.
- **Privacy as the default setting:** Privacy ensures that sensitive patient data are preserved in all states spontaneously despite the fact that the person does not do anything; their privacy stays intact [21]. With reference to traditional structures, the conversion and safety of statistics are accomplished through the intervention of the human directly.
- **Privacy embedded design:** The integration of IoT structural system and DT design encompass that privacy has become the core characteristic offering.
- **Proactivity:** Proactive one's antedate vulnerabilities and threats to critical healthcare data of a person and trying to avoid privacy threats from happening before reacting to breaches after it was happened [22].
- **Robustness:** Ensuring robust safety features are available in a common location to preserve security and privacy featured the life cycle of information technology structures.
- **Visibility and transparency:** This mechanism ensures the gathering, transformation, evaluation, movement and distribution of patient healthcare sensitive data are stored always and made available to all users and vendors for carrying out their appropriate functions [23].

8.5 Challenges in cloud-based digital twin in e-healthcare

The cloud allows small- and large-scale information to be transmitted over the network, making it easier to connect them. Owing to worries regarding data protection, clients must have complete faith in cloud-based security services. Since computers use traditional networks to link almost anything wirelessly, servers are extremely susceptible coming from external attacks or modifications. While academics work to identify viable answers to privacy and security problems, these two components are frequently studied separately, as discrete variables. Nevertheless, we suggest that improvements in privacy and security will indeed be achieved if the factors are combined and explored as a universal system, through the use of a focus on transparency, reliability and durability. Phishing, espionage, jammer, crypto-attacks, wormhole attacks and other security concerns exist in Cloud-based systems.

Organizations performance, healthcare industry protocols, safety and confidentiality, and healthcare systems have all changed as a result of this. For the very first moment in decades, cloud-based technologies make remote healthcare systems possible. Physicians nowadays can instantly watch, examine, treat and recommend without anyone ever trying to confront the individual in person. However, in order for the incorporation of cloud-secured-enabled DT in e-healthcare solutions to be effective, various issues must be examined and solved. Because of the influx of patients, generating and sharing healthcare information has grown difficult. The main concerns and challenges with cloud-secured-enabled DT in e-healthcare solutions are therefore found and addressed further below.

- Management tasks: A hybrid method combines cloud services, health institutions, as well as other necessary assets. Whenever a cloud security-enabled DT e-health system is adopted, management of resources is vital to responsible for acquiring, minimizing duplication, maximizing productivity and potentially reducing delay. To achieve sustained efficiency increases and/or minimize loss of efficiency, the resource management solution should be continuously adjusted.
- To overcome scarcity, healthcare files can be accessed in cloud computing or other similar devices, allowing the patient as well as other clients to track their condition and acquire and utilize patient data at any location and at any time. Clients have genuine complaints about saving their private data, despite the fact that decisions may be taken about how to manage saved information on the web. In order for information obtained to be accessed and has been used by various healthcare professionals, it should be maintained in accordance with established standards and regulations. A common data standard procedure, on the other hand, is still to be developed. Moreover, patients ought to have control over the data and the ability to be flexibly rid of it, thereby maintaining that the data are private.
- e-health replaces or adds detectors, diagnostic supplies and operational procedures to current health systems in the context of the transformation period. Modern hardware and methods are seldom easy to integrate. It should be done slowly and thoughtfully, and all essential staff must still be properly trained. All new systems and interfaces must also be retrograde compatible with the system that is being replaced or updated.
- Interoperability and standardization are both difficult due to the difficulties of standardizing heterogeneous data. The various factors of heterogeneity cloud-based e-health systems encompass a series of technology, firmware, software platforms and other parts, which adds to the complexities and creates compatibility concerns. Therefore, as a result, guidelines should be defined to simplify compatibility and overcome these obstacles.
- Prospective owners perceive inventions as compatible with particular values, background knowledge and requirements if they are compatible. Healthcare professionals' perceptions of e-health systems based on cloud computing ought to be commensurate with the demands of their jobs, which include the desire to actually encourage patients as well as other interested parties to accept and understand where to utilize such technologies.

8.6 Conclusion

The health sector has gained from DT in areas such as organ endowment, surgical procedure teaching as well as de-risking techniques. Though there is widespread welfare available to the society through the use of DT, the security threats of using the DT have to be discovered. In cloud-protected e-health systems, important privacy and security concerns are covered. Every cloud-secured DT-based e-health software system is distinct, requiring appropriate security and privacy strategies and topologies to safeguard this from threat while not compromising the service's purpose and functions. Cloud technology's significant importance's are transforming lives by linking an infinite number of gadgets. With innumerable gadgets transferring and receiving large amounts of data wirelessly, security and privacy have not been this susceptible as they are nowadays. As a result, experts must continue to generate and upgrade current secrecy and privacy solutions for cloud-secured-enabled DT in e-healthcare.

References

[1] Yang D., Karimi H.R., Kaynak O., and Yin S. Developments of digital twin technologies in industrial, smart city and healthcare sectors: a survey. *Complex Engineering Systems 2021*, 1, 3. https://dx.doi.org/10.20517/ces.2021.06.

[2] Barricelli B., Casiraghi E., and Fogli D. A survey on digital twin: definitions, characteristics, applications, and design implications. *IEEE Access*, 2019, 99, 1. 10.1109/ACCESS.2019.2953499.

[3] Rivera L.F., Jiménez M., Angara P., Villegas N.M., Tamura G., and Müller H.A. Towards continuous monitoring in personalized healthcare through digital twins. In: *Proceedings of the 29th Annual International Conference on Computer Science and Software Engineering*, 2019, pp. 329–335.

[4] Prithi S., Poongodi T., Sumathi D., and Suresh P. Real-time remote health monitoring using IoT sensors. In: Tripathi S.L., Balas V.E., Mohapatra S.K., Prakash K.B., and Nayak J. (eds.), *Electronic Devices, Circuits, and Systems for Biomedical Applications*. London: Academic Press, 2021, pp. 481–501 (Chapter 23), ISBN 9780323851725, https://doi.org/10.1016/B978-0-323-85172-5.00006-X.

[5] Wadhwa M. ICT interventions for improved health service quality and delivery in India: a literature review. In: *CSD Working Paper Series: Towards a New Indian Model of Information and Communications Technology-Led Growth and Development*, 2019.

[6] Domínguez-Mayo F.J., Escalona M.J., Mejías M., *et al.* A strategic study about quality characteristics in e-health systems based on a systematic literature review. Hindawi Publishing Corporation. *The Scientific World Journal* 2015, 2015, Article ID 863591, http://dx.doi.org/10.1155/2015/863591.

[7] Rojas Arce J. L. and Ortega Maldonado E. C. The advent of the digital twin: a prospective in healthcare in the next decade. In: *Advances in Production Management Systems. Artificial Intelligence for Sustainable and Resilient Production Systems*, 2021.

[8] Bagaria N., Laamarti F., Badawi H.F. *et al.* Health 4.0: digital twins for health and well-being. In: El Saddik A., Hossain M., and Kantarci B. (eds.), *Connected Health in Smart Cities*. Cham: Springer, 2020. https://doi.org/ 10.1007/978-3-030-27844-1_7.

[9] Liu Z., Su J., and Ji L. Detection and characterization of E-Health Research: A Bibliometris (2001–2016), *Scientometrics Recent Advances*, 2019, DOI: 10.5772/intechopen.88610.

[10] Aashish B. and. Saikat G. Leveraging digital twin technology in the healthcare industry – a machine learning based approach. *European Journal of Molecular & Clinical Medicine*, 2020, 7(6), 2547–2557.

[11] Damjanovic-Behrendt. A digital twin-based privacy enhancement mechanism for the automotive industry. In: *2018 International Conference on Intelligent Systems (IS)*, 2018, pp. 272–279, doi: 10.1109/IS.2018.8710526.

[12] Casadei R., Pianini D., Viroli M., and Weyns D. Digital twins, virtual devices, and augmentations for self-organising cyber-physical collectives. *Applied Sciences.* 2022, 12(1), 349. https://doi.org/10.3390/app12010349

[13] Erol T., Mendi A., and Dogan D. The digital twin revolution in healthcare. In: *2020 4th International Symposium on Multidisciplinary Studies and Innovative Technologies (ISMSIT)*, 2020, pp. 1–7. 10.1109/ISMSIT50672.2020.9255249.

[14] Ferdousi R., Laamarti F., Hossain M.A., *et al.* Digital twins for well-being: an overview [version 1; peer review: 1 approved with reservations]. *Digitaltwin* 2021, 1, 7. https://doi.org/10.12688/digitaltwin.17475.1.

[15] Khatoon N., Roy S., and Pranav P. A survey on Applications of Internet of Things in healthcare. In: Khatoon N., Roy S., and Pranav P. (eds.), *Internet of Things and Big Data Applications. Intelligent Systems*, vol. 180. Cham, Switzerland: Springer Nature, 2020, pp. 89–106.

[16] Kalyani G. and Chaudhari S. An efficient approach h for enhancing security in the Internet of Things using the optimum authentication key. *International Journal of Computers and Applications* 2019, 42, 306–314.

[17] Thakare V. and Kumbhar M. Internet of Things (IoT) in hospitals of India: a literature review and research direction. *UGC Care List Journal* 2020, 68, 132–137.

[18] Garcia L., Parra L., Jimenez J.M., Lloret J., and Lorenz P. IoT-based smart irrigation systems: an overview on the recent trends on sensors and IoT systems for irrigation in precision agriculture. *Sensors* 2020, 20, 1042.

[19] Iman A., Madi A.A., and Addaim A. Proposed architecture of e-health IoT. *IEEE* 2019, 19, 1–7.

[20] Garg A. and Diksha N.M. A security, and confidentiality survey in wireless Internet of Things (IoT). In: Balas V., Solanki V., and Kumar R. (eds.), *Internet of Things and Big Data Applications: Recent Advances and Challenges*, vol. 180. Cham, Switzerland: Springer Nature, 2020, pp. 65–88.

[21] Abouelmehdi, K., Beni-Hssane, A., Khaloufi, H., and Saadi, M. Big data security and privacy in healthcare: a review. *Procedia Computer Science* 2017, 113, 73–80.

[22] Jimenez J.I., Jahankhani H., and Kendzierskyj S. Healthcare in the cyberspace: medical cyber-physical system and digital twin challenges. Digital twin technologies, and smart cities. In: *Internet of Things (Technology communication Computing)*. Cham, Switzerland: Springer Nature AG, 2020, pp. 79–92.

[23] Diamantopoulou V., Argyropoulos N., Kalloniatis C., and Gritzalis S. Supporting the design of privacy-aware business processes via privacy process patterns. In: *Proceedings of the 2017 11th International Conference on Research Challenges in Information Science (RCIS)*, Brighton, UK, 10–12 May 2017; pp. 187–198.

Chapter 9

Digital twin in prognostics and health management system

S. Malathy[1], C.N. Vanitha[1] and Rajesh Kumar Dhanaraj[2]

9.1 Introduction

Dr. Michael Grieves coined the phrase "digital twin" (DT) in 2002. It is a digital depiction of physical assets, business processes, people, or locations. It aids firms in improving their performance by displaying the visualization of complicated assets and processes. Between the actual thing and its digital representation, DT can perform bi-directional automated data exchange:

- A DT is defined as a physical tool model which will contain complete information about a system/device and can act together with an existing database and live messages [1].
- It is also defined as a type of simulation which is based on expert knowledge and real data obtained from the existing system in order to attain more accurate results at various chronological and geospatial scales.
- It is also referred as a virtual model which depends on a physical system that can track the situation, continuance, and strength of the actual system in real time.
- It is incorporated with multiple physical components which are scaled up to multiple levels with a probabilistic simulation of a system that combine the best existing models with accurate sensor updates and history to match the reality of the concerned application domain.

DT uses four technologies as shown in Figure 9.1:

1. The Internet of Things (IoT),
2. Extended Reality (XR),
3. Cloud, and
4. Artificial Intelligence (AI).

[1]Department of Computer Science Engineering, Kongu Engineering College, India
[2]School of Computing Science and Engineering, Galgotias University, India

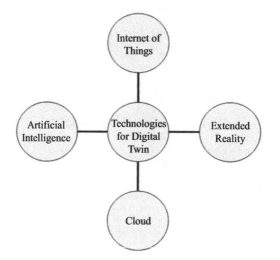

Figure 9.1   Technologies for DT

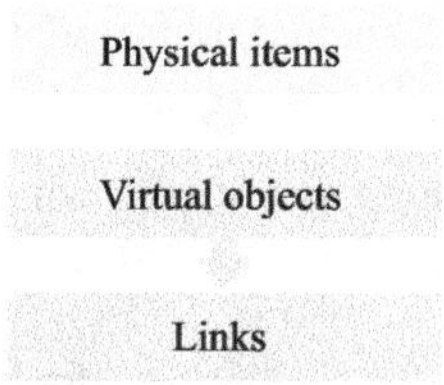

Physical items

Virtual objects

Links

Figure 9.2   Components of DT

The DT consists of three components as listed below as illustrated in Figure 9.2.

1. Physical items,
2. Virtual objects, and
3. Links between them.

Since then, DTs have grown in popularity as a hot research issue with plans to use them in a variety of industries, as well as smart cities and health. The DT was introduced in diverse domains with varying expectations in the early phases of its use in industry.

9.2   Pile of DT

The three piles of the DT are illustrated in Figure 9.3 as follows [2–4]:

1. Digital mirror (physical infrastructure).
2. Digital data flow.
3. Digital virtual thread to distribute the cloud.

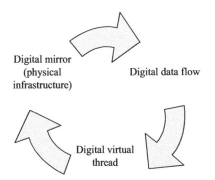

Digital mirror (physical infrastructure)

Digital data flow

Digital virtual thread

Figure 9.3 Pile of DT

9.2.1 Digital mirror (physical infrastructure)

A digital mirror is a mathematical representation of an existing or planned physical thing, with only one way information flow between the physical thing and the system.

9.2.2 Digital data flow

The data of a physical system can affect the state of a virtual unit automatically. The speed and granularity (resolution) of monitoring determine the effectiveness of data shadowing or data flow.

9.2.3 Digital virtual thread

The digital virtual thread is a structure in the various parts are combined together to offer a full view of the physical system all through the entity's working cycle.

9.3 A complete DT model

The complete DT encompasses a five-dimensional model which consists of the following [5,6] as depicted in Figure 9.4.

1. Physical section.
2. Digital section.
3. Linkage.
4. Data.
5. Service.

DT had only three dimensions in the early stages of development: physical, virtual, and connecting parts. Academicians believe that the DT is primarily concerned with those three parameters that can be extended beyond them to data and service as illustrated in Figure 9.3.

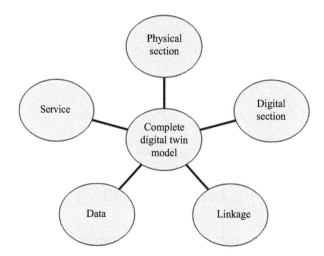

Figure 9.4   A complete DT model

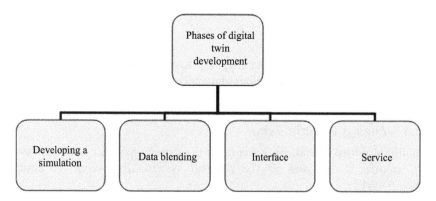

Figure 9.5   Phases of DT development

9.4   Phases of DT development

There are four phases of developing the DTs [7] is represented in Figure 9.5.

1.   Developing a simulation.
2.   Data blending.
3.   Interface.
4.   Service.

9.4.1   Developing a simulation

For the realization of DTs, modeling and simulation are essential. Industry, smart cities, and healthcare have a plethora of research publications on modeling frameworks, methodologies, and technologies, some of which are illustrated in Figure 9.6.

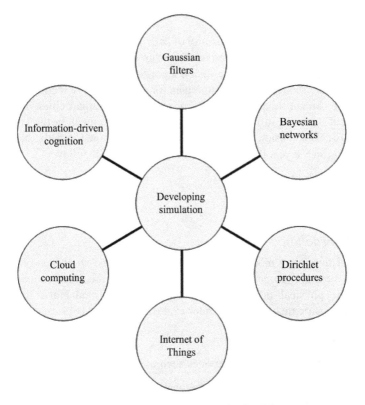

Figure 9.6   Technologies used by DT for health management

9.4.1.1   DT in health management

DTs for health management in the industrial sector are developed based on a hybrid model comprising Bayesian networks, Gaussian filters, and the Dirichlet procedure of mixing models [8]. Based on real-time models and simulation approaches, it is also created with a deep DT incorporation model of the invention line between the substantial and digital production lines [9]. DT in the healthcare industry is also developed by combining the concept of IoT and cloud computing platforms, which could provide considerable progress in patient rehabilitation [10].

9.4.1.2   DT in smart cities

The concept of virtual reality is used to simulate complex missions in a virtual city in order to generate personal DTs with information-driven cognition, with the goal of creating a personalized information system in the future [11]. It is also created by combining a space syntax-based lane grid model, a simulation for urban mobilization, a simulation for detecting the direction of the wind flow and some supplied geospatial data [12].

9.4.2   Fusion of data

The DT system contains a great quantity of data. It is essential to have a robust data fusion capability. There are numerous data from several sensors, necessitating the usage of data processing and data fusion algorithms [13]. As a result, data fusion can be considered one of the key strategies for realizing a DT model. Assume DT contains live camera footage and location information in smart cities. To deal with these data, it's crucial to use the right data fusion techniques in the DT city framework [14]. Data fusion technologies, according to some experts, can be categorized into three levels [15] as given in Figure 9.7 are as follows:

1. Fusion at information level.
2. Fusion at attribute level.
3. Fusion at choice level.

9.4.3   Interaction

It is critical that many modules of DTs connect with one another in order for the system to function properly. It is vital to evaluate the interconnection status between the physical infrastructure-based production model and its DTs, for example, to ensure that the DT is under exclusive control [16].

9.4.4   Service

The DT is employed in various services such as

1. Healthcare and prognostics management.
2. Continuous condition monitoring.
3. Decision based on events and triggers, etc.

For instance, in a production process, it could be intended to give customers advice on which tools to use. It should continuously check the system's health state in actual operating conditions to be aware of a fault. The ontology that represents robotic control services is widely used in robotics. Because mathematical models for procedure simulation, pathway simulation, and other tasks are already available

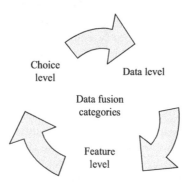

Figure 9.7   Data fusion categories

as cloud services, calling them should be simple for the automatic system [17]. Furthermore, the service design should include numerous elements, such as clever implementation, precise forecasting, and dependable control.

9.5 DT applications in healthcare

The uses of DTs in healthcare that have been addressed in recent studies have been addressed in this section. DT applications in healthcare are focused on personal health management and precision medicine. The key technology and applications required to apply DT approaches to personal health and well-being are outlined. The issues raised in the function of the DT are also discussed. DTs had a lot of achievements in the field of metropolitan healthcare management, particularly in the areas of water treatment and hospital management. The following is a list of the relevant applications.

9.5.1 Healthcare system

By combining city modeling and simulation, a DT model is created for the public health emergency system in a smart city.

For the hospital system, a DT paradigm included IoT, AI algorithms, and cloud computing technologies [18]. This system might offer real-time monitoring of the patient status and protect them in real time, according to the benefits of DT technology. A DT model that incorporated machine learning methods, deep learning algorithms, and some physical models to provide a map and predict physiological circumstances in the future [19]. The results suggest that this structure was effective in determining the patient future trajectories based on the clinical data collected.

9.5.2 Recovery of the patient

The data-driven technologies (e.g., machine learning) [30–32] and DTs are used to create a unique system for not only continually tracking patient health but also virtually evaluating the implementation and progress of medical therapies. They went into greater detail about the definition of internal structures for DTs in the context of continuous monitoring and individualized data-driven medical treatments [20]. A personal DT model is created based on real-world clinical data and omics features that could aid clinicians in properly protecting patients [21].

9.5.3 Precision medicine

Precision medicine has been a prominent issue for researchers as the Internet and communication technology have advanced.

9.5.4 Research in pharmaceutical development

A DT-based pharmaceutical quality control laboratory is created which could be used to forecast the performance of a new drug [22]. Recent research has explored the early stages of DTs in cardiovascular care, as well as the challenges and potential that lie ahead [23]. They emphasized the importance of combining mechanistic and statistical models to accelerate cardiovascular research and achieve precision medicine vision.

9.5.5   Drug administration

A methodology that combined DT and cloud computing service is employed to successfully track the health state of elderly patients and acceptable medication use, based on the properties of DT [24].

9.5.6   Disease treating ways

A DT model based on vast clinical data to cure liver disease is developed [25]. The DT concept can also be used for medication discovery, management, and treatment of various diseases. The tissue engineering processes were studied using a DT framework along with the skeletal tissue engineering procedure to compare their framework to other data-driven models [26]. Finally, the results suggest that the DT's and model's performance should meet regulatory requirements.

9.6   Challenges in DT implementation

Initially, a DT could only represent a single item or component, but as AI technology has advanced, DTs may now represent an entire complicated system, process, or location. The use of a DT to represent multiple hospital business operations aids in the optimization and improvement of the overall ecosystem. It simulates a variety of aspects of a hospital, including the mobility of doctors, patients, and equipment, as well as real-time tracking of systems, assets, and people. The AI model can simulate increased efficiency by using real-time data from all hospital data points. The model algorithm can combine the results of imaging and non-imaging laboratory diagnosis and give them to the physician in a way that will assist him in making a better decision.

The DT technique has been shown to be effective in a wide range of industries. Since DTs are often built on a variety of technologies, practical implementation will lead to a number of obstacles to overcome before it may be used in manufacturing or other fields [27].

9.6.1   Infrastructure for information technology

These aids may be necessary for DTs to function properly. The advancements in 5G technology may be helpful in this regard. To assure the performance of DTs, fast data transport and data processing speeds are required.

9.6.2   Data utilization

A high-quality, uninterrupted, and continuous stream of data is required for DTs. IoT technology has the potential to generate a vast amount of data. The accuracy of the data will have an impact on the performance of DTs, particularly in the areas of data analytics and processing. As a result, it is critical to ensure that the DT technology's input data is effective and of high quality.

9.6.2.1 Security

With the advancements in cloud computing and service, a vast amount of personal data is being stored on the cloud. As a result, security and privacy must be considered, particularly in smart cities and smart health. As a result, data encryption and intrusion detection systems will become critical components of DTs.

9.6.3 Consistent modeling

There is no common DT model for the modeling and simulation of specific events because the technology is still in its early phases of development. It would be easier for users who want to use a DT model to cope with specific situations if there was a common strategy.

9.6.4 Modeling of domains

Because of the characteristics of DTs, it is critical for a DT model to combine data from several domains. As a result, if these data cannot be transported rapidly, DTs will face significant challenges in the future.

Healthcare is one of the industries that have been identified as being affected by DT technology. The DT concept was first proposed and applied in product or equipment prognostics in the healthcare business. By adopting a more data-driven approach to healthcare, lives can be enhanced in terms of medical health, sports, and education. Because of technological advancements, it is now possible to create individualized models for patients that are constantly modifiable based on tracked health and lifestyle indicators. This could eventually lead to a virtual patient with a full description of a patient's current health status rather than relying solely on earlier records. Furthermore, the DT allows for the comparison of individual records to the population as a whole, making it easier to detect trends in great detail.

DTs are being used in the healthcare business to improve personalized medication, healthcare organization performance, and the development of novel drugs and technology. Although simulations have been around for a while, medical DTs are a significant step forward. The DTs will generate meaningful models based on data from omics, wearable devices and patient records, allowing patients, clinicians, and healthcare organizations, as well as medication and device manufacturers, to connect the dots across processes.

Although it is still early days, breakthroughs in real-time data inputs, machine learning, and augmented/virtual reality are propelling the field of DTs forward swiftly. As a result, DTs may have a significant impact on diagnosing and treating patients, as well as realigning the incentives for better health.

9.7 Role of DT in healthcare

Tailored medicine for individuals, enhancing healthcare institutions, and drug and medical instruments research incorporated with DTs are beginning to affect healthcare today. In reality, various types of DTs span numerous use cases and categories, and it is one of the inter-domain use cases that make DTs so strong [29].

9.7.1 Medicine that is tailored to the individual

DTs have a lot of potential in terms of building easier medical treatments for people based on their sole genetic composition, behavior, anatomy, and other aspects. As a result, academics are beginning to scale DTs from smaller to mass customization platforms that are comparable to today's advanced customer information platforms. Each patient's historical and real-time data aids the ML system in predicting future health issues. The model alerts the patient for prescriptions, dietary habit modifications, and medical consultation based on the patient's lifestyle, blood sugar data, daily food habits, etc.

As a result, DT uses AI-equipped models to generate more tailored and better treatment plans based on a significant amount of rich data from multiple IoMT devices [28]. Using insights from previous data, each patient's unique DT can assist in determining the best therapy, forecasting the result of a certain operation, and managing their chronic disease. Consider the case of a heart failure patient who requires cardiac resynchronization therapy (CRT) via pacemaker implantation. Few people do not respond to the therapy due to varying heart features. Furthermore, in order to avoid future risks, the placement of the proper patients must be accurate.

A DT of the patient's heart is built using MRI, ECG, and blood pressure data, and it aids cardiologists in defining the position of leads and digitally testing with placement before intervention surgery.

Another example is cancer treatment decision support using the proper therapy. The doctor can use the patient's imaging data, genetic data, and test results to determine the best treatment option, which could be hormone therapy, surgery, or radiation therapy. DT analyses physiological and behavioral data to detect chronic disease at an earlier stage which will be very useful for dealing with larger populations.

9.7.2 Development of virtual organs

- Virtual hearts that may be personalized to specific patients which help to understand the evolution of diseases over time or to detect how it will respond to new medications, therapies, or surgical procedures are being developed by a number of companies. Starting with the company's ultrasound equipment, Philip Heart Model simulates a virtual heart.
- Siemens Healthineers has been developing a heart based on DT technology to help with pharmacological therapy and cardiac catheterization simulations. After analyzing one of the customers' processes and operations, Siemens Healthineers built a DT model representation for their radiology department. By eliminating long wait times, effectively managing emergency services, optimum utilization of lab and medical equipment, staffing requirements, and managing device downtime, this simulation optimizes the process and improves the patient experience. As a result, hospital management can oversee

the whole infrastructure—from patients to clinicians to data to workflows—from a single platform.

- FEops, a European firm, has already commercialized the FEops Heartguide technology after receiving regulatory permission. It improves the investigation and treatment of structural heart disorders by combining a specific replica of patient heart with AI-associated anatomical analysis.
- In 2014, Dassault Systèmes launched the Living Heart Project, a crowd-sourcing project to create a virtual twin of the human heart. Medical researchers and surgeons, medical device makers, and medication companies have collaborated on the initiative as an open-source partnership.
- Meanwhile, the Living Brain project at the business is helping to guide epilepsy therapy and follow the evolution of neurodegenerative illnesses. Similar projects have been conducted for the lungs, knees, eyes, and other systems by the company.

9.7.3   Medicine based on genomic data

- Researchers have mapped the RNA of mice to create a DT that can anticipate the effects of various doses of arthritis medicines. The goal is to use RNA to personalize human diagnosis and therapy. The researchers discovered that roughly 40% to 70% of the time, medicine does not work.
- Human T-cells, which play a critical role in immunological defense, are also being mapped using similar techniques. These maps can aid in the early detection of many common ailments, when treatment is more successful and less expensive.

9.7.4   Healthcare apps

The pandemic has aided the emergence of digitized health services which use AI to assist individuals to identify and treat simple medical ailments.

The Healthcheck App from Babylon Health, for example, transforms health related data into DTs. It deals with data that is manually entered, such as symptom trackers, health histories, and mood swings. It also works with the data collected automatically through workout equipment and wearables like the Apple Watch. The DT can give basic information or aid in prioritizing and contacting clinicians to manage more serious or persistent conditions.

9.7.4.1   Customizing medicine therapy for each individual

DTs are being developed to help people with chronic pain get the most out of their medications. Age and lifestyle are used to tailor the DT in order to forecast the impact of pain drugs. Furthermore, patient comments on the efficacy of various doses are used to regulate DT accuracy.

9.7.4.2   Examining entire body

Most DT systems rely on current technology to collect the necessary data, but Q Bio's innovative platform begins with a full-body scan. The business claims that it can complete a full-body scan in 15 min with no radiation or breath holds, and that it can do so using new statistical physics models that are more accurate than traditional MRI for many diagnoses. Q Bio is also working on integrating data from anatomy, lifestyle, genetics, medical history, and chemistry to improve these models.

9.7.5   Surgery scheduling

- A Boston hospital tied up with Dassault Systèmes' digital heart to get up surgical process planning and assessment. They can also use DTs to create the cuff shape between the heart and the arteries.
- Sim&Size is a DT developed by Sim&Cure to assist brain surgeons in treating aneurysms based on simulations to increase the safety of the patients. Aneurysms are enlargements of the blood vessels that can cause a clot or stroke.

DTs can help surgeons plan and conduct less invasive surgeries that use catheters to place custom implants. Individual patient data is used to tailor simulations that run on an Ansys-embedded simulation program. The requirement for follow-up surgery has been drastically reduced based on preliminary results.

9.7.6   Increasing the effectiveness of healthcare organizations

- DTs have the potential to improve the way healthcare companies give treatment. It will describe the process of modeling how a company operates in order to improve underlying operations.
- Process mining can be used to uncover variances in business processes across most sectors. These strategies may be supplemented by new healthcare-specific tools.

9.7.7   Improving the experience of caregivers

Caregivers can use DTs to capture and locate information communicated among physicians and specialists. When a person visits their regular primary care physician, for example, the doctor will understand the patient details and their medical history along with the prescriptions. When a patient visits a specialist, they also repeat similar questions again and again.

A DT can develop a specific model for a patient and then utilize technologies like natural language processing to decipher all of the repeated questions and help to summarize the clear situation of the patient.

This kind of action will save time and increases the accuracy of gathering and displaying information such as specific drugs, status of health, and other facts that clinicians need to make therapeutic decisions.

9.7.8   Increasing productivity

The GE Healthcare Command Center is a large-scale project to virtualize hospital infrastructure and investigate the effects of a variety of decisions on entire organizational performance. The various modules used for analyzing changes in staffing, operational strategy, capacity, and care delivery models are included, as well as modules for determining which measures to take objectively. They have created a module to evaluate the effect of different bed arrangements on optimize surgical schedules, improve facility architecture, care levels, and optimize staffing levels. This enables managers to experiment with different ideas without needing to do a pilot. This platform is already being used by dozens of companies, according to GE.

9.7.9 Critical treatment window shrinking

Siemens Healthineers has been collaborating with the Medical University of South Carolina to improve the daily routine in the hospital environment by analyzing and redesigning the system workflow and process enhancement methodologies. They are working to shorten the time it takes to treat stroke victims, for example. This is significant because early therapy is crucial, but it necessitates the proper operation of multiple mechanisms.

9.7.10 Healthcare delivery system based on value

Many countries are looking into a new scheme to better connect new pharmaceuticals, therapies, and treatments with outcomes due to rising healthcare costs. One option that is gaining traction is value-based healthcare. The core premise is that participants, such as pharmaceutical corporations, will only be compensated in proportion to their influence on the outcomes. This will necessitate the formation of new forms of interactions between various participants in the healthcare delivery system. The underlying infrastructure for managing the details of building these new forms of arrangements could be provided by DTs.

9.7.10.1 Resilience of supply chains

The epidemic demonstrated how vulnerable today's supply systems can be. Due to shutdowns and limitations imposed by nations such as China, healthcare organizations experienced immediate shortages of necessary personal protective equipment. DTs implemented in the supply chain can assist healthcare businesses in better understanding how to plan for new occurrences, shutdowns, and shortages by modeling their supply chain relationships. In an emergency, such as the recent pandemic, this can help with planning and talks with government officials.

9.7.11 Rapid hospital erection

DTs could potentially speed up the design of medical facilities that must adapt to quick changes, such as those witnessed during the pandemic. A DT platform is created to assist and organize healthcare construction specifics. In earlier days it is difficult to have new facilities erected in remote parts of the world. The platform aids in the coordination of design, procurement, and construction activities.

9.7.12 Streamlining interactions in call center

Customer support personnel may find it easier to identify and converse with patients using DTs. A huge insurance company used a TigerGraph graph database to combine data from multiple sources to build a complete health history for each of its members to give a clear picture of the member's current and past medical state. This kind of approach will help to reduce call management time by 10%, which will have a huge impact on income for an organization.

9.7.13   Development of pharmaceuticals and medical devices

DTs can help in the development, monitoring, and testing of novel medical equipment and pharmaceuticals in a variety of ways. For example, Food and Drug Administration (FDA) in the United States has begun a large campaign to encourage the adoption of various sorts of digital techniques. Regulators in these countries are developing rules to be followed for using modeling and simulation as evidence in the approval of novel drugs and devices.

9.7.13.1   Software as a medical instrument

In European countries, FDA is developing regulations that will allow various medical companies to certify and sell authorized software as medical instrumentation. The basic concept is to create a separate DT for each patient using various data sources such as ultrasound, genetic tests, lab tests, and imaging equipment. Furthermore, DT can aid in the software-related optimization of various medical devices such as automated insulin pumps, innovative brain treatments, and pacemakers.

9.7.14   Detecting the dangers in drugs

DTs are being used by pharmaceutical researchers to investigate the heart risks of various medications. This could be a more cost-effective way to enhance drug safety for individual pharmaceuticals and new drug combinations than testing them manually. Recently a basic model of DT for few medications has been developed. Extending the same in the future for large amount of drugs will help to cut down the cost of developing, testing, approving, and launching new medications.

9.7.15   Simulating the new production lines

Siemens collaborated with a number of vaccine producers to develop and evaluate the production line configurations of several vaccines. Novel mRNA vaccines are delicate, and they must be synthesized precisely by using micro and nano-sized particles. Because of DTs, the process of designing and validating the devices manufactured and process scaling has reduced the launch time from a year to five months.

9.7.16   Improving the device availability

A few organizations have announced the launch of a predictive maintenance service that gathers data from various sources of medical imaging devices. The company hopes that DTs would increase uptime and assist engineers in customizing new equipment to meet the needs of various clients. It also intends to apply the same concepts to all of its medical equipment.

9.7.17   Post-sales surveillance

- As part of a procedure known as post-market sales surveillance, regulators are taking the initiative to place a greater emphasis on device producers monitoring the performance of the equipment after it has been sold.
- This necessitates either hiring costly specialists to preserve the equipment or incorporating DT capabilities into the device itself.
- Most of the device manufacturers will include performance testing on their devices in order to secure a waiver from these new standards.
- This paved the way for smaller clinical environments to be built closer to patients, allowing for faster diagnosis.

9.7.18   Human variability simulation

The ideal human is frequently shown in skeletons and atlases. Real-life persons, on the other hand, often have tiny variances in their muscles or structure of bones that go undiscovered. Because of this medical device manufacturers struggle to understand how frequent anatomical variances affect the fit and function of their products.

Virtonomy has created a library of typical variants to assist medical device manufacturers in conducting tests to see how these new variations impact the performance and safety of new devices. They are simulating traits that indicate general variances in a group rather than individuals in this situation.

9.7.19   A lab's DT

Thousands or millions of options must often be tested in a highly controlled environment in modern medication development. The use of a DT of the lab can aid in the automation of these facilities. It can also aid in the prioritization of tests in reaction to new information. Experiments could also be more reproducible across labs and across lab employees using DTs.

9.7.20   Improving drug distribution

Virtual Human System project carried out by Oklahoma State researchers has utilized a DT to optimize medicine administration models of simulated lungs. They discovered approximately twenty percent of several medicines reached their intended target. The DTs enabled them to modify the particle size of the concerned drug and combination properties, resulting in a 90% increase in delivery efficiency.

9.8   Benefits

- Remote visibility of systems, assets, and processes.
- Knowing the behavior of physical devices.
- Better decision-making.
- Increasing productivity and profitability via automation.

- Increasing operational efficiency.
- Generates more accurate results for business decisions based on dynamic changes in situations.

References

[1] Barricelli R, Casiraghi E, and Fogli D. A survey on digital twin: definitions, characteristics, applications, and design implications. *IEEE Access* 2019;7: 167653–71.

[2] Yaqoob I, Salah K, Uddin M, Jayaraman R, Omar M, and Imran M. Blockchain for digital twins: recent advances and future research challenges. *IEEE Network* 2020;34:290–8.

[3] Brecher C, Buchsbaum M, and Storms S. Control from the cloud: edge computing, services and digital shadow for automation technologies. In *Proceedings of the 2019 International Conference on Robotics and Automation (ICRA)*; 2019. p. 9327–33.

[4] Schuh G, Dölle C, and Tönnes C. Methodology for the derivation of a digital shadow for engineering management. In *Proceedings of the 2018 IEEE Technology and Engineering Management Conference (TEMSCON)*; 2018. p. 1–6.

[5] Tao F, Sui F, Liu A, *et al.* Digital twin-driven product design framework. *International Journal of Production Research* 2018;57:3935–53.

[6] Wu C, Zhou Y, Pereia Pessôa MV, Peng Q, and Tan R. Conceptual digital twin modeling based on an integrated five-dimensional framework and TRIZ function model. *Journal of Manufacturing Systems* 2020;58:79–93.

[7] Schluse M, Priggemeyer M, Atorf L, and Rossmann J. Experimentable digital twins – streamlining simulation-based systems engineering for industry 4.0. *IEEE Transactions on Industrial Informatics* 2018;14:1722–31.

[8] Yu J, Song Y, Tang D, and Dai J. A digital twin approach based on non-parametric Bayesian network for complex system health monitoring. *Journal of Manufacturing Systems* 2020;58:293–304.

[9] Gao Y, Lv H, Hou Y, Liu J, and Xu W. Real-time modeling and simulation method of digital twin production line. In *Proceedings of the 2019 IEEE 8th Joint International Information Technology and Artificial Intelligence Conference (ITAIC)*; 2019. p. 1639–42.

[10] Jimenez JI, Jahankhani H, and Kendzierskyj S. Healthcare in the cyberspace: medical cyber-physical system and digital twin challenges. In *Digital Twin Technologies and Smart Cities*. New York, NY: Springer; 2020. p. 79–92.

[11] Du J, Zhu Q, Shi Y, Wang Q, Lin Y, and Zhao D. Cognition digital twins for personalized information systems of smart cities: proof of concept. *Journal of Management in Engineering* 2020;36:04019052.

[12] Dembski F, Wössner U, Letzgus M, Ruddat M, and Yamu C. Urban digital twins for smart cities and citizens: the case study of Herrenberg, Germany. *Sustainability* 2020;12:2307.

[13]   Xie Y, Lian K, Liu Q, Zhang C, and Liu H. Digital twin for cutting tool: modeling, application and service strategy. *Journal of Manufacturing Systems* 2020; 58:305–12.

[14]   Shirowzhan S, Tan W, and Sepasgozar SME. Digital twin and CyberGIS for improving connectivity and measuring the impact of infrastructure construction planning in smart cities. *International Society for Photogrammetry and Remote Sensing* 2020;9:240.

[15]   He B, Cao X, and Hua Y. Data fusion-based sustainable digital twin system of intelligent detection robotics. *Journal of Cleaner Production* 2021;280:124181.

[16]   Ait-Alla A, Kreutz M, Rippel D, Lütjen M, and Freitag M. Simulation-based analysis of the interaction of a physical and a digital twin in a cyber-physical production system. *IFAC-PapersOnLine* 2019;52:1331–6.

[17]   Xu W, Cui J, Li L, Yao B, Tian S, and Zhou Z. Digital twin-based industrial cloud robotics: framework, control approach and implementation. *Journal of Manufacturing Systems* 2020;58:196–209.

[18]   Karakra A, Fontanili F, Lamine E, and Lamothe J. HospiT'Win: a predictive simulation-based digital twin for patients pathways in hospital. In *Proceedings of the 2019 IEEE EMBS International Conference on Biomedical & Health Informatics (BHI)*; 2019. p. 1–4.

[19]   Barbiero P, Torné RV, and Lió P. Graph representation forecasting of patient's medical conditions: towards a digital twin. arXiv preprint arXiv 2020:200908299.

[20]   Rivera LF, Jiménez M, Angara P, Villegas NM, Tamura G, and Müller HA. Towards continuous monitoring in personalized healthcare through digital twins. In *Proceedings of the 29th Annual International Conference on Computer Science and Software Engineering*; 2019. p. 329–35.

[21]   Fagherazzi G. Deep digital phenotyping and digital twins for precision health: time to dig deeper. *Journal of Medical Internet Research* 2020;22:e16770.

[22]   Lopes MR, Costigliola A, Pinto R, Vieira S, and Sousa JMC. Pharmaceutical quality control laboratory digital twin – a novel governance model for resource planning and scheduling. *International Journal of Production Research* 2019;58:6553–67.

[23]   Corral-Acero J, Margara F, Marciniak M, *et al.* The "Digital Twin" to enable the vision of precision cardiology. *European Heart Journal* 2020;41:4556–64.

[24]   Liu Y, Zhang L, Yang Y, *et al.* A novel cloud-based framework for the elderly healthcare services using digital twin. *IEEE Access* 2019;7:49088–101.

[25]   Subramanian K. Digital twin for drug discovery and development – the virtual liver. *Journal of the Indian Institute of Science* 2020;100:653–62.

[26]   Harari YN. *Homo Deus: a Brief History of Tomorrow.* UK: Random House; 2016.

[27]   Yang D, Karimi HR, Kaynak O, and Yin S. Developments of digital twin technologies in industrial, smart city and healthcare sectors: a survey. *Complex Engineering Systems* 2021;*1*(1)):3.

[28]   Erol T, Mendi AF, and Doğan D. The digital twin revolution in healthcare. In *2020 4th International Symposium on Multidisciplinary Studies and Innovative Technologies (ISMSIT)*, pp. 1–7. IEEE, 2020.

[29]   George Lawton, "21 ways medical twin will transform the healthcare", www.venturebeat.com, July 4, 2021.

[30]   Malathy S, Santhiya M, Vanitha CN, and Karthiga RR. Diabetes disease prediction using artificial neural network with machine learning approaches. In *ICECA 2021, 5th International Conference on Electronics, Communication and Aerospace Technology*, 2–4 December, 2021.

[31]   Vanitha CN and Malathy S. A multi-syndrome pathology for breast cancer through intelligent learning. *IEEE Xplore Digital Library*, DOI:10.1088/1757-899X/1055/1/012073.

[32]   Vanitha CN and Malathy S. Optimizing wireless sensor networks path selection using resource levelling technique in transmitting endoscopy bio-medical data. *IEEE Xplore Digital Library*, DOI:10.1088/1757-899X/1055/1/012071.

Chapter 10

Deep learning in Covid-19 detection and diagnosis using CXR images: challenges and perspectives

S. Suganyadevi[1], V. Seethalakshmi[1], K. Balasamy[2] and N. Vidhya[1]

The COVID-19 pandemic is endangering the health and lives of people in 223 nations and territories. When dealing with the Coronavirus, early discovery and isolation are the most important measures to take. X-rays, computed tomography and magnetic resonance imaging can show the presence of Covid-19, making infection detection a cinch. Chest X-rays (CXR) of people infected with Covid-19 are shown to have certain abnormalities and it is one of the frequently used imaging modalities. The digital twin monitors people's data, compares them to documented patterns, and analyses illness symptoms. Furthermore, the data might be used to create a digital modelling of a typical healthy patient, which aids in the definition of new healthy criteria. There are a variety of ways to use deep learning to find diseases in X-rays from previous efforts. Initially, 6,000 chest X-rays were collected from publicly available sources. These pictures will be recognized by a radiologist as evidence of Covid-19 sickness. Approximately 15% of children worldwide are killed by pneumococcal disease. Recognized and sorted pneumonia, healthy, and Covid-19 all come from the modified VGG16 deep learning (DL) technique. The convolutional neural network (CNN) is a deep neural network that incorporates both external and internal characteristics and is used by the identification model to identify pixels. The findings indicate that medical professionals should reconsider the use of X-ray images in the treatment of certain diseases and that more research into evaluating X-ray technology is required. The suggested detection approach performed better when compared to chest X-rays for pneumonia and non-pneumonia conditions.

10.1 Introduction

Coronaviruses are a type of virus that can lead to infection and, as a result, illness, extending from coughs and colds to severe sicknesses similar to Severe Acute

[1]Department of Electronics and Communication Engineering, KPR Institute of Engineering and Technology, India
[2]Department of Artificial Intelligence and Data Science, Bannari Amman Institute of Technology, India

Respiratory Syndrome and Middle East Respiratory Syndrome. Further Covid-19 has a 3.4% mortality rate, making it potentially fatal. A severe lung infection may be fatal due to Covid-19 to damage to the digestive system and respiratory failure [1]. Digital twins are a converging technique in which a digital clone of any living or non-living thing is created. At the moment, digital twins are widely employed in Industry 4.0, where they aid in optimizing machine performance through preventive and predictive maintenance [2]. By boosting medical treatment with digital tracking and developing human body modelling, the usage of digital twins in healthcare is transforming clinical operations and healthcare administrators. These techniques are extremely beneficial to researchers investigating illnesses, novel medications and medical gadgets [3]. Nevertheless, advanced twins will assist the medical services framework by offering life-saving developments for sale to the public quicker, at lower costs and with more noteworthy security for the patient. Early diagnosis and automated identification of Covid-19 allow for rapid ventilation of critically ill patients in high-tech hospitals, as well as illness progression monitoring. Pneumonia, like Covid-19, may be lethal for infants under two and seniors over 65 [4]. It has a wide range of symptoms and is highly contagious. Headway pneumonia within the respiratory system X-ray and chest X-ray may both account for pulmonary oedema like pneumonia in immunosuppressed people or newborns, which has been discovered to be more fatal than pneumonia and causes Acute Respiratory Distress Syndrome (ARDS). AI has now been applied in an assortment of utilizations, including detection and localization, classification, and image segmentation, using deep learning algorithms [5]. An ML structure is utilized to foresee Covid-19 from CXR pictures.

Not at all like the old-style approaches for clinical picture characterization which follow a two-venture methodology (hand-created including extraction + recognition), we utilize a start-to-finish DL structure that straightforwardly predicts the Covid-19 illness from crude pictures with practically no need for element extraction [6]. CNN is displayed to beat the traditional. The proof of the fast and squeezing innovative development joined with the overall rising legislative endeavours prompts the end that the medical care area is as of now confronting the effect of I4.0, really going eHealth on the way to Healthcare 4.0. AI approaches in the greater part of PC vision and clinical picture examination assignments as of late. Profound advancing oftentimes insinuates a framework wherein profound convolutional neural associations are employed for customized frame component extraction, which could be accomplished by the process named convolution [7]. Typically, significant learning suggests more significant associations than commendable AI ones, utilizing tremendous data [8]. Figure 10.1 shows a few example pictures of Coronavirus, and typical, pneumonia x-beams.

Covid-19 infected people may be identified by analysing chest X-ray pictures utilizing an AI method for machine learning, CNNs [9]. CNNs learn about qualities from the data rather than depending on people to extract them. Deep CNN has been shown to be effective in a variety of applications, including the detection of skin cancer, arrhythmia, brain illness and breast cancer in X-ray images, to name just a few. The cause of respiratory disease epidemics by contacting your mucous

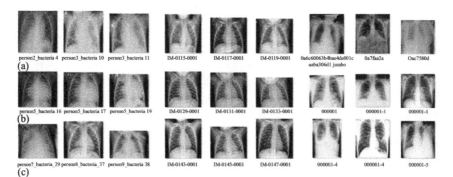

Figure 10.1   *X-ray images of (a) Covid-19-induced pneumonia, (b) healthy and (c) other viral-induced pneumonia*

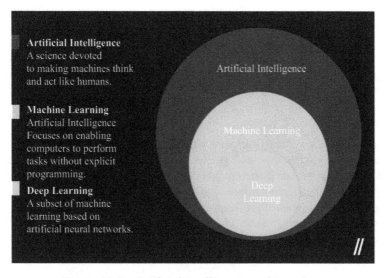

Figure 10.2   *Artificial intelligence and its subsets*

membranes, you may infect yourself with the Covid-19 virus [10]. Medical services suppliers create and catch gigantic measures of information containing incredibly significant signs and data, at a speed far more astounding than what conventional techniques for investigation can process [12]. Figure 10.2 shows the general definition of AI and its subsets.

A virus may enter a healthy cell and use the cell's genetic material to produce new strains of the virus. The number of infected cells increases as the Covid-19 viral population grows. Covid-19 may be detected via X-rays since practically all hospitals have these. Because of the fast spread of Covid-19, the medical community in many nations is scrambling to catch up, and accurate genetic testing for the disease is all but non-existent [13]. There is one benefit to using a scanner for CXR: even though the test results come back negative, the scan may reveal illnesses in their early stages. One drawback to the scanner's analysis is that a radiology professional is necessary and the process takes time. It is imperative that infected users be constantly aware of their surroundings. CXR and CT-Scan are more helpful in detecting Covid-19 and pneumonia than RT-PCR because they offer a sharper image of the alveoli. A wide range of investigations have used X-ray imaging of the lungs [14]. Using CXR images, we observed that a CNN may assist radiologists in diagnosing Covid-19 infections. Figure 10.3 represents the general classification of machine learning model. Table 10.1 provides some general applications of neural networks.

10.1.1   CNN

A convolutional neural network (ConvNet) is a type of deep neural network that is often used to evaluate visual images in deep learning. It employs a method known as Convolution. Convolution is a mathematical expression of two functions that yields a third function that explains how the form of one is affected by the other [15]. Here, two pictures which can be addressed as grids are duplicated to give a result that is utilized to remove highlights from the picture [16]. There are two fundamental parts to CNN engineering. A convolution device that isolates and distinguishes the different highlights of the picture for examination in an interaction called as Feature Extraction [17].

10.1.2   ANN

ANN is a data taking care of perspective that is charged up by the brain. ANNs, like people, learn by models. An ANN is intended for a particular solicitation, similar to model affirmation or data plan, through a learning collaboration. Progressing for the most part incorporates acclimations to the synaptic affiliations that exist between the neurons [18]. The model of artificial neural organization can be indicated by three elements, namely interconnections, activation functions and learning rules.

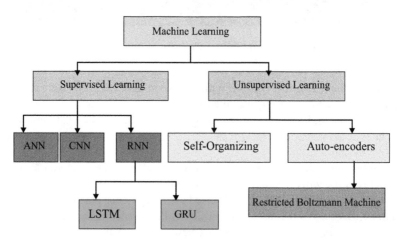

Figure 10.3   General classifications of machine learning

Table 10.1   Type of neural network comparison

Type of neural network	Applications
Perceptron (P)	Classification and encode database
Feed forward (FF)	Image compression, handwritten character recognition, pattern recognition, machine vision, sonar target detection and voice recognition
Radial basis network (RBN)	Function estimation, categorization, time-series analysis and system control
Deep feed-forward (DFF)	Financial forecasting, image compression, pattern classification, machine vision and ECG noise filters
Recurrent neural network (RNN)	Transcription, music composition robot control, time series forecasting, voice recognition, time series fault detection, rhythm learning and language processing
Long/short-term memory (LSTM)	Speech recognition and writing recognition
Gated recurrent unit (GRU)	NLP, polyphonic music modelling and speech signal modelling
Autoencoder (AE)	Classification, clustering and feature compression
Variational autoencoder (VAE)	Interpolate between sentences and automatic image generation
Denoising autoencoder (DAE)	Dimensionality reduction and feature extraction
Sparse autoencoder (SAE)	Handwritten digits recognition and feature extraction
Markov chain (MC)	Statistics, speech recognition, queuing theory, information and communication system
Hopfield network (HN)	Enhancing X-ray images, optimization problems and medical image recognition
Boltzmann machine (BM)	Collaborative filtering, regression, dimensionality reduction, classification and feature learning
Restricted Boltzmann machine (RBM)	Filtering, business and economic examination, classification, risk detection and feature learning
Deep belief network (DBN)	Recovery of documents or images and non-linear dimensionality reduction
Deep convolutional network (DCN)	Face recognition, road signs, cancers, image recognition, drug discovery, video analysis, time series prediction, natural language processing, fault detection and checkers game
Deconvolutional neural networks (DN)	Super-resolution images, estimating the depth of a surface from an image estimation of optical flow
Deep convolutional inverse graphics network (DC-IGN)	Manipulations of human faces
Generative adversarial network (GAN)	Create new human poses, convert photos to emojis, age your face, improve resolution, translate clothing and predict video
Extreme learning machine (ELM)	Feature learning, classification, clustering, sparse approximation and regression
Echo state network (ESN)	Time series prediction and data mining

(Continues)

Table 10.1   (Continued)

Type of neural network	Applications
Deep residual network (DRN)	Image classification, language recognition, object detection, speech recognition and semantic segmentation
Kohonen networks (KN)	Dimensionality reduction (DR), coastal water management and evaluation and prediction of water quality
Support vector machines (SVM)	Face finding, handwriting recognition, text classification and bioinformatics
Neural Turing machine (NTM)	Robotics, video captioning and construction of an artificial human brain

10.1.3   RNN

Recurrent neural networks are a vital variation of neural organizations vigorously utilized in natural language processing [19]. RNN has an idea of memory which recalls all data concerning what has been identified till time step *t*. RNNs are called repetitive on the grounds that they play out a similar assignment for each component of a grouping, with the result being relied upon past calculations.

10.1.4   LSTM

Hochreiter and Schmidhuber introduced "long short-term memory" models in 1997. LSTM is like an RNN version that could overcome the shortcomings of RNNs that do not perform well, such as when dealing with long-term dependencies [20]. A memory cell is introduced into LSTM networks. They can work with data that has memory gaps. When the statement's context changes, the memory cell remembers some of the prior data and should be able to add some new data as well. We can see from the above that time delay can be considered with the RNN model, once our RNN fails while we had a big amount of applicable data and we need to extract pertinent data from it, LSTMs are the technique to go. In addition, unlike LSTMs, RNNs are unable to recall data from the past [21].

Advantages: LSTMs further avoid the problem of gradient vanishing or exploding. In 1999, an LSTM with a forget gate was invented, allowing the cell memory to be reset. Gers *et al.* [22] enhanced the original LSTM and declared it the standard structure of LSTM networks. LSTMs, unlike deep feed forward neural networks, have feedback connections. They may also process data sequences rather than just single data points, such as vectors or arrays. As a result, LSTMs are very beneficial for evaluating speech or video data.

10.1.5   GRU

Since LSTM and GRU both have similar designs and generate comparable outcomes, LSTMs are a type of gated recurrent unit. GRUs having only three gates and it does not keep track of their internal state [23].

10.1.6 Deep autoencoders

An autoencoder is one of the neural network models that can detect structure in data in order to produce a compressed version of the data input. It's been trained to transfer the data from the input to the output. It has a hidden layer on the inside that defines the code used to characterize the input [24]. The network has comprised an encoder ($h = f(x)$) and a decoder ($r = g(x)$) which provides a reform. Several multiple varieties of the general autoencoder architecture exist with the objective of ensuring that the compact interpretation represents the purposeful characteristics of the original data input. Typically, the biggest challenge when working with auto-encoders is obtaining our model to learn a considerable and categorize latent feature recognition [25]. Autoencoders train how else to get compressed data based on attributes such as correlations among input vectors collected during training. Nevertheless, these algorithms are often only able to produce data that is comparable to the class of observations recorded during training. Autoencoders can be used for anomaly detection, data-denoising image in painting and retrieval of information [26].

10.1.7 Deep Boltzmann's machine

The initial training algorithm for Boltzmann machines [27] needed randomly initialized Markov chains to encounter their equilibrium distributions in predicting the data-dependent and data-independent requirements that an integrated pair of binary variables both would be seen on. It is a totally undirected model, unlike a deep belief network (DBN). There is only one hidden layer in an RBM. There are multiple hidden layers in DBM [28]. A DBM is a network of random binary units that are symmetrically connected. It has a visible group of units $v\epsilon\{0, 1\}^D$ and a hidden group of unit's $h\epsilon\{0, 1\}^P$. A state's energy $\{v, h\}$ is calculated as follows in (10.1):

$$E(v, h;\theta) = -\frac{1}{2}v^T Lv - -\frac{1}{2}h^T Jh - Wh \tag{10.1}$$

Advantages: DBMs have the ability to acquire increasingly complicated internal representations, making them a viable solution to solve image and voice recognition challenges. Higher-level models could be generated from a huge number of unlabelled sensory data inputs, with only lesser labelled data necessary to modify the model for the chores at hand. Not at all like DBMs has the estimation induction method remembered hierarchical criticism for extra to a bottom-up pass, empowering DBM to more readily communicate vulnerabilities about equivocal data sources and henceforth manage them all the more powerfully.

Challenges: One unfavourable feature is that sampling from a DBM is difficult. It is important to utilize MCMC across all layers to generate a sample from a DBM. Using stochastic maximum likelihood to train a DBM almost always fails. A number of strategies for joint training have been developed. Table 10.2 provides different applications and its neural network.

Table 10.2 Result assessment for CXR images

Author	Image count	Model	Accuracy	Sensitivity	Specificity
E. E.-D. Hemdan et al. [1]	50	COVIDX-Net	90.00	100.00	100.00
A. Narin et al. [2]	100	ResNet-50	98.00	96.00	100.00
I. D. Apostolopoulos et al. [3]	1427	MobileNet V2	96.78	98.66	96.46
A. E. Hassanien et al. [4]	40	Machine learning (SVM classifier)	97.48	95.27	99.70
H. S. Maghdid et al. [5]	170	AlexNet	98.00	100.00	96.00
M. Farooq et al. [6]	13,975	COVID-ResNet	96.23	100.00	97.00
I. D. Apostolopoulos et al. [7]	3,905	MobileNet V2	99.18	97.36	99.42
N. E. M. Khalifa et al. [8]	5,863	ResNet-18	99.00	98.97	98.97
M. Karim et al. [9]	16,995	MADE-based CNN model	91.60	92.45	96.12
A. I. Khan et al. [10]	1,300	Coronet	89.60	93.00	98.20
P. Afshar et al. [11]	864	COVID-CAPS based on Capsule Network	95.70	90.00	95.80
S. Minaee et al. [12]	5,071	ResNet-18ResNet-50SqueezeNetDenseNet-121	98.00	97.50	95.00
P. K. Sethy et al. [13]	381	ResNet-50	95.33	95.33	95.34
Y. Zhang et al. [14]	11,663	COVID-DA based on ResNet-18	97.00	88.33	98.15
Y. Oh et al. [15]	502	ResNet-18	88.90	96.00	96.40
M. Yamac et al. [16]	6,286	CheXNet based on DenseNet-121	95.90	98.50	95.70
L. Wang et al. [17]	13,975	COVID-Net	93.30	91.00	91.50
M. Ahishali et al. [18]	5,824	CheXNet-based on DenseNet-121	99.49	99.43	99.81
A. Abbas et al. [19]	51,960	Self-supervised decomposition	97.54	97.88	97.15
M. S. Boudrioua et al. [20]	3,300	DenseNet 121, NASNetLarge and NASNetMobile	98.00	100.00	99.50
P. Manapure et al. [21]	50	GRU neural network	91.00	100.00	80.00
M. A. Al-antari et al. [24]	1,312	YOLO predictor	97.40	85.15	99.05
L. Brunese et al. [26]	6,523	VGG-16	98.00	96.00	99.05
S. Q. Salih et al. [29]	1,262	Modified AlexNet	85.00	90.74	95.57
S. Chatterjee et al. [31]	1,302	ResNet18, ResNet34, InceptionV3, InceptionResNetV2 and DenseNet161	80.00	85.10	88.90
K. K. Singh et al. [33]	1,419	Depth wise separable convolution network	98.94	96.00	95.00
M. A. Elaziz et al. [34]	1st dataset:18912nd dataset:1560	MobilNet	Acc., for 1st dataset:96%, acc., for2nd dataset: 98%	1st dataset: 98.752nd dataset:98.91	98
X. Mei et al. [36]	905	Inception_ResNet_V2	99.4	84.3	82.8

10.2   Related work

Several DL architectures are constructed rapidly to identify the Covid-19 virus using X-ray CXR pictures. Wang *et al.* formed COVID-Net to recognize Covid-19 in CXR. This data set includes Covid-19 infection, pneumonia, and a healthy chest radiograph (non-Covid-19 infection).

The overall accuracy of this pneumonia classification is 84.5%. Radiologists may now rapidly identify Covid-19 in CXR using the COVIDX-Net deep learning algorithm [29]. Figure 10.4 shows some general applications of deep learning in medical imaging.

10.2.1   Detection/localization

The machine vision local area, then again, is especially worried about object location in enormous pictures, for utilizations, for example, picture-related search machines or natural diagnostics, where the point could be to distinguish tumours and different irregularities in photos of human tissue consequently [30]. Distinguishing objects adds to the trouble [30]. Objects like those on which the NN was prepared in 2011 are probably going to show up in picture districts that produce exceptionally dynamic result units. Finally, the first deep learning system won a competition for visual object detection in photos with several million pixels. There are two sorts of profound learning-based object location. The area proposition-based calculations are one model. Utilizing a particular pursuit procedure, this strategy extricates a few sorts of patches from input photographs [31]. From that point forward, the prepared model decides if each fix contains various things and groups them as indicated by their district of interest (ROI). The article identification in different ways was finished involving the relapse strategy as a one-stage network [33, 34]. These techniques use picture pixels to straightforwardly find and distinguish bouncing box arranges and class probabilities in complete pictures [32].

10.2.2   Segmentation

DL also won the initial pure image segmentation competition in 2012 [35], using a GPU-MPCNN ensemble once more. Two Electron Microscopy stacks were pertinent to the newly permitted massive brain schemes in Europe and also in the United

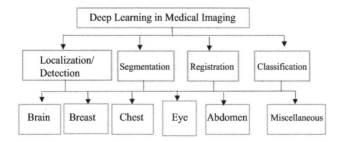

Figure 10.4   Applications of deep learning in medical imaging

States. Human experts, on the other hand, require many hours to months to illustrate the images: Which sections of the image represent neuronal membranes? What aspects of the scene are merely background? Turaga *et al.* (2010) recommend automating this process. Poudel *et al.* recommended another Recurrent Full Convolutional Network (RFCN) that can distinguish and isolate physical constructions by gaining picture portrayal from the entire 2D cut stack and using between cut spatial reliance through inward memory cells. When consolidated into a solitary design for start-to-finish preparation, it fundamentally lessens calculation time, improves the division cycle and empowers ongoing applications [34]. Isensee *et al.* proposed a technique for characterizing a totally computerized handling pipeline that utilizes an assortment of U-Net constructions to fragment the cardiovascular design at each stage in the heart cycle by joining division and illness. To see the ROI containing LV, Liao *et al.* made an identifier that was coordinated with a Neural Network (NN) classifier [36]. The ROI's LV is then split using hypercolumns. To estimate the volume, the 2D segmentation outcomes are combined with multiple pictures. These techniques employ end-to-end learning and directly labels the actual work.

10.2.3   Registration

In clinical research, deformable image registration is vibrant. To begin correct anatomical identifications, image registration is required. Although intensity-based feature selection approaches are commonly employed in medical image registration, they do not ensure perfect anatomic site correlation. Hand-crafted features like Gabor filters and geometric moment invariants are very popular, although they do not perform well with all sorts of image data [37]. Many AI-based approaches for picture registration have recently been used. Because it does not require prior knowledge or hand-crafted characteristics, deep learning may be more promising than conventional learning-based methods. It employs a hierarchical deep architecture to quickly and effectively infer complex non-linear relationships. STN, which was recommended in 2015 and studies to spatially modify feature maps in a way that is favourable to the task of interest, is a basic component of most DLIR techniques. Despite the fact that they are not intended specifically for image registering, but slightly to provide networks with the ability to learn features in a way that is insensitive to rigid and deformable changes, they had formed the foundation for most unsupervised registration algorithms. In a number of multi-modal registering approaches, Generative adversarial network image translation networks (e.g. Cycle-GANs) [38] learn to map the appearances change across sectors, that is among images from multiple methods. [39] analyses the design of recommended systems for DL-based clinical image registration, classifying and evaluating them according to their design and learning principles (i.e. supervised, semi-supervised or unsupervised).

10.2.4   Classification

Image classification, as a fundamental task in computer vision, is critical in computer-aided diagnosis. The classification of an input image or a sequence of images as containing one (or a few) of preset diseases or devoid of diseases is a simple usage of image classification for medical image analysis. Skin disease identification in dermatology and eye disease identification in ophthalmology, including diabetic retinopathy, glaucoma and corneal disorders, are examples of common clinical uses of picture classification tasks [40]. This topic also includes the classification of pathological pictures for various infections for example breast and brain cancer. In the fields of image analysis, document and digit recognition, conv nets have dominated. They've recently been applied in traffic signal identification, which outperforms the natural human recognition system. Furthermore, the inclusion of GPUs accelerated data preparation and recognition. Convolutional Neural Network (CNN) Architecture [97] is used as like feature extractor in almost all of the Covid-19 detection models, and Softmax or Sigmoid is used as a classifier. A sigmoid layer was also used by some researchers to augment CNN [41].

10.2.5 Application

In a lot of CAD applications, deep learning has emerged as one of the most essential technologies for medical image interpretation. DL models are able to recognize hidden associations in complex visual data or link them to goal diagnosis or disease tracking with great success. Artificial intelligence, quantitative statistics, optimizations, biology, pattern classification and many other branches of study are all influenced by it and it incorporates them all [42]. In recent days, image classification and its applications have made significant advances in the field of deep learning. However, academics have worked hard to develop a number of effective CNN models that have reached excellent accuracy and even outperformed human recognition ability. But on the other hand, using the CNN architecture in medical image interpretation became one of the deep learning's most appealing approaches [43].

Deep learning, a major AI research topic, permits end-to-end techniques to accomplish desired outcomes without any need for human feature extraction using data input. DL architecture had been extensively utilized for hitches such as pneumonia recognition from CXR, arrhythmia identification, retina image segmentation, skin cancer categorization, chest cancer detection, brain disorder classification and lung segmentation. As a result, this paper proposes an alternative diagnostic method for detecting Covid-19 cases that make use of available resources and advanced deep learning algorithms DNN, particularly CNN, which recently launched imaging techniques such as classification performance in a variety of medical applications, including diabetic retinopathy, tuberculosis and tumour diagnosis [39,40].

The inception framework's deep architectures include InceptionResNetV2, InceptionResNet201 and ResNetV2. The accuracy of Covid-19 was confirmed by comparing 50 X-ray pictures, 25 of which included Covid-19 and 25 of which did not. Covid-19 can be recognized using the VGG19 and DenseNet models [40]. However, the InceptionV3 model fails to identify Covid-19 at all and classifies only healthy data properly.

According to Kumar *et al.*, Covid-19 may be recognized via X-ray imaging. It made use of an extremely deep convolutional neural network. This model's accuracy was 96.32% when trained on data from GitHub and Kaggle. Ozturk *et al.* used

CXR to build a model termed DarkCovidNet to categorize Covid-19. To appropriately classify Covid-19, healthy and pneumonia cases, here suggest the DarkCovid-Net model. The model correctly classified 87.02% of cases in multiclass situations and 98.08% of cases in binary situations. Ioannis *et al.* used two datasets to train two deep-learning models.

The originally set of 1427 X-beams comprises 504 healthy images, 700 bacterial pneumonia data and 220 Covid-19-infected images. The second gathering of photos includes 500 pictures of sound individuals, 720 pictures of viral and bacterial pneumonia and 225 pictures of Covid-19. The rates of precision for courses 2 and 3 were 98.75% and 93.48%, individually. Khan *et al.* created CoroNet to differentiate Covid-19 from CT and CXR. This Xception model was prepared to utilize ImageNet. Table 10.2 gives the outcome assessment of different CNN methods for X-beam pictures. Table 10.2 gives some best-in-class models with execution measurements.

Figure 10.5 provides the Recent Research investigations related to Covid-19 diagnosis models with accuracy, sensitivity and specificity summary for X-ray images. Classification precision, sensitivity, specificity, accuracy, F1-score, etc., are selected metrics that could be employed for assessing the enforcement of architecture. On the basis of 618 pulmonary CT images, the early network is capable to differentiate Covid-19 images from pneumonia and adults (i.e. 175 healthy people, 225 individuals with

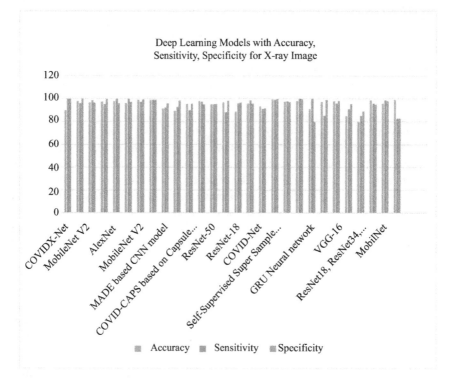

Figure 10.5 Various deep learning models with accuracy, sensitivity and specificity for X-ray image

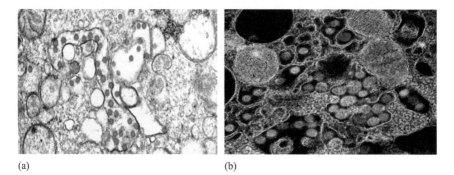

(a)   (b)

Figure 10.6   The Covid-19 virus was imaged using (a) a false colour scanning
electron microscope and (b) a transmission electron microscope

pneumonia and 219 patients with Covid-19). The COVNet architecture achieved 90.3% accuracy, 0.962 AUC and 96.2% specificity for recognizing Covid-19. This model has an overall delicacy of 85.2% (Covid-19 vs. bacterial pneumonia) and a total delicacy of 94.2% (healthy vs. Covid-19). B. Ghoshal and colleagues developed a probabilistic deep literacy classifier using Covid-19 X-ray pictures.

The Bayesian conclusion raises the standard VGG16 model's discovery accuracy from 84.6% to 93.1%. According to Zhang and colleagues used to diagnose Covid-19 from CXR. This model was trained using 1008 pneumonia patients and 70 pictures from Covid-19 instances. It had a perceptivity of 96.0%, a particularity of 71.2% and an AUC of 95.2%. Figure 10.6 provides Covid-19 image taken from an electron microscope.

10.3   Proposed model

VGG16 is a convolutional neural network architecture. In general, it is regarded as one of the most well-known model designs to have been built to date [9]. For the most distinctive feature of VGG16, a 3 × 3 filter with steps and a 2 × 2 filter with skip connections were employed, rather than the huge number of hyper-parameters that would have been needed to accomplish this goal. With the aid of convolutional layers, the pooling layers are positioned in the same way throughout the architecture. A softmax handles the output after two completely linked layers have been completed. The number 16 in VGG16 refers to the number of weighted layers. This network has around 138 million parameters, making it large [12]. In this video, CNN and transfer learning are shown. CNNs are alike to neural networks, rather than CNNs have at least one layer of convolution. Equation (10.1) describes the first layer of a basic brain organization. Figure 10.7 provides the workflow of our proposed approach.

$$Z^{[1]} = g(W^{[1]}a^{[0]} + b^{[1]}) \tag{10.2}$$

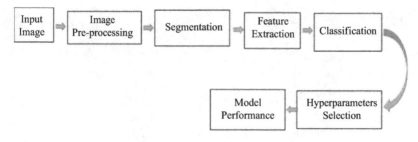

Figure 10.7   Workflow of the proposed model

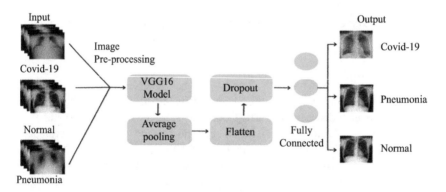

Figure 10.8   Modified VGG-16 for Covid-19 classification

The initial or information layer, which handles the stresses of the main layer and is also the inclination, is the current level. We replaced rising activity with fusion activity by refreshing a two-dimensional weighted network with three-dimensional channel tensor loads for the VGG19 Convolution Layer. Equation (10.2) shows a direct comparison in the main channel of a "c" final layer for each "x" channel:

$$Z^{[1]}_{(i,j,k)} = (x * W^{[1]})(i,j,k) + b^{[1]}_{(k,1)} \tag{10.3}$$

$$Z^{[1]}_{(i,j,k)} = \sum_{(l,m,n)}^{3} W^{[1]}_{c(l,m,n,k)} a[0]_{(i+l,j+m,n)} + b^{[1]}_{(k,1)} \tag{10.4}$$

All three sections are compared, and the final conclusion is taken into account for every piece. While k is the image of the channel that is currently utilized in the form of the line, section and channel numbers 1 to n, respectively, it is still the picture that symbolises the channel. Look at the similarity of the two equations. Similar to the convolution operation of (10.3)'s lattice increase 2. A good example of this is seen in (10.4). In this case, the () symbol, which is used to identify convolution, is employed in a novel manner.

Figure 10.8 represents the VGG-16 model. Whether it comes to arithmetic and measurement, cross-relationship has capabilities that are comparable to

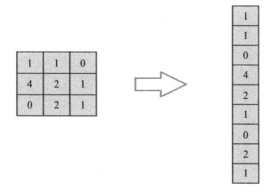

Figure 10.9   Flattening technique

cross-relationship. Nevertheless, in DL literature, cross-relationship has been commonly tangled with the name convolution. Figure 10.9 depicts the layers of information, convolution, pooling, completely associated and yielding in their various configurations. CXR pictures are referred to as information layer images.

The progression of the channel window on the communications system is shown by the use of steps. Following the convolution process, the following layer in the stacking is a pooling layer, which is utilized to diminish the time it takes to complete various tasks. It examines typical pooling skills including regular, standard, least and most pooling. A case in point of individuals max pooling. It is significant to note that there is another layer that is the fully connected layer closely related to the pooling layer. Like the levelled adaptation layer before it, this layer has a network of connections between every neuron in the brain.

The findings of the model are also impacted by the classes that were utilized in its construction but to a lesser amount.

The output of this research has been classified into four unique groups as a consequence of the findings:

- The radiology scans of patients who tested negative for Covid-19 are included in this collection.
- It is probable that these patients had additional pneumonic diseases based on the statistics.
- This collection contains radiology scans of Covid-19 but did not have any other pneumonic illnesses.

10.3.1   Image pre-processing

There are two phases to image pre-processing:

Step 1: To begin, all images were measured for base height and width using a tape measure. As a result of this finding, all dataset photos were scaled to reflect this aspect ratio. The smallest aspect ratio of our work is 640 × 640. As a consequence, all of the photographs in the collection have been reduced to 640 × 640 pixels.

Step 2: Resized photos are pre-processed in accordance with ImageNet specifications. The VGG16 model is a free and open-source model that supports over a thousand different picture formats. The VGG16 Massive induces the updating of cutting-edge algorithms by using pictures from VGG16 that have been divided into subsets and combined into a single image. This work takes advantage of an organization that was developed on ImageNet in order to construct an organization for our dataset. Move learning is a technique of constructing an organization on a new dataset by using a previously prepared organization on VGG16 as a model for the new dataset. Therefore, the normalized photos obtained in step 1 are smaller images than those captured in step 2. This is seen in VGG16. If you are working with VGG16 data, divide each pixel by 255, remove the VGG16 standard deviation from the mean and divide again. Every picture in our dataset receives the same treatment.

10.3.2   Data augmentation

Training images that have been artificially made using a variety of processing methods, including randomized spin, shifts, shears and flips, as well as contrast, hue and saturation, among many others. Image augmentation often results in a $3\times$ to $4\times$ increase in the present data test sample.

With the use of a technology known as "augmentation," it is feasible to significantly improve the amount of images available. The distributions of healthy people's images, viral-induced pneumonia images and Covid-19-induced person images were derived from data sets. The number of images collected from two data sets in each image class for each image class. It represents a big deviation from the norm. A model is said to overfit when it is unable to summarize sufficiently on a short dataset, and so exactness is not an appropriate presentation metric in this situation. In order to avoid overfitting, regularization approaches such as till-well are used in this investigation. It was decided to improve the amount of Covid-19 data and additional classes in order to avoid the model being overfit. The Gaussian blur and the turn are two techniques that were employed in this study to increase the quantity of information available.

10.3.3   CNN with transfer learning

In this examination, convolutional neural networks (CNNs) are created in this research by transferring learning from one task to another. In order to build the Deep CNN with stored loads, we utilized ImageNet as a foundation and then layered on top of it the dataset we needed for this study. This would be advantageous since the vanishing inclination problem makes it impossible to use machine learning to develop the foundation layers of an organization, which would be a benefit.

Furthermore, the organization has learned fundamental skills such as the recognition of shapes, edges and so on. Therefore, the previously constructed model gets information from the current dataset. Because just the final tiers of the structure must be constructed, this approach decreases the amount of time required for calculations. Furthermore, in terms of computation speed and accuracy, the lingering CNNs are now outperforming other organizational structures, such as VGG, beginning and thick organizations, according to the latest research. In order to identify Covid-19, the proposed approach is separated into two phases, each of which has its own lingering network. When it came to training their personnel, both companies relied on mobile learning solutions.

The last layers of the architecture are rewritten in order to the increased classes in the dataset. Convolutional layers are used to store and analyse this data, which is then used to predict which classes will be present. It has been determined that the pre-processed data for this dataset has been locked and that only the final neural layer is ready to transform those different highlights into suggestions for the dataset's classes.

10.3.4   ChestXRay20 dataset

The Chest ray Dataset has 6,163 CXR images, consisting of 3,884 photos of pneumonia, 1,349 images of Healthy and 930 photographs of Covid-19 test pictures. The dataset contains 3,884 pneumonia images, 1,349 healthy images and 930 Covid-19 images. Pneumonia, healthy and Covid-19 images are all included in this data-gathering process. Each and every Covid-19 image was included in this data-gathering effort.

According to our board-certified radiologists, only anteroposterior images are suitable for Covid-19 prediction in our practise. Upon reviewing the photographs, our board-certified radiologist determined that there was no Covid-19 radiological evidence. You will then be able to provide the community with a more specific collection of data. We used the same image to produce both the test and training sets for this exercise. It has been previously stated that the augmentation technique was employed on the training set in order to add 330 Covid-19 samples to the set. In order to ensure that each patient's image was associated with just one of the instruction or test sets, notably, radiologists have found areas that are positive for Covid-19.

10.4   Experiments and result discussion

We used three different CXR datasets in this study: (i) Covid-19 vs. healthy, (ii) Covid-19 vs. pneumonia and (iii) Covid-19 vs. non-Covid-19.

Case 1: Covid-19 vs. healthy

Deep learning was used to differentiate the false positives from the actual ones and deep learning was used to do so. This was accomplished by comparison of the CT dataset of Covid-19 infected persons and healthy people. Preparation, review and testing are the three sub-datasets that make up this data collection. All of the photographs were used for instructional purposes, with just 3% of the images being used for evaluation. On the other hand, we only used 9% of the time we spent preparing images for approval, out of a total of 90%.

The Coronavirus validation dataset is intended for use in the creation, endorsement and testing of the Coronavirus vaccine. The dataset dispersion for healthy patients, on the other hand, is used for preparation, approval and testing. Following the ordering of the dataset, we may apply the DL techniques that had been recommended with the infected dataset. The accuracy with which catastrophic charts are created, approved and validated is essential. Upon reaching age 13, we attained the finest outcomes for the suggested approach, which was resorted to with a red touch on getting ready precision and endorsement precision, respectively. The recommended technique automatically eliminates overfitting by terminating the experiment at an early stage. The projected model's display has been determined by the disarray network. Thus, we were able to determine the adaptability and uniqueness of the model. Furthermore, the radiologist may use the VGG model to display shading in order to make expert and specific conclusions depending on the clarity of the pictures. We can see when this methodology was utilized, the proposed model accomplished a general precision of 88.53% while additionally giving specialists a superior comprehension of the profound learning model's expectations.

Case 2: Covid-19 vs. pneumonia

The major aims of this investigation exist to detect Covid-19 positive individuals as well as instances of pneumonia. Should a case of pneumonia arise, we will refer to CXR scans recorded roughly 2–3 years ago, when the Covid-19 pandemic was still a long way off. When it came to patients with positive Covid-19, we followed the same guidelines as we did in Case 1. The dataset split is utilized for preparing, screening and licencing purposes for people with pneumonia, as well as for getting ready, testing and approval purposes for patients with positive.

We were able to determine the most effective settings. Affectability and explicitness were given to positive Covid-19 examples in this section. In accordance with the findings, the suggested approach can able to identify Covid-19 images (including true positives) 96.55% of the time. The proposed model correctly differentiates Covid-19 cases with 96.55% accuracy. We utilized photographs to organize and show the patches on the lungs' surface. CT and CXR images of chest Covid-19-infected people may reveal these results.

Case 3: Normal vs. non-COVID

Patients with Covid-19 and without Covid-19 were compared and identified with this paper, using CXR and CT image data. Patients with Covid-19 and without Covid-19 were comprised in the ChestXRay20 image set. In this study, the disarray network assessed both affectedness and explicitness independently of one another. A Covid-19 individual may have an effect factor of 94.26%, according to these statistics. The radiologists' development of our model has been shown to be more trustworthy as a result of the more exact representation of our model that CT scans provide to them. DL approaches were pragmatic in order to identify the parts of the lungs that were affected by the illness. After preparation, the suggested CT-scan methodology may be accustomed to correctly discovering Covid-19 CXR images using the proposed CT scan methodology (Figures 10.10–10.12).

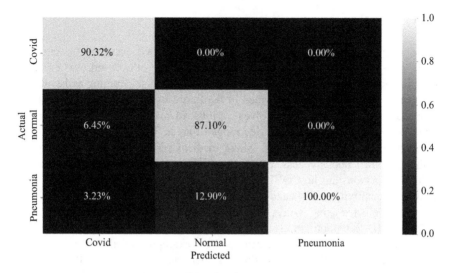

Figure 10.10 A confusion matrix for predicting Covid-19

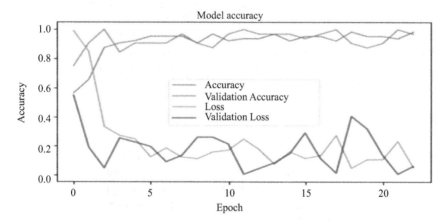

Figure 10.11 Accuracy and training loss for Covid-19, pneumonia and healthy CXR

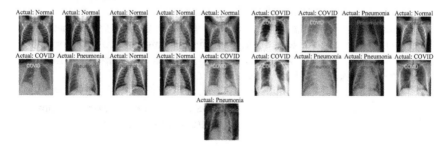

Figure 10.12 A sample Covid-19 prediction result

10.5 Conclusions

When it came to identifying Covid-19 disease in CXR pictures, we employed modified VGG16 architecture. COVID Xray6k, on the other hand, was created in order to check Covid-19 tags with the help of a radiologist. Training and evaluating forecasting models will be performed in the future using the Covid-19 binary bitwise classifier. Industry 4.0 involves various advancements and developments, which are being carried out in a wide range of areas. In this chapter, we centre on the medical care or clinical area, where medical services are being altered. We evaluated their responsiveness, validity, receiver operating characteristics and area under the curve using the COVIDXray5k dataset. These algorithms have a specificity and sensitivity of 90% and 98%, respectively. This demonstrates that Covid-19 may be detected using X-rays. The research comprises 930 Covid-19 images and 6,000 COVID-free photographs from a public database, for a total of 930 Covid-19 photographs. On this page, you can see two examples of alignment times and responses to Covid-19 ray processing. Further trials using Covid-19 images are required in order to properly assess the correctness of these models. According to Covid-19 recognized specialists, organs that have been infected with viruses will be imaged for future study. We want to develop a system that makes use of a variety of organizational practises. We will utilize artificial intelligence to construct research that will be focused on the factors that cause infection in humans (blood group, RNA arrangement and age). The accuracy of the project's input will be increased in the next phase, and CT scans will be added to the project's input in order to provide more accurate results.

References

[1]   Hemdan, E. E.-D., El-Shafai, W., and Sayed, A. (2022), CR19: a framework for preliminary detection of Covid-19 in cough audio signals using machine learning algorithms for automated medical diagnosis applications. *Journal of Ambient Intelligence and Humanized Computing*. https://doi.org/10.1007/s12652-022-03732-0.

[2]   Narin, A., Kaya, C., and Pamuk, Z. (2021). Automatic detection of coronavirus disease (COVID-19) using X-ray images and deep convolutional neural networks. *Pattern Analysis and Applications: PAA*, 24(3):1207–1220. https://doi.org/10.1007/s10044-021-00984-y.

[3]   Apostolopoulos, I. D. and Bessiana, T. (2020). Covid-19: automatic detection from X-ray images utilizing transfer learning with convolutional neural networks. *Physical and Engineering Sciences in Medicine* 43:635–640. https://doi.org/10.48550/arXiv.2003.11617.

[4]   Elsharkawy, M., Sharafeldeen, A., Taher, F., *et al.* (2021). Early assessment of lung function in coronavirus patients using invariant markers from chest X-rays images. *Science Report* 11:12095. https://doi.org/10.1038/s41598-021-91305-0.

[5] Maghdid, H.S., Asaad, A. T., Ghafoor, K. Z., Sadiq, A. S., and Khan, M. K. (2020). Diagnosing COVID-19 pneumonia from X-ray and CT images using deep learning and transfer learning algorithms. https://doi.org/10.48550/arXiv.2004.00038.

[6] Narayan Das, N., Kumar, N., Kaur, M., Kumar, V., and Singh, D. (2020). Automated deep transfer learning-based approach for detection of COVID-19 infection in chest X-rays. *Ingenierie et recherche biomedicale: IRBM = Biomedical Engineering and Research,* Advance online publication. https://doi.org/10.1016/j.irbm.2020.07.001.

[7] Nayak, S. R. Nayak D. R., Sinha U., Arora V., and Pachori R. B. (2021). Application of deep learning techniques for detection of COVID-19 cases using chest X-ray images: a comprehensive study. *Biomedical Signal Processing and Control* 64:102365, ISSN 1746-8094, https://doi.org/10.1016/j.bspc.2020.102365.

[8] Loey, M., Manogaran, G., Taha, M., and Khalifa, N. (2021). Fighting against COVID-19: a novel deep learning model based on YOLO-v2 with ResNet-50 for medical face mask detection. *Sustainable Cities and Society* 65:102600. https://doi.org/10.1016/j.scs.2020.102600.

[9] Suganyadevi, S., Renukadevi, K., Balasamy, K., and Jeevitha, P. (2022). Diabetic retinopathy detection using deep learning methods. In: *2022 First International Conference on Electrical, Electronics, Information and Communication Technologies (ICEEICT)*, pp. 1–6. https://doi.org/10.1109/ICEEICT53079.2022.9768544.

[10] Rong, G., Zheng, Y., Chen, Y., Zhang, Y., Zhu, P., and Sawan, M. (2021). COVID-19 diagnostic methods and detection techniques: a review. *Reference Module in Biomedical Sciences*, B978-0-12-822548-6.00080–7. https://doi.org/10.1016/B978-0-12-822548-6.00080-7.

[11] Afshar, P., Heidarian, S., Naderkhani, F., *et al.* (2020). COVID-CAPS: a capsule network-based framework for identification of COVID-19 cases from X-ray image. *Computer Vision and Pattern Recognition.* https://doi.org/10.48550/arXiv.2004.02696.

[12] Minaee, S. *et al.* (2020). Deep-COVID: predicting COVID-19 from chest X-ray images using deep transfer learning. *Computer Vision and Pattern Recognition*, arXiv:2004.09363.

[13] Sethy, P. K. and Behera, S. K. (2020). Detection of Coronavirus disease (COVID-19) based on deep features. Preprints, 2020030300 (doi: 10.20944/preprints202003. 0300.v1).

[14] He, K., Zhang, X., Ren, S., and Sun, J. (2016). Deep residual learning for image recognition. In *Proceedings of the IEEE Conference on Computer Vision and Pattern Recognition*, pp. 770–778.

[15] Ibrahim, D. M., Nada M. E., and Amany M. S. (2021). Deep-chest: multi-classification deep learning model for diagnosing COVID-19, pneumonia, and lung cancer chest diseases. *Computers in Biology and Medicine* 132:104348.

[16] Minaee, S., Kafieh, R., Sonka, M., Yazdani, S., and Soufi, G. J. (2020). Deep-COVID: predicting COVID-19 from chest X-ray images using deep transfer learning. *Elsevier-Medical Image Analysis.* https://doi.org/10.1016/j.media.2020.101794.

[17] Wang, X., Deng, X., Fu, Q., *et al.* (2020). A weakly supervised framework for COVID-19 classification and lesion localization from chest CT. *IEEE Transactions on Medical Imaging* 39(8):2615–25. http://dx.doi.org/10.1109/TMI.2020.2995965.

[18] Loannis, D. A. and Mpesiana, T. A. (2020). Covid 19: automatic detection from X ray images utilizing transfer learning with convolutional neural networks. *Springer-Physical and Engineering Sciences in Medicine*, 43:635–640. https://doi.org/10.1007/s13246-020-0865-4.

[19] Panwar, H., Gupta, P., Siddiqui, M. K., Ruben, M.-M., and Singh, V. (2020) Application of deep learning for fast detection of COVID-19 in X-rays using nCOVnet. *Chaos, Solitons & Fractals* 138:109944. https://doi.org/10.1016/j.chaos.2020.109944.

[20] Yadav, A., *et al.* (2021). Automatic detection of COVID 19 infection using deep learning models from X-ray images. In *2021 IOP Conf. Ser.: Mater. Sci. Eng.* 1099 012050, doi:10.1088/1757-899X/1099/1/012050.

[21] Ouchicha, C., Ammor, O., and Meknassi, M. (2020). CVDNet: a novel deep learning architecture for detection of coronavirus (Covid-19) from chest x-ray images. *Elsevier – Chaos, Solitons and Fractals* 140:110–245. https://doi.org/10.1016/j.chaos.2020.110245.

[22] Gers, F. A., Jurgen, S., and Fred, C. (2000). Learning to forget: continual prediction with LSTM. *Neural Computation* pp. 2451–2471.

[23] Balasamy, K. and Shamia, D. (2021). Feature extraction-based medical image watermarking using fuzzy-based median filter. *IETE Journal of Research* 1–9. 69(1): 83–91, https://doi.org/10.1080/03772063.2021.1893231.

[24] Mugahed A. A.-A., Han, S.-M., and Kim T.-S. (2020). Evaluation of deep learning detection and classification towards computer-aided diagnosis of breast lesions in digital X-ray mammograms. *Computer Methods and Programs in Biomedicine* 196:105584, https://doi.org/10.1016/j.cmpb.2020.105584.

[25] Balasamy, K., Krishnaraj, N., and Vijayalakshmi, K. (2021). An adaptive neuro-fuzzy based region selection and authenticating medical image through watermarking for secure communication. *Wireless Personal Communications* 123:2817–2837. https://doi.org/10.1007/s11277-021-09031-9.

[26] Togacar, M., Ergen, B., and Comert, Z. (2020). COVID-19 detection using deep learning models to exploit social mimic optimization and structured chest X-ray images using fuzzy color and stacking approaches. *Elsevier Computers in Biology and Medicine* 15:566–581. https://doi.org/10.1016/j.compbiomed.2020.103805.

[27] Ackley, D. H., Hinton, G. E., and Sejnowski, T. J. (1985). A learning algorithm for Boltzmann machines, *Cognitive Science* 9(1); 147–169. https://doi.org/10.1016/S0364-0213(85)80012-4.

[28] Suganyadevi, S., Shamia, D., and Balasamy, K. (2021). An IoT-based diet monitoring healthcare system for women. *Smart Healthc Syst Des Secur Priv Asp.* https://doi.org/10.1002/9781119792253.ch8.

[29] Brunese, L., Mercaldo, F., Reginelli, A, and Santone, A. (2020). Explainable deep learning for pulmonary disease and coronavirus COVID-19 detection from X-rays. *Computer Methods and Programs in Biomedicine* 196:105608. Published online 2020 Jun 20. doi: 10.1016/j.cmpb.2020.105608.

[30] Suganyadevi, S., Seethalakshmi, V., and Balasamy, K. (2021). A review on deep learning in medical image analysis. *International Journal of Multimedia Information Retrieval* 1:19–38. https://doi.org/10.1007/s13735-021-00218-1.

[31] Jain, G., Mittal, D., Takur, D., and Mittal, M. K. (2020) A deep learning approach to detect Covid-19 coronavirus with X-ray images. *Elsevier – Biocybernetics and Biomedical Engineering* 40:1391–1405. https://doi.org/10.1016/j.bbe.2020.08.008.

[32] Balasamy, K. and Suganyadevi, S. (2021). A fuzzy based ROI selection for encryption and watermarking in medical image using DWT and SVD. *Multimedia Tools and Applications* 80:7167–7186. https://doi.org/10.1007/s11042-020-09981-5.

[33] Sethy, P. K., Behera, S. K., and Ratha, P. K. (2020). Detection of coronavirus disease (COVID-19) based on deep features and support vector machine. *International Journal of Mathematical, Engineering and Management Sciences* 5(4):643–651. https://doi.org/10.33889/IJMEMS.2020.5.4.052.

[34] Sahlol, A. T., Yousri, D., Ewees, A. A. *et al.* (2020). COVID-19 image classification using deep features and fractional-order marine predators' algorithm. *Science Report* 10:15364. https://doi.org/10.1038/s41598-020-71294-2.

[35] Cireşan, D., Meier, U., Schmidhuber, J. (2012). Multi-column deep neural networks for image classification, arXiv:https://arxiv.org/abs/1202.2745.

[36] Fan, H., Mei, X., Prokhorov, D., and Ling, H. (2018). Multi-level contextual RNNs with attention model for scene labeling. *IEEE Transactions on Intelligent Transportation Systems* 19(11):3475–3485. doi:10.1109/TITS.2017.2775628.

[37] Gopalakrishnan, T., Ramakrishnan, S., Balasamy, K., and Murugavel A. S. M. (2011). Semi fragile watermarking using Gaussian mixture model for malicious image attacks. In: *2011 World Congress on Information and Communication Technologies*, pp. 120–125.

[38] Ramakrishnan, S., Gopalakrishnan, T., and Balasamy, K. (2011). A wavelet based hybrid SVD algorithm for digital image watermarking. *Signal & Image Processing An International Journal* 2(3):157–174.

[39] Aceto, G., Persico, V., and Pescape, A. (2020). Industry 4.0 and health: Internet of Things, big data, and cloud computing for healthcare 4.0. *Journal of Industrial Information Integration* 18:100129, ISSN 2452-414X, https://doi.org/10.1016/j.jii.2020.100129.

[40] Gaba, D. M. (2004). The future vision of simulation in healthcare. *Quality and Safety in HealthCare* 13(suppl_1):i2–10. https://doi.org/10.1136/qshc.2004.009878

[41] Holden, R. J., Carayon, P., Gurses, A. P., *et al.* (2013). SEIPS 2.0: a human factors framework for studying and improving the work of healthcare professionals and patients. *Ergonomics* 56(11):1669–1686. https://doi.org/10.1080/00140139.2013.838643.

[42] Lasi, H., Fettke, P., Kemper, H. G., Feld, T., and Hoffmann, M. (2014). Industry 4.0. *Business & Information Systems Engineering* 6(4):239–242. https://doi.org/10.1007/s12599-014-0334-4.

[43] Paul, S., Riffat, M., Yasir, A. *et al.* (2020). Industry 4.0 applications for medical/healthcare services. *Journal of Sensor and Actuator Networks* 18(1):100129. https://doi.org/10.1016/j.jii.2020.100129.

Chapter 11

Case study: digital twin in cardiology

K. Sathya[1] and Vani Rajasekar[1]

11.1 Introduction

Even the skilled surgeons face difficulty in choosing the right treatment for their patients. Doctors and surgeons tailor their diagnosis and treatment patterns based on the patient's current situation. When doctors and surgeons are unaware of the underlying cause of the medical problem, they opt for broad-spectrum treatment and many times are left with unanswered questions which cost the life of a patient. With the advancement of technology and digitalization in every field of science, healthcare is not an exception. Healthcare evolved through various stages like surgery, biopsy, laparoscopy, and nano-robotic surgery to name quite a few. Cyber-physical systems came into existence with the concept of integrating computer systems and physical objects. Precision medicine is the new medical model being put into practice. It focuses on the lifestyle, genetics, and environmental conditions of a patient and even studies molecular diagnostics and imaging analysis to precisely diagnose a patient and choose the most suitable treatment.

Then came the digital twins, an advancement of cyber-physical systems [1]. The digital twin is still thriving in many fields of science to help human in identifying, studying, and examining real-world objects which would not have been possible in the absence of its digital twin.

11.2 Digital twin

Digital twin is the new technological methodology to develop a digital counterpart of physical objects. The twin is developed digitally based on the characteristics obtained from the real object. The concept of digital twin has three types namely as shown in Figure 11.1:

1. Digital twin prototype (DTP)
2. Digital twin instance (DTI)
3. Digital twin aggregate (DTA)

[1]Department of Computer Science and Engineering, Kongu Engineering College, India

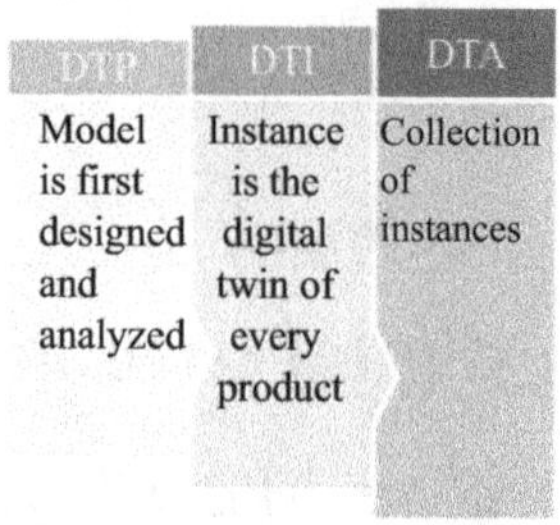

Figure 11.1   Types of digital twin

Digital twin prototype – Prototype is the phase where the model is first designed and analyzed. The prototype models the physical object. Prototyping helps in the simulation of the physical object even before the physical object was produced. The prototyped model will then be analyzed and checked for promptness before the original product is produced.

Digital twin instance – Instance is the computer model (digital twin) of every product being produced. The instances are useful for further examination and help in collecting data from the physical object.

Digital twin aggregate – DTA is the collection of instances. Instances are used in collecting information and data which can then be used in interrogating the physical objects and studying the characteristics of the physical objects in the research-controlled environment.

This chapter explains various digital twin heart development models developed around the globe.

11.3   Issues in cardiology

The medical field has been in constant evolution to cope up with the new found diseases. New medical techniques help physicians in diagnosing the early stages of diseases and modern medicine improves the human body in many ways [2].

Mathematical modeling, image analysis, and disease prediction using neural networks are a great boon to human life [3,4]. However, cardiovascular diseases are the most common and fatal diseases leading to the frequent cause of death. The heart is the most critical organ of the human body and needs immediate attention in case of any heart-related diseases. Most heart diseases are harder to predict at early stages and thus when the symptoms show up, doctors are left with fewer choices of treatment.

Treatment techniques might be the same for all patients, but still, not all patients recover at the same pace and in the same way. For example, not all cardiac patients successfully have their pacemakers implanted in their bodies. Most of them fail to get a synchronized heartbeat from a pacemaker. These differences arise from various background reasons like genetics, lifestyle, and physiological features of the organ and so on [5].

Surgeries performed on the heart has higher risk rates next to neurosurgery compared to other parts of the body. Before surgeons open up the human body to operate on the heart, they must be very well aware of the condition of the organ, the underlying problem, and the solution to the cause. They operate with higher uncertainty which may lead to unexpected scenarios during the surgery. Medical imaging of the organ and other test results might project a different picture of a patient's heart that might not accept the chosen treatment.

11.4 Digital twin heart

To study the heart before choosing the right treatment and to rule out the possible failure cases of treatment, it is important to have a model of the patient's heart that imitates the natural heart of the patient in every aspect including the physiological feature, disease diagnosed, molecular composition and so on [6,7].

Researchers at the Medical University of Graz and Graz University of Technology developed a computer model with mathematical analysis [8]. The computer model is said to be the twin of the patient's heart and can be used to simulate the treatment and study for its impact on the twin heart as shown in Figure 11.2. With this approach, doctors can predict what happens to the heart after the treatment and helps in choosing the right treatment. Pre-simulation of therapy on the twin heart can drastically improve the success rate of many cardiology diseases.

11.5 Development of digital twin heart

Precision medicine in cardiology (precision cardiology) is a new approach to treating and preventing cardiovascular disease that takes into account individual

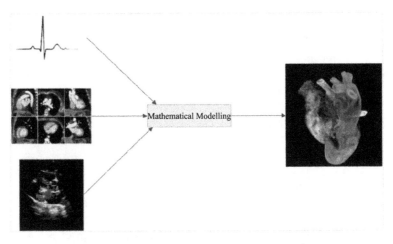

Figure 11.2 Construction of a digital twin heart

differences. A digital twin is a computer model that virtually represents a physical entity. It blends physics, physiology, population data, and patient-specific measures with AI algorithms to update and interrogate the model [9]. The healthcare business is the most likely to be impacted by digital twin technology because it allows for the creation of continuously-adjustable patient-specific models based on recorded health and lifestyle data that can predict a patient's needs [10].

The development of technologies for continuously updating a digital representation of a patient's heart anatomy, function, and physiology throughout time is required to realize the cardiac digital twin. This switches the focus of data analysis from a single picture of a patient during a single scanning session to how measurements change over time as a disease advances or in response to a medication. This enables ongoing learning, prediction, and validation of digital twins throughout time.

To make the digital twin a reality, researchers will need to thoroughly analyze photos and integrate repetitive clinical measures from a patient over time into a single digital depiction of the patient. Millions of factors must be calculated in order to replicate a heartbeat in the computer. Complex mathematical techniques, sophisticated algorithms, and special hardware capable of billions of computations per second are required.

11.6   Philip's HeartModel[A.I]

Precision, accuracy, and granularity are vital in the digital society we live in. Clinical medicine is more difficult than ever before. As a result, we must work really hard. Your heart is as important to your health as it is prone to illness. It is estimated that around 17.7 million people die every year from cardiovascular diseases (CVDs), accounting for over a third of all fatalities globally. Early identification and prediction of CVD development are critical for improving treatment outcomes and saving lives. Despite major advancements in medical imaging methods such as MRI, CT, and ultrasound, finding the best treatment regimens for CVD patients remains difficult.

Medical photos give a plethora of information, but reconstructing and interpreting the architecture of a patient's heart from a series of 2D images is tough. Nonetheless, knowing the nature of a CVD and developing and guiding therapies requires this stage. The fact that each heart is unique adds to the intricacy. The use of generic, rigid anatomical models based on average population data is thus limited.

HeartModel[A.I] is a clinical application developed by Philips that allows cardiologists to analyze many heart functions to diagnose and treat patients with CVD [11]. Based on a collection of 2D ultrasound scans, it creates 3D views of a patient's left heart chambers automatically. HeartModel[A.I] also assess the efficiency with which the heart pumps blood, which is a key sign of potential heart failure.

AI stands for Anatomical Intelligence. AI analyses a patient's ultrasound data and uses adaptive system intelligence and 3D anatomical models to provide more consistent and repeatable outcomes. Advanced organ modeling, image slicing, and proven quantification are used in ultrasound to assist make tests easier to execute and more repeatable while offering new levels of clinical information to address the economic and clinical concerns of today's healthcare system.

11.6.1   Building the HeartModel[A.I]

HeartModel[A.I] is built in a two-stage namely, learning stage and personalization stage.

11.6.1.1   Learning stage

When scan images of a heart are loaded into HeartModel[A.I], it is not just a digital shell. It has prior knowledge of the heart's overall structural arrangement, how the heart's position changes inside a picture, and how the heart shape changes. This information is fed into the model by training it on over a thousand ultrasound pictures of a wide range of heart shapes and sizes. The process of HeartModel[A.I] construction is shown in Figure 11.3 (sourced from Philips HeartModel[A.I] Whitepaper).

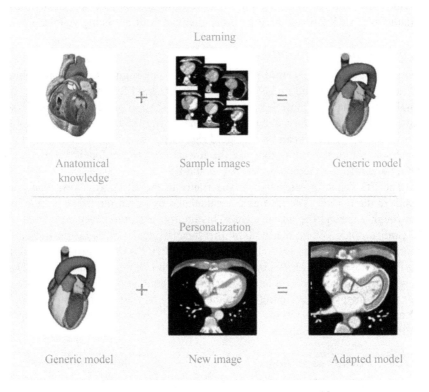

Figure 11.3   Construction of HeartModel[A.I]

11.6.1.2   Personalization stage

HeartModel[A.I] converts the basic model built in the learning stage into a customized one based on the unique scan images of a patient's heart.

This method's strength is that it combines scientifically validated knowledge of cardiac architecture with modern data analytics. The HeartModel[A.I] program, on the other hand, is not meant to adapt to substantial structural changes like those observed in congenital abnormalities, nor is it designed to adapt to very odd-shaped hearts like those with a massive aneurysm. A versatile editing interface is offered for such odd forms.

11.6.2   Image acquisition

With the LV and LA centered along the volume axis, HeartModel[A.I] has been taught to detect the heart in a 3D volume collected from the conventional apical 4-chamber window. While HeartModel[A.I] will work in pictures that differ somewhat from this imaging window, substantial variations should be avoided because of HeartModel[A.I] was not trained in these conditions. The 3D volume's field-of-view should be large and deep enough to encompass the full LV and LA chamber, but not too wide or deep, lest the frame rate suffers. HeartModel[A.I] was created and tested on photos that showed at least 14 of the 17 ASE segments. The use of images with less than 14 segments in the HeartModel[A.I] application and for LV volume measurement can be avoided, since the volume accuracy would be extremely variable with such a major portion of the chamber wall not being visible.

11.6.3   Phase detection

Because of the present HeartModel[A.I] application is designed to measure volumes at End-Diastole (ED) and End-Systole (ES), the ED and ES frame recognition is the initial step in the algorithm. It is best to measure the ED present in the first frame immediately to the mitral valve closure, or measuring the ED in the frame that has the greatest LV, and ES can be measured right after the aortic valve closure in the first frame, or in the frame that has the lowest LV. HeartModel[A.I] uses an estimating and refining method to define ED and ES.

The ED frame is calculated as the frame in the ECG waveform that corresponds to the R-peak. The ES frame is calculated by observing tissue motion in an area roughly around the mitral plane. This motion is significantly correlated with the cardiac phase. When the tissue in this location achieves its height limit along the transducer plane, the ES frame is calculated. In 99% of the instances analyzed ($N = 120$), these ED and ES estimations were within one frame of the actual ED and ES when compared to a complete cycle study. By comparing the frames before and after the estimates and selecting the frame with the biggest and lowest volume, the ED and ES frames are refined. The HeartModel[A.I] border detection technique is used to calculate the volumes.

11.6.4   Border detection

Border detection follows up after the phase detection. It involves two different stages as mentioned earlier.

11.6.4.1   Knowledge-based identification

(a)   Heart localization:
   The overall pattern of the complete heart, which corresponds to the form of the model, is identified in the picture at the coarsest scale, and is then positioned, orientated, and scaled inside the volume at the discovered spot.
(b)   Chamber alignment:
   The position, orientation, and scale of each chamber in the model (LV, LA, RV, and RA) are calculated at a finer spatial scale, and the chambers are then changed such that each structure better corresponds to the places.

11.6.4.2   Personalization

(a)   Regional alignment:
   Small localized sections inside each structure are recognized at the tiniest spatial scale, and the model's borders are modified to best correspond with the patient's heart image.
(b)   Blood-pool border alignment:
   Because the innermost endocardial border, or blood-tissue border, has greater shape variation than the other borders, it is only initialized after Step 3 and has more flexibility than the other layers when it comes to locally altering this border to best fit with the patient's heart image.

While the model is pushed and pulled to align with the image throughout the pattern-fitting process, the model's integrity is also maintained, thus the final modified model may be regarded as a compromise between the patterns recognized in the image and the previous knowledge imposed by the model.

11.6.5   Validation

Several hundred images were used to evaluate the performance of HeartModel[A.I] for the goals of measuring the LV at ED and ES, as well as the LA at left ventricular end-systole. The inner and outer LV endocardial boundaries, as well as the LA boundary, are created by the completely automated HeartModel[A.I] algorithm was compared to manual segmentations done by multiple clinical specialists in the studies. In terms of geographic origin, heart size, disease, heart shape, and imaging quality, the studied images were pretty uniformly distributed. Several centers across the world have looked at the HeartModel[A.I] algorithm. The results show that the algorithm is extremely reliable and precise at adjusting to a wide range of heart sizes and shapes in images of various qualities.

11.6.6   Tuning the model

The algorithm of the HeartModel[A.I] program detects two LV endocardial boundaries, and the user must decide where the final single border should be positioned relative to these two borders. This relative placement is regulated by graphical sliders in the user interface – one for ED and one for ES. The default relative location can be set by the user, and it may differ depending on an institution's or user's desire for where boundaries should be drawn. Despite vastly differing tracing techniques in the clinical world, the flexibility to modify the HeartModel[A.I] application to fit the particular preferences of users allows the HeartModel[A.I] application to produce applicable fully-automated or minimally edited findings.

The user can choose between two editing options: a global or regional edit. The global edit entails modifying the ED or ES slider value, or the relative placement of the single LV endocardial boundary relative to the algorithm-detected inner and outer borders. The user adjusts the border on a more localized basis using control points put along the contour during regional editing. The HeartModel[A.I] program may be used on hearts that have a particularly distinctive or irregular form thanks to regional modification.

11.6.7   Uses of HeartModel[A.I]

The HeartModel[A.I] application is a completely automated model-based segmentation approach for LV and LA measurement that was created to address the variability that exists in today's clinical practice. Rather than recognizing a single boundary, the HeartModel[A.I] algorithm identifies two endocardial boundaries – one at the blood–tissue interface and the other at the compressed myocardium – and allows the user to select a single endocardial border based on their clinical judgment or practice. The resulting single endocardial border recognized by the user is both accurate and resilient over a broad variety of heart shapes and picture quality since the two detected boundaries are simply and reliably identified in an image. The HeartModel[A.I] program offers confident regular clinical use of 3D ultrasound images by combining powerful segmentation algorithms with a simple workflow and user interface that allows for rapid and easy visualization and modification.

11.7   "Living Heart" Project

Cardiologists, cardiac medicine researchers, medical device designers, Governmental regulatory bodies, and cardiology academicians have come together as part of the Living Heart Project to design and validate extremely realistic individualized digital twins of a patient's heart [12]. The twin model can be used as a cohesive framework for heart health medicine, and thus widely used for learning medical skills, development of medical devices, screening, diagnostic testing, and allowing for the accelerated translation of ongoing and prospective cutting-edge advancements into improving the quality of medical service.

This project is fueled by burgeoning participants that are catalyzing the collaboration in designing and developing reliable heart models as well as the exploration of innovative digital therapeutics. The United States Food and Drug Administration (FDA) has inked a five-year joint research agreement in starting this project. It evaluates the test results, performance of pacemakers implanted into the patient body and provides a basis for more customized selective medical care to the patient.

New cardiovascular device approvals with the help of digital evidence from heart simulation will be investigated in pioneering research using the Living Heart simulated 3D heart model. The investigation will have in silico clinical trial without the need for animal clinical trials and it evaluates the efficiency and effectiveness of those devices. This novel innovation has an efficient and cost-effective impact on patient health by minimizing the distrust of medical devices and delays in treatment.

11.7.1 Members of the "living heart"

11.7.1.1 Researchers

Decades of critical study have already yielded a wealth of knowledge on the functioning of the human heart. Spectroscopic techniques are widely used to disclose the geometrical anomalies and biological functioning required for a more full knowledge of the heart's mechanics. Additional study is needed to understand the complexity of abnormal functioning of the heart, in cases like congenital heart diseases and the way they work with implanted assistive devices and artificial objects. Based on medical images of abnormal hearts, input from CVD patients, 3D model of the heart may bring all of this information together and assist potential research in new surgical and therapeutic areas.

As the project proceeds, academic and clinical experts collaborate to monitor, analyze, and influence the development of cardiac models. Their ideas for model improvement, novel applications, technology implementation, and verification of data largely help in simulating the organ models more closer to the real ones that can consistently replicate clinically observed behavior.

11.7.1.2 Industries

Cardiovascular device and service firms are increasingly seeing computer simulation as a critical design tool. They can imagine what they cannot see, mimic in vivo settings, study extensively about the design model, modify their ideas, and choose the best medical care for the patient in a faster and more effective way with the aid of computer simulation. This kind of innovation leads to more realistic designs in a cost-effective manner, quicker testing, and speedy introduction of services into the medical field.

The project's data is being gathered in a pre-competitive way without being specific to a device or disease to ensure product knowledge and patent protection. Companies are testing the concept to see whether it can be used in their fields.

11.7.1.3 Medical practitioners

The large sums of money spent on CVD research, both governmental and private, are never transformed into clinical realities. The difficulties of investigating novel and creative treatment alternatives must be budget friendly and meet the requirements of regulations at the heart of this problem. When properly polished and verified, in silico approaches have shown to be more reliable to deliver profound knowledge of basic functioning and offer a risk-free environment for forecasting by adequately refining and validating the models which would have been not possible otherwise. When realistic simulation of heart function is paired with the understanding and advice offered by accurate simulation of heart function, determining the right therapeutic therapy for CVD can be considerably strengthened. Clinicians are taking part in The Living Heart Project to see if such simulation tools are ready for today's challenges and to help drive the development of cutting-edge technology and apps that will improve patient care even more [13,14].

Doctors and surgeons contribute to this project to provide a patient-oriented diagnosis and treatment in a reliable manner. Clinicians give valuable recommendations to largely utilize the simulation models in diagnosing and treating CVD by tailoring the needs of the patient in a unique way.

As the research advances, clinicians collaborate to monitor and assess the model's evolution. Their recommendations, which are based on real-life patient experiences, ideas for applicability to specific disease states, and/or ideas for model augmentation or refinement based on clinical data, all help the development of realistic simulations that reliably replicate observed behavior.

11.7.1.4 Regulatory

Regulation requirements are an important part of the construction of medical devices. The FDA has ramped up measures to use the simulation models in cost effective treatments. It also funds other projects like the construction of a respiratory simulation and Medical Device Design Tools (MDDTs). The FDA acknowledges that simulating models is more critical for the design of medical devices, medical treatments, and services and the approval of medical devices in the market. Simulation is also thought to lower animal testing and clinical trial expenses, enhance bench testing, and give a better knowledge of in vivo behavior in situations when traditional techniques of evaluating devices are not feasible. The FDA is studying ways to use simulation to promote regulatory science through different efforts, including sponsorships and active engagement in groups such as the Medical Device Innovation Consortium (MDIC).

The most difficult task facing any medical regulatory organization is determining the safety of new gadgets without resorting to expensive and intrusive human testing. As the research advances, regulatory science stakeholders collaboratively monitor and assess the model's evolution. Their input is crucial in determining the heart model's mechanical and material qualities, defining test methods, and devising validation strategies for specific applications.

11.8 Impact of digital twin

Digital twins have a lot of potential in terms of making it simpler to tailor medical treatments to people based on their unique genetic composition, anatomy, behavior, and other aspects. As a result, academics are beginning to call on the medical community to work together to scale digital twins from one-off studies to mass customization systems that are comparable to today's advanced customer data platforms.

11.8.1 Organ simulation

Virtual hearts that may be personalized to specific patients and updated to understand the evolution of illnesses over time or the response to new medications, therapies, or surgical procedures are being developed by a number of companies. FEops, a European firm, has already commercialized the FEops Heartguide technology after receiving regulatory permission. It improves the investigation and treatment of structural heart disorders by combining a patient-specific copy of the heart with AI-enabled anatomical analysis.

11.8.2 Genomic medicine

Swedish researchers have mapped the RNA of mice to create a digital twin that can anticipate the effects of various types and dosages of arthritis medicines. The objective is to use RNA to customize human diagnosis and therapy. The researchers discovered that roughly 40–70% of the time, medicine did not function. Human T-cells, which play a critical role in immunological defense, are also being mapped using similar approaches. These maps can aid in the early detection of many common ailments, when treatment is more successful and less expensive.

11.8.3 Personalized health data

The epidemic has aided the emergence of digital health services that use artificial intelligence to assist individuals to identify and treat minor medical ailments. Babylon Health's Healthcheck App, for example, converts health data into digital twins. It uses manually supplied data, such as health histories, as well as a mood tracker, symptom tracker, and automatic data collection from fitness gadgets and wearables. The digital twin can give basic front-line information or assist in guiding priorities and contacts with clinicians in order to address more serious or persistent diseases.

11.8.4 Personalized treatment

Digital twins are being developed at the Empa research facility in Switzerland to help individuals with chronic pain get the most out of their medications. Age and lifestyle are used to design the digital twin in order to forecast the effects of pain drugs. Furthermore, patient comments on the efficacy of various doses are used to calibrate digital twin accuracy.

11.8.5 Improving the medical service

A digital twin can model the patient and then utilize technologies like natural language processing (NLP) to decipher all of the data and cut through the clutter to summarize what is going on. This saves time and increases the accuracy of gathering and displaying information such as particular drugs, health conditions, and other facts that clinicians need to make therapeutic choices.

11.8.6 Software-as-a-medical device

The FDA is developing regulations that will allow firms to certify and sell software-as-a-medical-device. The basic concept is to create a patient-specific digital twin using various data sources such as lab tests, ultrasound, imaging equipment, and genetic testing. Furthermore, digital twins can aid in the software optimization of medical equipment such as pacemakers, automated insulin pumps, and innovative brain therapies.

11.9   Issues in using digital twin in healthcare

11.9.1   Privacy issues

The fundamental barrier in both the creation and clinical translation of the digital twin is data access, which is hindered by infrastructural, legal, and sociological factors. Electronic health records and information systems are scattered, varied, and difficult to integrate. Information is frequently stored in an unstructured state, necessitating either human labor or more study into automated natural language processing methods. Specialized expertise and supercomputers may be required for simulations. Cloud infrastructures may be able to facilitate the delivery of digital twin technologies in this context. When managing the personal data required to build and evaluate digital twin technologies, consent and secrecy are essential factors. The EU General Data Protection Regulation (GDPR), which includes new legal obligations such as the right to withdraw permission and the right to be forgotten, has sparked debate over the expense and practicality of enforcing it. Any digital twin solution that has enough information in order to identify a patient must adhere to these guidelines, which also extend to observational studies and backups [15].

11.9.2   Ethical issues

1. As more clinical duties are handled by models, there is a risk that physicians will be replaced by machines. In some cases, machines may be able to match or even exceed doctors. In other circumstances, human specialists may lose abilities that are still essential when dealing with complex issues if they do not practice on the easy problems answered by the computer [16].
2. Distrust stemming from a "black box," in which algorithmic forecasts are not matched with a convincing explanation. Creating proof is one obvious method to build trust. Another option is to employ ways to depict the logic inside the box, such as clustering and association algorithms, which may aid in the identification of causes and mechanisms [17].
3. Personalization allows for greater participation in healthcare decisions. Patients will be able to better manage their condition by using the digital twin to learn more about their present and anticipated states, as well as potentially adopting healthier lifestyle recommendations. A well-informed patient will be able to have more efficient talks with clinicians and will be able to consent to and make decisions on diagnostic and therapeutic procedures more quickly [18].
4. In healthcare systems, models have the potential to introduce or worsen existing racial or social biases: if a group is misled in the training dataset models, that group may get sub-optimal treatment [19].

11.10   Conclusion

The key to increasing the therapeutic effect of digital twin technologies is to build confidence among academics, physicians, and the general public. Expectations should not be inflated by research communities. Claims concerning generality and potential effect should be supported by robust methodology, external cohorts to verify inference validity, and measurement of prediction uncertainty. Any model is a simplified portrayal of reality that has a restricted scope and is based on assumptions. The potential is to handle these restrictions properly, with models that can detect data discrepancies and data that can be used to constrain and test model assumptions.

The digital twin, being a new field, requires rules, gold standards, and benchmark testing. Scientific groups and regulatory agencies have issued standards for determining the level of rigor required for computational modeling. Twenty-seven such guidelines and standards are useful tools because they allow regulators to assess computational evidence and industry to comprehend regulatory requirements for computational models, reducing a significant portion of the risk and uncertainty involved in the generation of these new technologies. They can even boost and simplify their translational impact by adhering to such recommendations throughout model building, since the quality and resilience of the models and their output will improve. The reach of these early multi-stakeholder consensuses comprising industry, academics, and regulators needs to be expanded.

Citizens, care providers, clinicians, and researchers must be educated on the applications and prospects of digital twin technologies in order for them to be adopted and accepted. University education systems should also allow for information interchange at the early phases of a career: medical students ought to have some computational training, and biomedical engineers should receive cardiology instruction during their studies. Eighty-eight postgraduate training programs should also help to overcome the residual cultural and linguistic divides between fields.

References

[1] Baillargeon B, Rebelo N, Fox DD, Taylor RL, and Kuhl E. The living heart project: a robust and integrative simulator for human heart function. *European Journal of Mechanics-A/Solids.* 2014;48:38–47.

[2] Barbiero P, Torné RV, and Lió P. Graph representation forecasting of patient's medical conditions: toward a digital twin. *Frontiers in Genetics.* 2021;12:652907.

[3] Barricelli BR, Casiraghi E, Gliozzo J, Petrini A, and Valtolina S. Human digital twin for fitness management. *IEEE Access.* 2020;8:26637–64.

[4] Boschert S and Rosen R. Digital twin—the simulation aspect. In *Mechatronic Futures.* New York, NY: Springer; 2016. p. 59–74.

[5] Chakshu NK, Sazonov I, and Nithiarasu P. Towards enabling a cardiovascular digital twin for human systemic circulation using inverse analysis. *Biomechanics and Modeling in Mechanobiology.* 2021;20(2):449–65.

[6] Corral-Acero J, Margara F, Marciniak M, *et al.* The 'Digital Twin' to enable the vision of precision cardiology. *European Heart Journal.* 2020;41(48): 4556–64.

[7]   Elayan H, Aloqaily M, and Guizani M. Digital twin for intelligent context-aware iot healthcare systems. *IEEE Internet of Things Journal.* 2021;8 (23):16749–57.

[8]   Gillette K, Gsell MA, Prassl AJ, *et al.* A framework for the generation of digital twins of cardiac electrophysiology from clinical 12-leads ECGs. *Medical Image Analysis.* 2021;71:102080.

[9]   Haag S and Anderl RJMl. Digital twin – proof of concept. *Transportation Letters.* 2018;15:64–6.

[10] Jones D, Snider C, Nassehi A, Yon J, and Hicks B. Characterising the digital twin: a systematic literature review. *CIRP Journal of Manufacturing Science and Technology.* 2020;29:36–52.

[11] Kanimozhi N, Keerthana N, Pavithra G, Ranjitha G, and Yuvarani S (eds). CRIME type and occurrence prediction using machine learning algorithm. In *2021 International Conference on Artificial Intelligence and Smart Systems (ICAIS)*; 2021, New York, NY: IEEE.

[12] Kavitha M, Saranya S, Adithyan KD, Soundharapandi R, and Vignesh A (eds). A novel approach for driver drowsiness detection using deep learning. In *AIP Conference Proceedings*; 2021. Melville, NY: AIP Publishing LLC.

[13] Levine S. Living heart: using predictive AI/VR models to reduce uncertainty in cardiovascular diagnosis and treatment. *Canadian Journal of Cardiology.* 2019;35(10):S79–S80.

[14] Malathy S, Vanitha C, Mohanasundari M, and Prasath HV (eds). Improved face recognition using convolutional neural network with unaided learning. In *2021 5th International Conference on Electronics, Communication and Aerospace Technology (ICECA)*; 2021. New York, NY: IEEE.

[15] Martinez-Velazquez R, Gamez R, and El Saddik A (eds). Cardio twin: a digital twin of the human heart running on the edge. In *2019 IEEE International Symposium on Medical Measurements and Applications (MeMeA)*; 2019. New York, NY: IEEE.

[16] Saranya S, Kanimozhi N, Kavitha M, Atchayaprakassh K, and Ragul K (eds). Authentic news prediction in machine learning using passive aggressive algorithm. In *2022 Second International Conference on Artificial Intelligence and Smart Energy (ICAIS)*; 2022. New York, NY: IEEE.

[17] Schneider R. HeartModel[A.I]. Removing the complexity of live 3D quantification. Koninklijke: Philips. 2015(V).

[18] Segars WP, Veress AI, Sturgeon GM, and Samei E. Incorporation of the living heart model into the 4-D XCAT phantom for cardiac imaging research. *IEEE Transactions on Radiation and Plasma Medical Sciences.* 2018;3(1):54–60.

[19] Tao F, Zhang H, Liu A, and Nee AY. Digital twin in industry: state-of-the-art. *IEEE Transactions on Industrial Informatics.* 2018;15(4):2405–15.

Index